ISLAMIC
TEXTILES

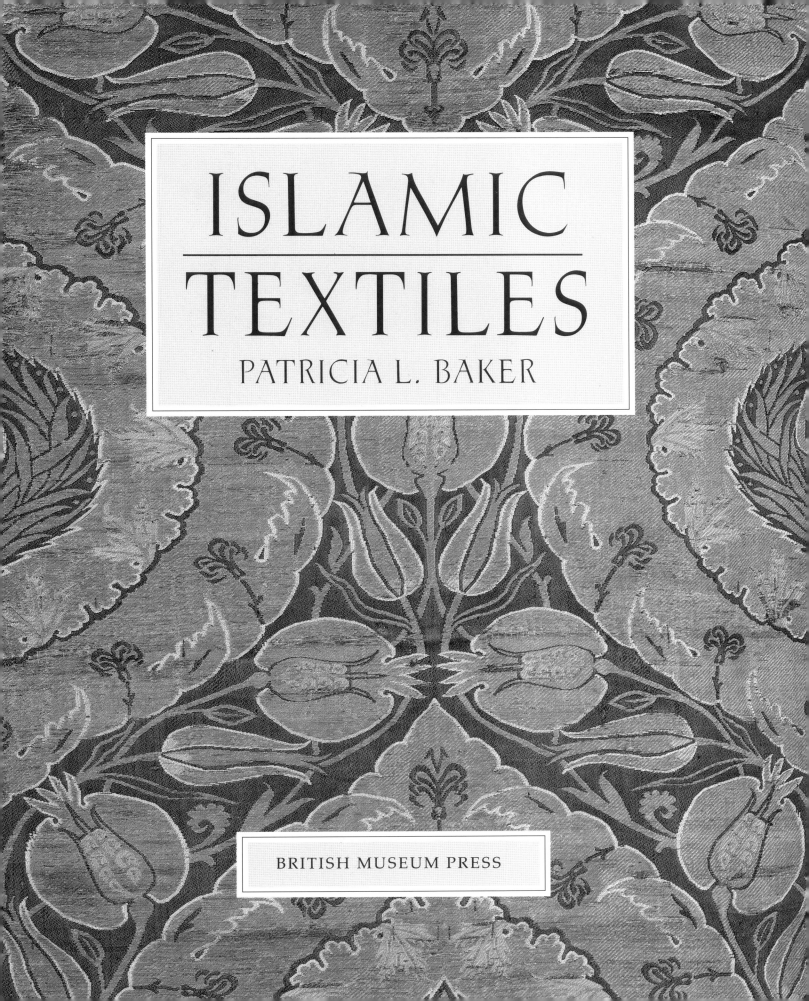

ISLAMIC
TEXTILES

PATRICIA L. BAKER

BRITISH MUSEUM PRESS

To Mary Shelton
and Ann Beresford-Bourke

© 1995 Patricia L. Baker
Published by British Museum Press
A division of The British Museum Company Ltd
46 Bloomsbury Street
London WC1B 3QQ

ISBN 0-7141-2522-9

British Library Cataloguing-in-Publication Data
A catalogue record for this book is available
from the British Library

Designed by Harry Green
Set in Palatino by
Rowland Phototypesetting Ltd
Bury St Edmunds, Suffolk
Printed and bound in Spain
by Imago Publishing Ltd

FRONTISPIECE Lady with castanet,
oil-painting, first half of 19th century,
Qajar Iran, dressed in various patterned fabrics
of the period.

TITLE PAGES Detail of silk lampas with ogival
lattice of tulips and pomegranates, probably
second half of 16th century. Surviving
fragments show that this pattern was produced
in at least two other colourways, featuring a
green and also a red ground. 127 × 65 cm.
(New York, 52.20.22)

CONTENTS

Preface
page 7

Introduction
page 9

1
Textiles, trade routes
and society
page 13

2
Early Islamic period I
Textiles as tribute
page 35

3
Early Islamic period II
Textiles at court
page 49

4
Mamluk textiles
page 65

5
Ottoman opulence
page 85

6
Safavid splendour
page 107

7
Textiles of Qajar Iran
page 125

8
Eighteenth- and
nineteenth-century
Ottoman fabrics
page 149

9
The contemporary
world
page 163

Bibliography
page 181

Illustration
acknowledgements
page 187

Index
page 189

PREFACE

Silk lampas curtain of two panels joined vertically, 15th century, Nasrid Iberia. Inclusion of the Nasrid dynastic motto, 'There is no conqueror but Allah', below the 'corniche' and down the central band indicates manufacture for the palace. The plaited Kufic script at top and bottom reads 'prosperity' and 'good fortune', while the Naskhi edging the square panels is 'Dominion belongs to Allah alone'. 4.38 × 2.72 m. (Cleveland, 82.16)

In recent years British Museum Press has published a number of books concerning aspects of Islamic art, such as painting, metalwork and tiles, while also extending its geographical coverage of ethnographic textiles. This publication will interest readers in both fields, for the phrase 'Islamic textiles' immediately brings to mind the rich silks and velvets of the sixteenth-century Ottoman and Safavid worlds, while visitors to the Islamic Middle East will be aware that among the mass of foreign textiles on sale something of regional manufacture has survived the great changes of the last century.

In the space of this volume it is impossible to describe all the types of fabrics, designs and techniques, past and present, throughout the region and to explore all the issues and questions. Readers may be disappointed that discussion of carpet manufacture and design is limited, but it should be remembered that there are numerous publications on Islamic carpets, while this is the first work of this kind on Islamic textiles; given the constraints of space and illustrations, it has proved possible only to mention recent discoveries or to emphasise the relationship in design between contemporary textiles and carpets. I have tried to provide a context for the textiles – cultural, historical, economic, philosophical, aesthetic, functional and technical – and to alert the reader to recent research and summarise current thinking. In this respect I must record my deep gratitude to all those who have so readily and generously shared their ideas and research findings. The first section deals with certain 'constant' factors referring to the importance of textiles in Islamic society and briefly describes the main materials and technical processes. Subsequent chapters follow in more or less chronological order, opening with a short historical survey of the major regional dynastic authority in the period under consideration. The final section brings the reader into the twentieth century, focusing on some of the most distinctive textiles produced in the region without any pretence of being a comprehensive survey, while highlighting certain issues and questions.

For their help and assistance regarding the respective textile collections my thanks go to Dr Anne Farrer and other members of the Department of Oriental Antiquities and Hero Granger-Taylor of the British Museum, as well as the curators and staff of the Victoria and Albert Museum, London; the Ashmolean Museum, Oxford; the Embroiderers' Guild, Hampton Court; the Whitworth Art Gallery, Manchester; the Art Institute, Chicago; the Brooklyn Museum, New York; the Cleveland Museum of Art, Ohio; the Metropolitan Museum of Art, New York; the Museum of Fine Arts, Boston; and the Textile Museum, Washington, DC. At the Royal Ontario Museum in Toronto, Canada, the kindness of Anu Liivandi-Palias and Jeannie Parker was much appreciated. Library staff at the British Library, National Art Library and the School of Oriental and African Studies, London University (SOAS), have been most considerate and long-suffering.

I owe a very special debt of thanks to Marianne Ellis and Jennifer Wearden for their advice and constant encouragement in this project. It was Jack Franses who first opened my eyes to the world of Islamic textiles, and then Dr Tarcan Yilmaz and Dr Hülye Tezcan who introduced me to the treasures of the Topkapi Saray Museum, Istanbul. I am so grateful to them and to others who have clarified certain matters: Ruth Barnes, Dr Beata Biedronska-Slotowa of Krakow National Museum, Elisabeth Crowfoot, Jacqueline Herald, Dr Colin Heywood of SOAS, Umar Hegedus and Khadije Knight, Peter Kelly, Dr Donald King, Deryn O'Connor, Silvia Sella of Geneva, and especially Dr Norman Indictor of New York and Diane Mott of the Museum of Fine Arts, Boston. The kindness and hospitality of Kesa Sakai in Washington, David and Edna Hampton in Toronto, Gülbikem Ronay of Unitur, Istanbul, Cynthea Rhodes in Cheshire, Fredi GlueXcksmann and June Hinton in London were undeserved.

It has been a pleasure working with my editor at British Museum Press, Nina Shandloff, and with Deborah Wakeling; my sincere thanks to them both, and to Charlotte Deane for her assistance over illustrations.

None of the above, of course, bears responsibility for the pages which follow, an attempt to do justice to the magnificent textiles produced in the Islamic Middle East over some 1,400 years. There is a Persian proverb I would ask the critical reader to remember: '*Zarbaft burida pamba kardan*'; I am indeed aware that I have 'attempted the impossible'.

NOTE

Arabic, Turkish and Persian terms may be transliterated in a number of ways; there is no one accepted system. As this publication is aimed at a general readership, the transliteration has been kept simple; the plethora of dots and dashes under and over the various letters can be irritating and confusing to the general reader, while the specialist reader knows the possibilities. Generally speaking the modern spelling has been followed for Turkish words but without specifying the undotted 'i'. For Arabic and Persian terms no vowel stress nor diacritical has been incorporated, but the letter *ayn* is rendered in the usual manner, ꜥ. The most common rendering for geographical and historical names has been given: thus, for instance, Mecca is used here rather than Makka, which is technically correct.

The Muslim calendar is based on the lunar (not solar) year of twelve months of some twenty-nine or thirty days' duration, commencing on the Prophet's departure from Mecca for Medina (1 Muharram 1 AH) which corresponds to 16 July 622. With the general reader in mind such dates have been kept to the minimum in this text. Although there is a growing usage of the Common Era abbreviation (that is, BCE and CE instead of BC and AD), I regret it has not been possible to follow the system here.

INTRODUCTION

For centuries Islamic textiles, whether they were the fine linens of medieval Egypt, the delicate muslins of Syria, the sumptuous silks and exquisitely soft velvets of Ottoman and Iranian production, or the rich variety of carpets, delighted customers in the Islamic world and further afield. Strictly speaking any survey of Islamic textiles should include fabrics produced in all those regions in which the majority of people live according to Islamic mores. The term could also be understood to refer to fabrics with specific Muslim content or ritual function. However, as with the phrase 'Islamic art' it is established convention to focus on the work, religious and secular, produced in Egypt and Syria, Anatolia and Iran; these pieces exemplify the aesthetic criteria against which all others from the world of Islam are measured. Thus the embroideries of Nigeria and the batiks of Indonesia, because they do not conform to this stylistic yardstick, are perceived not as Islamic but African and Asian respectively.

In the West it is held that the golden age of Islamic art was the post-medieval period (c. 1350–1650) after which there was an irrevocable decline. But while the textiles of this period represent for many the apogee in design, colouring and technical expertise, the later work is important reflecting the enormous changes during the nineteenth century when textile manufacture verged on extinction. The twentieth century has seen a certain revival as the public, home and abroad, has increasingly associated certain textiles with national and cultural identity, and officialdom has recognised that crafts sponsorship could help to stem rural depopulation.

Given the inherently fragile nature of textiles, we are fortunate in the number that have survived the ravages of time, climate, insect infestation – and human behaviour. The custom of cutting up fabrics and constant reuse ensured the destruction of much material. To the casual observer it may appear that the thousands of extant pieces are more than sufficient to build up an adequate picture of textile manufacture in the Islamic Middle East, but in fact these represent just a minute percentage of the total quantity, quality

and variety produced. Most of the Islamic textiles held in public and private collections were acquired in the late nineteenth century from dealers, and so indirectly represent the taste and interest of that era in the highly decorative and the 'exotic'. Today the focus is directed on work which may be described as 'contemporary tribal', while textiles specifically made to meet the local demand of town and village people have been largely ignored. So just as Kashan and Iznik ceramics do not typify the totality of Islamic pottery production, so these textile collections do not demonstrate the full range of manufacture.

Few pieces have been published with full details of structure, although it is now realised that without technical analyses Islamic textiles are extremely difficult to assign and date securely, as will be seen below (the Buyid controversy, p. 44). A number do possess inscriptions which give a date and place of manufacture, but not all are genuine. Leaving aside modern-day fakes, fraudulent attribution (as on the Burgo de Osma silk fragment opposite, p. 44) was a recognised problem in medieval Islamic times with market inspectors warning both traders and customers. Because their entry in European royal or church treasuries, tombs or reliquaries is recorded, occasionally a *terminus ante quem* dating relates to certain pieces. Moreover, textiles have been unearthed during archaeological excavations, but not all digs have been carried out in controlled circumstances, and excavators are rarely presented with an unambiguous dating stratigraphy.

However, there is a wealth of diverse information contained in Islamic literature. Geographers, travellers and court recorders all mention textiles, their production centres, their appearance and usage, while the everyday problems of buying and selling are recorded in market regulations and mercantile documents such as the eleventh- to twelfth-century Geniza letters, found in a Cairo synagogue in the 1950s. Literary works, too, are a rich source containing numerous analogies to textiles. The poet Farrukhi living in eleventh-century Central Asia went so far as to compare composing verse to weaving (Clinton 1972, p. 128):

Each thread of its warp was drawn from within me:

Each thread of its woof was painstakingly extracted from my soul; . . .

But while references abound, unambiguous and precise descriptions of technique and appearance are rare. Of course, representations in paintings, on ceramics, metalwork and so on of the Islamic world assist, but fabric texture and the patterning process implied are difficult to gauge from the image. With the advent of photography in the nineteenth century some of these problems were addressed.

Silk 'diasper' lampas, early 12th century, Iberia, found in the tomb of St Pedro de Osma (d. 1109). The paired warp is z-twist, while the weft has no discernible twist; the gold is on animal substrata. The woven inscription in the roundels specifies Baghdadi manufacture, but epigraphic details betray its Andalusian origins. (Boston, 33.371)

1

TEXTILES, TRADE ROUTES AND SOCIETY

'Timur Leng holding court', detail from a *Zafar-nama* manuscript, AH 872/AD 1467–8. The Central Asian ruler, who died in 1405, is shown surrounded by richly patterned tents, canopies and carpets. (Baltimore)

Today the Middle East is associated with the production of oil and petrochemicals, transported over vast distances to foreign consumers, but for centuries the region supplied Europe with silk, cotton and flax in raw or finished state, carpets, dyes and mordants, produced in the region or further afield. The historic – and financial – importance of this trade has left its mark in the languages of Europe. It may be obvious that 'cotton' comes from the Arabic *qutn* and 'taffeta' from the Persian *tafta*, but mohair and seersucker have similar antecedents: *mukhayyar* (Arabic: 'choice') and *shir-i shakar* (Persian: 'cream and sugar', referring to the fabric's colouring); whereas the fine quality of textiles produced in medieval Mosul and Damascus are commemorated in 'muslin' and 'damask'. Whenever we refer to a gala occasion, we are using the medieval Arabic word *khilʿa*, meaning a valuable honorific gift, usually consisting of a costly garment or rich fabric. Costume words were also adopted, such as 'sash', 'cummerband', 'chemise' (*shash*, *kumar-band*, *qamis* respectively) and 'caftan', as were some furnishing terms, for instance, mattress, divan and sofa, and the names for certain dyestuffs and colours: 'henna' from *hina*, 'crimson' from *qirmiz* and 'saffron' from *zaʿfaran*. Along with words technical and artistic ideas were exchanged as merchants and pilgrims, Christian, Jewish, Zoroastrian and Muslim, travelled through the Middle East to fulfil their obligations.

Any mention of the transportation of textiles through the Middle East evokes images of camel caravans travelling along the Silk Road. In fact there was no one 'road' from China to the east Mediterranean coast but two main routes, each with important branches. Few merchants travelled the complete length, which would have taken over two years. Instead they journeyed along a small section, buying and selling as they went. Trade along the Silk Road flourished from Han times (206 BC–AD 220) until the beginning of the tenth century, when disturbances in north-western China affected travellers' safety. There was a resurgence in the thirteenth to fourteenth centuries as Central Asia and Iran were brought under single regimes, but political insta-

13

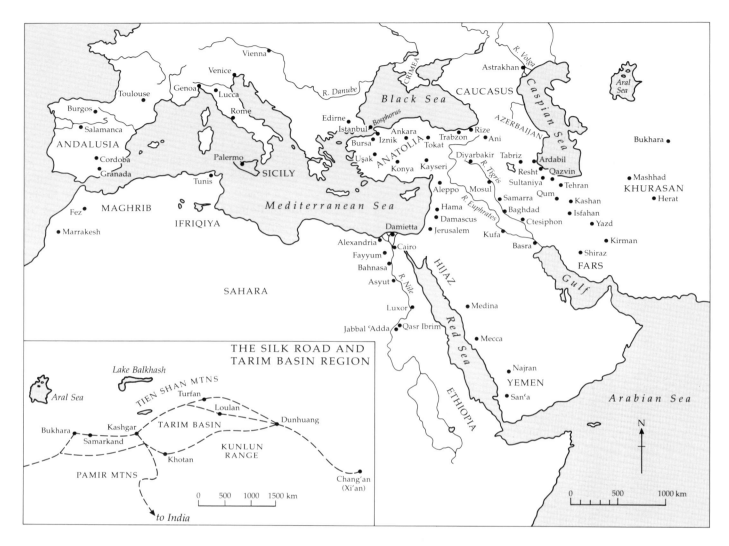

Map of the Islamic Middle East, with inset showing the Silk Road and Tarim Basin region.

bility in mid-fifteenth-century Iran again caused problems. The establishment of the Safavid regime (1501–*c.* 1735) largely rectified this, but Ottoman embargoes and Safavid discrimination against Sunni merchants in the 1680s resulted in trade caravans rerouted through Russia and Siberia.

Sea routes were also extensively used. Goods from the East were brought by sea (or along the Persian coastlands) to the Tigris and Euphrates, or alternatively to the southern coast of Arabia and up the Red Sea. By AD 1000 unrest in southern Iraq and hostility between the Baghdad and Cairo regimes caused most maritime trade to be diverted from the Gulf to the Red Sea, until the late fifteenth century when European merchants utilised the Portuguese 'discovery' of the Cape sea route.

Fabric production and trade dominated central and regional economies in the Islamic world for centuries. In the eighteenth century Cairo had lost most of its former mercantile importance, but still one-fifth of its artisans was involved in textile manufacturing and a quarter of shop-workers handled fabrics. Tributes in the early Islamic period were frequently paid in fabrics and clothing, and later regimes established profitable monopolies on raw materials like alum, silk and cotton. Official trade embargoes often included silk calculated to inflict maximum economic damage and sometimes other textiles. The sixteenth-century Ottoman sultanate, battling to control the Mediterranean, vainly tried to prohibit the sale of heavy cotton canvas to European merchants to forestall use on 'hostile' Italian sailing ships.

At court luxurious textiles and dress displayed the authority, prosperity and prestige of the regime, and so were frequently sent as diplomatic gifts between rulers. The acceptance of the *kiswa*, a special textile covering for the Ka'ba shrine, by the Meccan authorities publicly acknowledged the political predominance of the donor. Instead of handing out medals in recognition of service, the ruler generally bestowed gifts of clothing *(khil'a)*, whose value depended on the status of the recipient. Supporters of the regime were expected to wear a certain colour or item of dress, and neglect or refusal to do so signified withdrawal of allegiance. It was through dress that one gauged the wearer's social grade, profession and religious affiliation.

Textiles, it was believed, conveyed 'magical' powers. *Baraka* (blessings) were passed on by donning a garment of a saintly person, by possessing a fragment of it or, if possible, the Meccan *kiswa* or even a phial of the water used in its washing. Conversely curses could be effectively transmitted by concealing spells in the recipient's clothing.

Dress and furnishing fabrics were considered inflation-proof and always featured in trousseau lists, divorce settlements and wills. As one modern historian summed up: 'Cloth played the same part that automobiles and durable mechanical goods play today in the American middle-class standard of living' (Lapidus 1967, p. 31). The average Middle Eastern house until early this century was crammed with woven storage bags and sacks, mattresses, divans, cushions and pillows, rather than wooden furniture. Fabrics were extensively employed for insulation and as shields against dust and light. In a nomadic environment the actual dwelling was often textile: felt for the colder climates and woven goat-hair for warmer zones. In a courtly context tents were recognised as 'emblems of royal authority and luxury' (Ibn Khaldun, vol. 2), and commentators described the magnificent examples used to house the ruler and entourage on military campaigns, hunting trips, royal 'progresses' and audiences.

Every aspect of a Muslim's life is theoretically governed or guided by divine law, the *Shari'a*, and thus there is advice relating to dress, fabric and colour as well as guidelines on the issue of figural representation. But before exploring the relationship between textiles and Islamic law, it should be noted that five duties (the Five Pillars of Islam) are incumbent on every Muslim: the profession of faith, the performance of prayer, the giving of alms, fasting during the lunar month of Ramadan, and making the pilgrimage (*Hajj*) to Mecca at least once, if possible. The first duty is achieved by announcing with all conviction and sincerity the *shahada*, 'There is no god but Allah, Muhammad is the Messenger of Allah'. As the final Divine Revelation of Allah, the one, uncreated God, was communicated in Arabic to Muhammad (d. AD 632), this is the language of both the Quran and formal prayers. This Arabic formula when found on Muslim flags and prayer-mats represents a renewal of a personal and group commitment to the faith. Praying is carried out at certain times during the day, and while a prayer-mat or -rug is not essential it serves to define and isolate the space for the worshipper.

Of the other three Pillars the *Hajj* has always played an important role in

A *mahmal* (camel palanquin), late 19th century, used to convey the *kiswa*, historically the gift of the leading Muslim regime of the time, for the Ka'ba shrine to Mecca.

the dissemination of artistic, technical and philosophical information, but there are direct connections with textiles. Just prior to the *Hajj* season the old Ka'ba *kiswa* is replaced by a temporary white cover, cut up and distributed as mementoes for its *baraka*. The pilgrims themselves don special *ihram* dress at certain designated approaches to Mecca; this is worn for the rest of their visit.

For guidance a Muslim will turn to the Quran and then to the collections of the Prophet's pronouncements (*hadith*, generally translated as 'Tradition'); together these form the basis of Islamic law. The *hadith* was gathered and verified during the ninth century, and it is a responsibility of the ʿ*ulama* (Muslim theologians, jurists and teachers) to advise and adjudicate on the sometimes seemingly conflicting sayings. In the Sunni community there are four schools of legal interpretation: the Hanbali (prevalent in Saudi Arabia), the Maliki (Africa and South-East Asia), the Shafiʿi (Egypt and Syria) and Hanafi (Turkey and Central Asia).

Sunni *hadith* generally holds that all figural representations, human and animal, are proscribed. Considered as attempts to imitate the Creator in His work, they render the artist or designer liable to a terrible penalty on the Day of Judgement. Whether woven textiles are included in the proscription has been debated by the ʿ*ulama* through the centuries. In the early Islamic period figured fabrics were allowed, provided there was no aura of veneration (van Reenen 1990), but by the late fifteenth century the situation in the four Sunni law schools was as follows (Qastallani, vol. 8, p. 483):

> It is completely agreed that images are forbidden if they are in the round.
> And if they are on woven material, there are four judgements: [firstly,]
> the complete lawfulness according to the Tradition which declares 'except
> what is on woven material'; [secondly,] the absolute prohibition; [thirdly,]
> the lawfulness of them on cushions and the like, if the figures on the
> cushions are deformed and their heads are cut off; [lastly,] if they are
> not deformed it is unlawful and if they are in an inferior status [e.g. on
> the floor] they are allowed, but if they are hung they are prohibited.

The Shiʿi attitude (Paret 1968) takes into consideration the context and function of the textile, but in the past provided the textile was for domestic or active military use such patterns were generally acceptable.

There were similar discussions over silk. It is worn by the angels of Paradise (Quran, *sura* 76, v. 21) and so is 'meant for you in the Hereafter on the Day of Judgement' (Hanbali *hadith*), rather than to be enjoyed in this life: thus theologians prefer to wear other fabrics. Silk may be employed for men's wear, but the amount and positioning depend on the law school concerned. Hanafi interpretation, for instance, is generous in its view that garments may be made of pure silk, provided it is outer clothing, and indeed the royal robes of the Hanafi-guided Ottoman sultanate demonstrate how this provision was utilised. All four Sunni schools agree that silk mixtures (that is, silk warp and another yarn as weft) may be worn in battle, and indeed Maliki scholars allow such fabrics at all times. Three rulings advise against sitting or leaning on silk covers, but as Ottoman cushion velvets suggest, Hanafi interpretation permits the practice.

An aspect hardly ever considered is colour. White is considered in Islamic law as most fitting for Muslim men: according to Sunni *hadith*, 'Allah loves white clothes, and He has created Paradise white' (Dozy 1845, p. 6). With its associations of purity, brightness and loyalty it is the colour for *Hajj* and Muslim burial attire, except for those killed in battle who may be buried as they fell. The other colour associated with the angels and gardens of Paradise is green, and in time it came to be identified with the descendants of the Prophet and then as the colour of Islam. Eighteenth-century Europeans who were careless enough to wear green on the streets of Istanbul soon regretted it. As in the West, some hues have dual associations. Thus black, a sign of mourning and retribution particularly in the Shi'i Islamic world, is also considered powerful protection against the evil eye, as is turquoise-blue which since at least the fourteenth century has been a mourning colour in Central Asia.

Attitudes could and did change over time. In his youth the Prophet Muhammad had liked red but later he denounced it as Satan's colour, although his wife 'Aisha continued to wear it. In the late medieval Islamic world red was linked with Mars, the planet of war, blood, passion and love, and in both Seljuk and Ottoman convention it was the bridal colour; however, in Mamluk Egypt it was required dress for prostitutes. According to Sunni *hadith* yellow was worn by non-Muslims in the Prophet's lifetime, and so along with blue, red and black it was occasionally stipulated for outdoor dress of non-Muslims (*dhimmi*s). In eighth-century Islamic society yellow signified a hedonistic lifestyle, but 700 years later the wearing of yellow shoes was a privilege bestowed on certain Ottoman court officials.

Apart from the *'ulama*, who spoke out whenever they considered social and moral values were endangered by fashions, the ruler and his immediate household were deemed custodians and arbiters of good taste. Leaders such as the Egyptian Mamluk Sultan Qalawun (1280–90) were lauded in the chronicles for improving standards of (military) dress, and many actively encouraged textile workshops and established new ventures. Such patronage was seen as essential: if royal custom was withdrawn, decline in quality or even closure was considered inevitable. Some establishments had a specific courtly function, like the *tiraz* workshops discussed later, and if costly gold and silver thread was used in production, the work was closely supervised by high-ranking officials.

It was acknowledged that discerning taste was demonstrated by careful selection of specific brands of silks, linens and cottons for one's attire. Medieval etiquette advised against wearing contrasting strong tones and mixing fabrics of different textures, such as linen and cotton (al-Washsha in Serjeant 1972, p. 214).

Such advice carried no legal weight, but the local market inspector (*'amil al-suq* or *sahib al-suq*; later called *muhtasib*) saw that sumptuary laws were observed in public places. (Whether these regulations, stipulating the colour and type of fabrics and clothing to be worn in public by Muslims and non-Muslims (*dhimmi*s), were ever consistently enforced and with what impact has never been ascertained.) He watched for any flagrant violation of agreed practice (*hisba*) among traders and manufacturers. Two sales practices relating to textiles are prohibited in Islamic law: the *mulamasa* whereby merely touching the cloth made purchase compulsory; and the *munabadha*, or tossing the fabric to the customer before inspection, the act of catching being considered a binding commitment to buy. The *hisba* regulations were overwhelmingly concerned with quality and quantity control, and provide the modern

ABOVE Embroiderers working on the Ka'ba
kiswa. Since 1961 the *kiswa* has been produced in
Mecca. Quranic verses are reproduced in gold
and silver thread on black silk. Centuries earlier,
according to medieval writers, other colours
and fabrics were often employed.

LEFT Muslim pilgrims circumambulate the
kiswa-draped Ka'ba shrine. Male pilgrim dress
consists of two seamless lengths in any white
fabric except silk, one wrapped around the hips
and the other draped over the left shoulder.
There is no set requirement for female dress,
except that the face must be unveiled and, as
for men, back-less shoes are worn.

19

reader with intriguing insights into medieval tricks of the trade (Ibn al-Ukhuwwa, p. 43):

> Thread must be received [from the client] by weight for weaving and the cloth returned by weight, to avoid doubt. If it is claimed by the customer that the weaver has changed the thread and if he has a sample and the weaver declares it is the same, the muhtasib shall take them before persons of experience . . . If a man hires a weaver to weave a piece of cloth of certain dimensions and he weaves it differently . . . he deserves no hire [fee].

Dyers were reminded to charge only for dyestuff *actually* used, to work with permanent dyes and to record the owner's name on the cloth before dipping. The *muhtasib* was directed to check for tampering with yarn and textile bales – adding sand or water to increase the weight was a favourite ploy – and that the appropriate tax and quality seals were on each. He was empowered to reprimand publicly, and for subsequent misdemeanours to ban the culprit from operating and confiscate goods.

Merchants and craftsworkers had recourse to their guilds, which by the early fourteenth century had a distinct civic role (Floor 1975, Baer 1977). Apart from the training of apprentices, the awarding of journeyman status after training, and with the approval of 'masterpieces' the granting of 'master' titles and licences, the guild (*sinf*) offered its members protection on pricing, trading and competition, safeguarded technical knowledge, allocated essential materials, and maintained close contact with other guilds. In the small Ottoman town of Manisa, for instance, there were guilds for the cotton-yarn dealers, the weavers of fine cotton, and of coarser cloth, the fabric dealers, the dyers and the related guilds of the cap-makers, quilt-makers and tailors. The guild was responsible for collecting the various taxes (as on looms) and conveying members' anxieties to the central administration.

Under Islamic law spinners and weavers were classed alongside money-changers, tanners (and thus presumably some dyers), gold and silversmiths, singers and dancers: that is, their trade placed them in some ethical dilemma, say, exposure to ritually polluting stuffs (for example, the use of urine in tanning and the preparation of *ᶜasb* (ikat) fabrics). Conversely, the occupations of bleaching, tailoring and dealing in linen stuffs were highly commended by medieval Islamic philosophers. It is said that Khadija, the first wife of the Prophet, was a linen merchant.

It was understood that certain crafts required a greater level of skill than others. A block-printer was apprenticed for four years (Mukminova 1992), whereas a medieval trainee weaver was bound for four months. Nevertheless, the talent of individual weavers was recognised. Fourteenth-century *hisba* rules noted that a merchant should not pass off products from inferior looms as work of the superior workshop (Ibn al-Hajj in Serjeant 1972, n. 56, p. 46):

> Analogous to this is the case of a craftsman who is good at weaving, the public competing to put up the price of cloth attributed to him. So let him (the merchant) not sell anything manufactured by someone else as his work, even it be like it, or better.

Textile production was well established in the Arabian peninsula before the advent of Islam, wool, camel- and goat-hair being the staple yarns. Silk and linen were imported: silk from the Byzantine world, Iran and China, and linen from Egypt.

A bronze seal stamp, with foliated Kufic inscription (in reverse) naming the il-Khanid ruler Khudabanda Muhammad Uljaitu (r. 1304–17) and the *dar al-harir Abarquh* (silk workshop at Abarquh). Height 10 cm. (London, 765)

Wool

Although Sunni *hadith* records that the Prophet was first repelled by the strong smell of woollen garments, which incidentally suggests that potash washes to remove the natural lanolin were not then customary, wool (Arabic: *suf*; Turkish: *yün*; Persian: *pasm*) quickly became associated in the Islamic world with simplicity, honesty and piety. It was thus proper clothing for saintly theologians, just rulers and champions of the faith, perhaps lending its name to certain Muslim mystics: 'The Sufi is he that wears wool [*suf*] with purity of heart' (Abu ʿAli al-Radhbari in Nicholson 1906, p. 342).

For weaving the wool was usually carded, spun by distaff or wheel and

Shepherd cloaks drying outside the felt-making workshops of Afyon, western Turkey, 1992.

often plied, but there was a constant demand for felts. From the thick felts used for shepherds' cloaks, saddle-blankets and nomad *kibitka* ('yurt') tent covers to the very thin, they are made from sheep wool with some goat- and camel-hair. After bowing or beating to separate the fibres, the wool is scattered evenly over a reed matting, sprinkled with water and soap before being rolled up in the matting. The felt-makers then compress the roll with their feet or arms, or as in Afyon, Turkey, today primitive machinery is used. Decorative patterns are added by incorporating different-coloured wool threads or prepared felt shapes during the rolling process, or by sewing felt appliqués on to the finished surface. Finally the felt is rubbed smooth and washed to remove traces of soap.

Goat-hair

The fine underhair of the goat was always highly prized, as suggested by its Arabic name *mukhayyar* ('choice'). A particular favourite in sixteenth-century Istanbul (French 1972) was the costly moiré mohair cloth from Ankara (thus angora wool) and Kastamonu, while the raw wool and yarn were exported in quantity to Europe. The fine-quality *tirma* cloth was sought after by nineteenth-century Iranian ʿulama for their mantles, while the softest goat-hair was used for making Kirman shawls, which rivalled those of Kashmir.

21

بهانهٔ کتاب دیدن سخن می‌گفت و کتبی که در آن دکان بود یک یک پیکر

را از دست او می‌گرفتند و در پهلوی خود

ABOVE Detail from an Ottoman *Sur-name* manuscript, *c.* 1583, depicting members of the *kemha* fabric guild parading before the sultan in the Hippodrome, Istanbul. (Istanbul, H. 1344, f. 330b–331a)

'A scene in the bazaar (punishment of a book thief)', *Majalis al-ᶜUshshaq* of Husayn Bayqara, *c.* 1560 in Shirazi style, illustrates the sort of punishment meted out by a *muhtasib*. From ᶜAbbasid times, if not before, offenders wore a distinctive cap, known in Persian as the *kulah-i zangula*, or cap of bells. (Paris, suppl. Persan 775 f. 152v)

Cotton

Cotton (Arabic: *qutn*; Turkish: *pan(m)buk*; Persian: *pambah*) of some variety was being cultivated in the fourth century BC in the Gulf area, Ethiopia and Sudan, and the Levant. After picking, husking, deseeding and bowing, raw cotton was used for wadding (of quilts, mattresses and clothing). Spun on a distaff or wheel, it was then passed to yarn-twisters before going to the dyers and weavers. By the sixth century AD the eastern provinces of Iran were exporting large quantities to China, and with the spread of Islam cultivation began in Sicily and Iberia. Such scientific works as *Kitab al-Filaha* by Ibn Bassal (d. 1105) gave practical advice on growing (Lewis 1974, pp. 146–7):

> . . . watering should be stopped until it grows to the length of a finger or about a handsbreadth. Then it should be tended, pruned, straightened, and moved again and again, then watered, then singled and weeded, then watered, continuing this practice until the beginning of August. It should be watered every fifteen days. At the beginning of August watering should stop, for fear lest the plant go soft . . . giving no produce.

Egyptian and Syrian cotton production increased substantially after the tenth century, and then again in the mid-fourteenth century when farmers turned away from planting cereals, as consumption plummeted following severe outbreaks of the Black Death. Raw cotton was soon being exported in bulk to Italy and Spain, with Venice alone taking 8,000 bales (each weighing about 150 kg) in a good year. Woven cottons, too, found eager European customers until the French and English governments moved to protect their textile industries in the seventeenth century. Heavy import duties and much cheaper Indian chintzes meant Persian and Ottoman cottons could never compete on equal terms.

European preference for long-staple cotton in the early nineteenth century led to a temporary revival in sales. Cultivation quickly spread from Egypt through the Middle East, except in Iraq where local conditions favoured another variety. The twentieth century has witnessed active government support for cultivation and textile manufacture in Turkey, Iran and Central Asia, but in the latter inefficient pesticide and irrigation control has had disastrous environmental consequences for the Aral Sea region.

Linen

The cultivation of flax and trade in linen (Arabic: *qattan*; Turkish: *ketan*; Persian: *katan*) have long been associated with Egypt, the earliest-known fragment of Egyptian linen being datable to 5000 BC, although a recent archaeological find in Turkey indicates linen twining or weaving some 2,000 years earlier (*New York Times*, 13 July 1993). There were at least twenty-six varieties grown in medieval Egypt and south-east Iran. Other important centres were Tunis and Carthage in North Africa, Andalusia and Syria. However, excessive taxation in the early thirteenth century and later the withdrawal of royal patronage resulted in Egyptian production falling sharply in the post-medieval period and vast quantities of French linen flooding the market.

Planting of flax was carried out in April for harvesting a month or so later. The gathered flax stems were combed after drying, then soaked for ten to fourteen days to separate the hard core from the soft bast fibres. After re-drying, the bast fibres were recombed and spun.

Silk

Chinese histories record the smuggling of silkworms into the Tarim Basin region in AD 419, some 3,000 years after sericulture began in China, and indeed tenth-century Islamic historians write of silk production spreading westwards from that region. In or around AD 552, according to Byzantine chroniclers, silkworms were taken into Byzantine territory, hidden in the hollow walking-staffs of some travellers. Ten years later sericulture and silk-weaving became an Imperial monopoly, bringing mass unemployment to the silk-weavers of Tyre and Beirut. According to Arabic sources, the Persian silk-weaving industry was established by the Sasanian ruler Shapur, which could mean Shapur I (AD 240–72) or Shapur II (AD 309–79). An episode in the Iranian epic *Shah-nama* ('History of Kings') offers a clue: it tells how prosperity came to a city in south-west Iran after a magic worm was found in an apple by a girl. Putting it in her spindle-bag, she then completed twice her usual amount of cotton spinning that day. As she fed it, the worm grew as did her output, bringing wealth to the city. Attracted by such prosperity, Shah Ardashir (*c.* AD 226–40) captured the city only after pouring molten lead down the giant worm's throat, and of course silk-cocoon processing does involve heat in some form. Further tangential support for the earlier dating is a Diocletian edict of AD 301 which mentions Egyptian silk spinners and weavers.

Sericulture and silk-weaving spread with the Islamic conquests, moving, it has been argued, into Italy from Islamic Iberia in the early tenth century. Contemporary geographies and revenue returns suggest a surge in production from the thirteenth century until the Middle East virtually monopolised the silk trade with Europe. Then in the fifteenth century the development of water-power allowed Italian silk manufacturers to cut prices sharply, but they still preferred to use heavy Persian filaments for their warp, as reflected in such Genoese silk terms as *seta Ghella* (Gilan silk) and *seta Mazandroni* (Mazandaran).

By 1670 some 2.7 million kg of Persian silk were purchased by the East India Company alone, but political upheavals in the early eighteenth century and then outbreaks of the silkworm disease, pebrine, in the mid-1860s brought the Iranian industry to its knees. Disease-free eggs and some steam-driven spinning equipment were introduced, but by then European importers had found other sources.

Concerning Turkish production, Bursa in north-west Anatolia was a famous trading and weaving centre by 1504, producing over ninety quality silks. Sericulture in the region followed, and both production and weaving were important to the Ottoman economy for another three centuries. Then changes in dress in the early nineteenth century dramatically reduced domestic demand. Despite the introduction of machinery and certain protectionist measures, the industry never fully recovered. By 1913 only 6 per cent of local silk was being woven by the Bursa weavers.

Several Islamic commentators, such as al-Damiri (d. 1405), carefully studied the silkworm itself, reporting (Jayakar 1908, vol.1, p. 795):

> . . . it is fed on the leaves of the white mulberry-tree . . . until it becomes of the size of a finger, and changes (its colour) from black to white successively. This takes place mostly within the period of sixty days. It then begins to weave (a web) round itself, out of the substance it brings out from its mouth . . . the worm itself remaining confined in it for nearly ten days . . . if it is desired to have its silk, ten days after its finishing the process of weaving the cocoon, it is left in the sun for a day or part of a day, upon which it dies.

The cocoons could be covered in salt, so suffocating the pupa inside, or steamed but that required strict temperature control. They were then usually tossed into boiling water and sour milk (Wilson 1896), which facilitated reeling, removing the natural gum exuded by the silkworm. Three to eight filaments, each up to one kilometre long, were taken up at the same time either by hand-reels or more sophisticated reeling equipment. The filaments were then 'thrown' or stretched, before twisting and plying.

Metallic threads

For both weaving and embroidery gold and silver were used, with copper introduced in the nineteenth century. Wire was drawn from ingots and twisted around a fibre core of silk, linen or cotton to produce a pliable thread. It could also be beaten into flat leaf and gilded on to narrow strips of leather, animal gut or bark-paper to the same end; this method was probably introduced from China with the Mongol and Timurid conquests, from the thirteenth century onwards. Round wire and flattened 'foil' were also used but their relative inflexibility meant that these were generally 'laid' on to the surface of the textile and kept in place by binding warps, or by couching.

A silkworm. Kept in circular bamboo trays, the silkworms in Wuxi, China, are fed on mulberry leaves before they begin to form the cocoon.

An early eighteenth-century Persian administrative manual, the *Tadhkirat al-Muluk*, gives quite specific instructions regarding the quality of the metal for textile work (Minorsky 1943, p. 59):

> . . . gold used for plating [silver thread] is usually of 5 per cent. quality; when it is required that gold brocade (*zar-baft*) should be woven particularly rich in gold . . . the plating of the high quality is 10 per cent., and of the highest . . . 15 per cent.

Workshops utilising metallic threads were generally supervised by a court appointee, with rigorous security to prevent theft and illicit melting. This might also explain why tailors had to weigh the fabric as supplied, and then the finished garment, before the client.

Painting or stamping metallic pigments on to the fabric was used on certain Yemeni, Egyptian and Ottoman textiles, but no details are available on the precise method or methods employed.

Looms

In Islamic literature it was the third son of Nuh (Noah) who invented weaving and Idris (traditionally held to be the biblical Enoch) who first cut and sewed cloth into garments. According to Persian myth it was the second shah, Tahmuras, who introduced weaving, and his son, Jamshid, tailoring. For looms in this region the earliest pictorial evidence comes from pre-Dynastic Egypt (*c.* 5000–3100 BC), showing the horizontal loom with the warp lying tensioned parallel with the ground; the vertical type with the warp hanging at right angles to the ground was in use *c.* 1570–1070 BC.

The simple backstrap loom was undoubtedly employed throughout the Islamic world and is still used, particularly for domestic production of flat-weave rugs. It is not known when the single-heddle horizontal looms and band-looms (with a heddle supported on a tripod) were introduced, but certainly these have had a long history in the region. Such ground-pegged looms are often found in nomadic (pasturalist) groupings because they are easily dismantled, transported and set up, although uneven weave tension often results from such disruption.

Weir (1970) has noted that vertical looms, already rare in the 1930s, have now vanished from the Palestinian region. However, they may still be seen elsewhere in the Middle East, for example, in central Anatolia and central Asia, if only in carpet production. Often the warp is continuous, that is, passing round both upper and lower beams and, if required, over an intermediate beam placed well behind the frame, but usually the warps are fixed and wound round movable beams, permitting the unrolling and rolling of warps and length as work progresses. Medieval Egyptian sources mention a royal garment called a *badana*, which needed no further cutting or sewing once removed from the loom; this suggests a tubular weave, but the only concrete evidence is records of twentieth-century vertical 'tubular' looms in Syria and Palestine (Hald 1980).

Within this group the warp-weighted loom should be mentioned. It had no lower beam, the warp threads being tensioned by free-hanging weights; its disuse may be linked to growing use of cotton for the warp in early medieval times. Warp-weighting was also utilised with fixed frame horizontal looms for longer lengths; it is still found in the Levant region and in Iran (Weir 1970, Wulff 1966). On both the vertical and horizontal looms the weaver

Water-colour drawing of a Chinese drawloom, from 'Silk Culture and Manufacture', dating from the reign of Qing Emperor Kangxi (1662–1722). In modern Iran it is usual for the drawboy also to sit over the warp threads facing the weaver. (London, D. 1656–1904)

攀華
時態尚新巧
女工慕精勤
心手暗相應
照眼華紛紜
慇勤拋錦字
曲折續回文
更將無限思
織作雁背雲

could work in the tapestry-weave technique, used as early as the second millennium BC in Iran.

In the earliest looms interlacing of the warp and weft was done by hand, but in time mechanical means of separating the warp threads were developed to speed up the process of weaving. The new technology spread slowly across Asia, some regions being quicker to adopt and adapt it than others. Around the first millennium BC weft-patterned compound twill weaves (with a single set of warps) were being produced. The fixed frame horizontal loom with multiple heddles (or treadle loom) was employed in Egypt from the second century BC and thereafter throughout the Middle East, before appearing in Europe. As the south Caspian (Iran) term *pa-chah* ('foot-pit') for this type of loom suggests, the weaver sat on the floor with his feet in a pit operating the treadles. Again, the origins of the loom are unclear with textile historians suggesting both China and India.

The number of heddles or harnesses which can be fitted into the enclosed space is regulated by the size of the frame. The maximum which may be accommodated at any one time is about eighty, and some complicated repeat patterns require many more. The invention of the drawloom in or around the first century AD in China and/or Syria solved this problem. It speeded up the weaving operation of repeat-patterned textiles but entailed complicated pre-weave preparation. As required by the pattern design repeat, the warp was separated into small groups ('lashes') about three to six warp threads in each. While the weaver dealt with the treadles, throwing the weft and beating, an assistant, perched above the weaver, lifted and lowered groups (lashes) of pattern heddles into the frame as required. The system allowed intricate and detailed designs to be repeated quickly by calling down the relevant lashes. However, individual warp threads could not be selected; the French invention of the Jacquard mechanism around 1760 solved this problem.

Although the Islamic textile manufacturers were slow to exploit European eighteenth-century technology, the Jacquard system was imported by the mid-nineteenth century. The series of punched cards (each controlling a pattern harness) could be operated by a simple foot pedal, so making the drawboy redundant, yet allowing more intricate patterning and speeding up the making process. Its first use was confined to a few Ottoman state-controlled factories and certainly was not on the scale of Lyons's 18,000 looms working in 1812.

Mordants and bleaches

The most popular mordant in the Islamic world was alum (Arabic: *shabb*; Turkish: *şab*; Persian: *zaj*). Also used in tanning leather and felting, it worked well on silk and wool. For Iran, Anatolia and Egypt it was a valuable export commodity; in 1192 over 800,000 kg were sold by the Egyptian finance ministry which held the monopoly. Trade with Italy then declined, reportedly because Egyptian supplies were exhausted and the Genoese, in particular, turned to Anatolia, where Karahisar alone produced that amount every year. As substitutes, certain salts, such as iron and copper, and astringents containing a high level of tannic acid in the form of boiled liquor from turpentine, pistachio leaves and galls, or oak galls (known as Aleppo/Smyrna/Turkish galls and 'Dead Sea apples') could be used.

The mordant not only fixed the colour but allowed it to develop, and with additives gave a special tone. Thus pure alum with madder yielded a rich, fast red, but madder used with iron and alum resulted in a reddish-brown to blackish shade, with tin a pink, and with yoghurt a bright, brilliant red. Urine was used as a mordant solvent, but fabrics processed in this manner were considered somewhat impure. Thus the ⁿulama forbade newly-widowed women to wear ⁿasb (ikat) and any clothing dyed after weaving during this time of social seclusion (Lane 1874).

As the place-name Wadi Natrun suggests, the main supply of natron used for bleaching yarn came from this area between Cairo and Alexandria. Successive regimes controlled dealing to their advantage, selling in the late tenth century a *qintar* (62 kg) for 70 silver dirhams, at a basic cost of 2 dirhams.

Dyes

The cost of quality dyestuffs was high so, as *hisba* literature records, dyers were always tempted to substitute cheaper, inferior ones. Much of the dyeing process remained a guild secret, frustrating European traders (Hakluyt 1903), although they could glean basic information from Islamic pharmaceutical texts. The central regime at times actively supported the craft, so indicating its importance to the economy. Founding Ramla (Syria), the Umayyad Caliph Sulayman (715–17) first saw to the palace plans and then to the construction of the *Dar al-Sabbaghin* (Dye Workshop). Similarly, Rashid al-Din (d. 1318), the great administrator of the il-Khanid dynasty, established a dye-house as well as a mint, paper-making works and a weaving establishment.

European synthetic coal-tar ('aniline') dyes were introduced in the second half of the nineteenth century and soon were extensively used along with later chemical dyestuffs. At first the dyes were very fugitive but new shades entered the repertoire, varying from 'muddier' tones to vivid fluorescent hues in more recent years. At the same time the custom of dyeing small quantities as required was largely replaced by the processing of large quantities of industrially spun yarn (that is, regular thickness), so minimising subtle colour variations in the yarn.

Few pre-Islamic and Islamic textiles have been submitted to chemical analyses, but texts suggest certain dyes were extensively employed. Indigo (Arabic: *nil*; Turkish: *çivit*; Persian: *rang-i kirmani*, 'colour of Kirman province') was the preferred blue dye, grown in Yemen, Egypt, Palestine and Iran in three main varieties. Locust root was also used but *hisba* literature warned that its colour was inferior and fugitive. As for woad, sales declined dramatically in the medieval period. When indigo is combined with either henna or iron vitriol, a deep black is obtained. No mordant is needed. Ground leaves from *Indigofera tinctoria* are fermented in water overnight, then sieved out. The yarn or filament is immersed in the colourless liquor which when exposed to the air oxidises forming the blue indigotin. This very chemical reaction posed problems for block- and *qalam*-printers (*qalam*: pen) until the mid-eighteenth century.

Cultivation of indigo yielded a high return with harvesting every hundred days, but as irrigation required skill, costs were high. As late as the second quarter of the nineteenth century indigo growing in Egypt was under state control, bringing valuable revenue into government coffers, but large amounts still had to be imported from the Yemen and India to satisfy the constant demand.

Indigo dyer in Bait Abud,
Yemen, 1983.

The best-quality red dye came from three species of the insect *Coccus* genus: the *Kermo-coccus vermilio*, *Coccus ilicis* and *Porphyrophora hameli*, the first two living on two kinds of oak and the latter on *Dactylis litoralis* grass, found in the Caucasus. All were used extensively for silk-dyeing, and all were confused with each other in medieval Islamic literature. This ninth-century description links *qirmiz* dye with a worm (Persian *kirm*) (al-Jahiz in Serjeant 1972, p. 65, slightly amended):

> They claim that qirmiz is a grass in the root of which there is a red worm
> . . . Nobody knows this grass and [exactly] where it is to be found,
> except a sect of Jews who have charge of collecting it every year in . . .
> [the twelfth solar month].

Madder (Arabic: *fuwwa*; Turkish: *kizilkök*; Persian: *runas*), the dried crushed roots of *Rubia tinctorum*, was grown from Central Asia to Iberia and exported in quantity to India. It took three years for the plant to mature. For a good deep red on cotton or linen the material had to undergo repeated soakings in olive oil and alum/soda, and 'ageing' processes before the madder bath, while block-printing required careful cleaning with animal dung and water. Quicker and easier to use was cinnabar from Zanzibar giving an orange-red tone; henna and Brazil-wood were other cheap but fugitive alternatives. Incidentally, the term 'scarlet', meaning red-dyed woollen cloth, perhaps originates from the Arabic *siqlatun* (Persian: *saqallat*; Latin: *sigillatus*). In the eleventh-century Islamic world it usually referred to a silk, heavily patterned with a blue or, in Spain, red ground, and this earlier meaning is often forgotten by modern commentators on medieval sources.

All yellow dyes (and thus most greens) tended to be fugitive. The best-quality yellow tone came from saffron (Arabic: *za῾faran*; Turkish: *safran*; Persian: *za῾fran*), but its high cost despite being watered down 500,000 times consigned its use to expensive silks. Far more widespread were the dyes obtained from turmeric, sumac, pomegranate rinds, safflower (*Carthamus tinctorius*, known as dyer's saffron) and larkspur, barberry, vine-leaves and, particularly from the Yemen, *wars* (*Memecylon tinctorum*).

Double dyeing with first yellow (often buckthorn berries or larkspur flowers) and then indigo gave a wide range of green tones, with the cost of the two dyebaths and the dyestuffs reflected in the final price. Both buckthorn and larkspur in certain combinations yielded green tones when used in a one-dye bath process, as did the Persian *banafsh* (probably the *Viola odorata*).

Pattern dyeing and printing

The technique which entails covering the designated areas of fabric with wax, gum or clay paste which 'resists' or rejects the mordant or dye colour has been found on fragments of wool, and also linen, thought to be Egyptian of the second century BC and fifth to sixth century AD respectively. Perhaps the process was not extensively employed in the early Islamic world, but at least one late tenth-century world map was produced with wax and dyes on Egyptian *dabiq* (probably linen) cloth (Serjeant 1972, p. 140).

A resist technique found throughout the Middle East is tie-dyeing, as seen in so-called ikat (from the Malay) fabrics of medieval Yemen and later Central Asia, Syria and Turkey. Known as *abr(ant)* (Uzbeg: 'cloud') and *῾asb* (Arabic), most Middle Eastern examples are made by tightly wrapping warp threads, although some weft- and a few double- (weft and warp) ikats are known. In

ABOVE Fragment of silk plain weave, printed in the *jiaxie* technique, thought to be 8th-century Tang manufacture from Dunhuang, Tarim Basin. Similar textiles featuring Islamic design elements, probably dating from the 8th to the 10th centuries, have survived. (London, OA MAS 876)

the mordant/dyebaths the bound parts remain unaffected so the process of untying and wrapping different sections for the various colours can be repeated as wished. At the loom the tie-dyed warps are painstakingly adjusted as the design requires, for it is these (in this context) that create the finished patterned appearance. Resist-sewing or -tying finished cloth, although found, never achieved the same popularity in the Middle East as in India.

Neither did another pattern-dyeing method, known in China as the *jiaxie* technique, although several silk fragments have survived, including some from the Silk Road Tarim Basin region. In this process layers of cloth are clamped between two carved wooden boards, punctured with small pluggable holes for each individual pattern section. The relevant mordant for the dye is poured through and out of each section before that particular dyebath, and the process repeated as necessary; or if the dyes allow, the fabric is prepared with a common mordant bath, and then one by one the dyes are dripped through the relevant sections of the clamp-boards.

The first undisputed Chinese examples of woodblock-printing (on paper) are of the early eighth century (Tsien 1985), although blocks have been found in a second-century BC tomb context (Riboud in Eastwood 1990). Prints, again on paper, from the Islamic world date from AD 900, but inks not dyes were used on these. Most medieval printed cottons found in Egypt are classified as Indian (Pfister 1938; Gittinger 1982; Eastwood 1990), but it is known that printing blocks were used in the Mamluk territories at least as early as the fourteenth to fifteenth century and were in extensive use throughout the Islamic world from the seventeenth century. Typically, the craftsworker uses a brush, pen (*qalam*) or stamp to supply a mordant to specific areas, which will then retain the dye colour in the post-dye wash. When completed, the fabric is immersed into the relevant dyebath, washed to remove surplus dye, and then the whole process is repeated as many times as different colours require.

Embroidery

The vast and rich variety of Islamic embroidery has been largely ignored by art historians. From one end of the Islamic world to the other decorative stitching was used to embellish the surface of small items of personal clothing to enormous furnishing lengths. On one level it was always cheaper to make or purchase embroidery than a patterned silk; on another it offered the worker complete freedom of creativity, whereas a drawloom weaver was constrained by the pattern lashes. Medieval documents record that commercial (male) embroiderers were lowly paid, and even in early twentieth-century Iran payment was calculated solely on the difference in weight between the fabric as received and on completion. Male embroiderers became increasingly associated with luxury gold and silver work, as on the prestigious Meccan *kiswa*, presumably because the close (male) supervision required for the bullion prevented Muslim women being employed in such workshops. Until recently in Central Asia it was believed that women embroiderers 'polluted' metal thread. In this context it is interesting to note that US research into nuclear production found women workers during menstruation excreted acids through the palms of their hands.

Despite commercial work receiving such poor financial recognition, the gift of a personally embroidered item was taken as a great honour. Thus the Persian term *tarazidan* ('to embroider') was adopted to describe the courtly honorific decorative bands (*tiraz*) worked on clothing and other fabrics of the early medieval period. Today quilted and embroidered (now often machine-work) coverlets are still considered important embellishments of both the circumcision and marriage beds.

Distinguishing commercial work with domestic embroidery is wellnigh impossible, and rarely can work be assigned securely to a region. Confusion in stitch terminology, past and present, raises other problems, and even with magnification to inspect the front *and the back* of the fabric the exact stitch variation and combination may be difficult to identify.

2

EARLY ISLAMIC PERIOD I
TEXTILES AS TRIBUTE

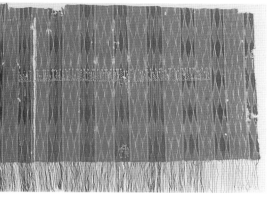

ABOVE Cotton plain-weave warp ikat (reverse), early 10th century, Yemen. Both warp and weft are of z-spun cotton, while the embroidery thread is two-plied, s-spun. Its fringed edge suggests use as a shawl or waist-sash. 45 × 74 cm. (Washington, DC, 73.213)

OPPOSITE Silk plain weave, 9th–10th century. Perhaps *Abu Qalamun* fabrics looked like this. The cream ground has been transformed with tiny woven details (by 'flying shuttle'?) in six colours of silk. Red- and also yellow-gold wrapped round silk cores are extensively used. Although fragments of this were acquired in Egypt, one art historian argues for Baghdad production. 16.8 × 10.5 cm. (Cleveland, 50.526)

The history of the early Islamic period is complex, but as some textile inscriptions and patternings, often designed and made centuries later, allude to events in this period, it may be useful to highlight certain episodes. On the Prophet's sudden death in AD 632, one of his close companions was elected by the elders to act as caliph (*khalifa*: 'deputy') to lead the community, and this procedure was followed three more times. These first four caliphs are known as the Rashidun (Rightly-Guided) caliphate, and under their leadership substantial territorial inroads were made into Byzantine Syria and Egypt, and Sasanian Iraq and Iran. Their names are proudly recorded on many later military flags.

The selection of ᶜAli, the cousin and son-in-law of the Prophet, as the fourth caliph in AD 656, was disputed by the governor of Syria, Muᶜawiya of the Umayyad family. On ᶜAli's assassination in 661 he assumed the caliphate, which then remained in his family until AD 750. These events marked a break within the Muslim community, with the supporters of ᶜAli (*shiᶜat ᶜAli*: the party of ᶜAli) on one side and those who accepted Muᶜawiya as caliph on the other. The Shiᶜis believed then as now that the Prophet had transferred spiritual and temporal authority to ᶜAli and his descendants through his wife Fatima, one of Muhammad's daughters; thus textiles which carry inscriptions proclaiming the importance of ᶜAli and Fatima are associated with Shiᶜi communities. Those Muslims who accepted Umayyad rule maintained that the prophetic succession ended with Muhammad, and that they (Sunnis as they became known) were acting in accordance with the *sunna* (example) of the Prophet.

Under the Umayyads (661–750) these boundaries were pushed forward along the North African coastline and deep into the Iberian peninsula, and in the east to the borders of the Chinese Empire. With tribute pouring into the state coffers the caliphal court increasingly adopted Byzantine and Sasanian ceremonial and, as will be seen, drew heavily on established artistic repertoires for design and patterning.

35

Beset by intertribal disputes and severe unrest in the eastern provinces, the Umayyad regime was ousted by the ʿAbbasid family, but a survivor set up court in Islamic Iberia. Umayyad rule continued there until 1013 and in time the North African Almoravid dynasty (1070–1146) took control. Authority then passed to the Almohad family and then the Nasrid dynasty in southern Spain (1239–1492).

Meanwhile, the ʿAbbasid regime quickly transferred the state administration from Syria to Iraq, founding and finally settling in Baghdad. With the move into former Sasanian territory, the influence of Iranian culture grew at court. Trade and industry particularly in textiles flourished, and science and technology developed apace. But within a century the western provinces had broken away, and in the eastern regions powerful hereditary governorships paid only nominal allegiance to the ʿAbbasid caliph. From 945 the Shiʿi Buyid family was the power behind the throne until replaced in 1055 by the Seljuk tribal confederation, Sunni in persuasion. Originally from Central Asia, the Turkic-speaking Seljuk leaders in Iran extended their influence westwards and into Anatolia after defeating the Byzantine army in 1071. It was into this political arena that the Crusaders marched. However, the Muslims feared the graver threat from the east; in 1258 the Mongols stormed Baghdad and forced the ʿAbbasid caliph into exile.

As Islam spread, communities and regions entered into agreements with the Prophet and his successors, which specified the taxes and tribute payable in return for protection and assistance. One of the first involved the Jews and Christians in southern Arabia who contracted to send textiles made in Najran in part payment, and this arrangement continued into early ʿAbbasid times. Whether these celebrated striped fabrics of southern Arabia resembled in any way a special Yemeni textile called *washi*, avidly collected by several Umayyad caliphs, is not known.

The Arabic word *washi* has several meanings, from the abstract ('decorative' and 'patterned') to the specific ('worked with embroidery'). The royal passion for this textile continued well into the ʿAbbasid period with the legendary Caliph Harun al-Rashid leaving some 4,000 *washi* garments on his death in 809. However, its precise character and appearance remain unclear, although we know it was also manufactured at Kufa, Alexandria and Herat. Textile historians generally accept Lamm's suggestion (1937) that *washi* was silk, linen or cotton patterned in an ʿasb or ikat technique, and indeed several ninth- to eleventh-century ikat fragments have survived, the earliest so far known dated 270 AH/AD 883–4, made in Sanʿa.

Textiles from Coptic lands

Egypt sent tribute in the form of robes (*jubba*s), Coptic tunics (*qibti*s), cloaks (*burnus*) or turban cloths (*ʿimama*s) and shoes. Its linen and wool fabrics had long been highly prized, and two Rashidun caliphs continued the pre-Islamic custom of draping the Kaʿba shrine with Egyptian fabrics, as did the Umayyad caliph Muʿawiya (661–80).

Well over 20,000 textile fragments, perhaps as many as 100,000, in public and private collections are classified as 'Coptic'. Most are decorative medallions or bands, cut from linen (or wool) tunics (dalmatics), which sometimes had as many as eleven of these patterned units. The tunic was typically constructed in one piece, woven from one sleeve edge to the other, so that

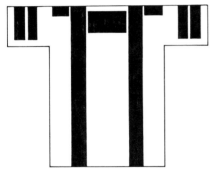

A schematic diagram showing one of four main pattern banding distributions found on Coptic tunics.

when folded the warp ran horizontally and the decorative woollen bands in dovetail tapestry weave fell vertically. According to an early fifth-century Syrian bishop, customers chose and could design the decorative patterns: certainly the subject-matter is extremely varied. Some have a religious connection, featuring Coptic crosses, figures of saints, worshippers in the *orans* posture. Others draw on Classical Mediterranean mythology with depictions of Orpheus, the Judgement of Paris, Dionysus, and so on. Animal and bird forms amid sturdy vegetal scrolls were popular, and there was clearly a fashion for interlaced knots and plaits with no figural representation.

Earlier in the twentieth century it was assumed such textile production ceased with the Islamic conquest of Egypt in AD 641, but by the 1960s it was realised this theory was untenable and that manufacture was not necessarily confined to Egypt. Only a handful may be firmly dated or securely provenanced, and few have been scientifically analysed. Recent research (Carroll 1988, De Moor 1993) has shown the importance of considering weave details and dye materials as well as iconography. In itself stylisation or total absence of figural motifs does not prove manufacture immediately post-conquest, for the Muslim proscription on the representation of living forms was formulated around a century later (van Reenen 1990). Stylisation of motifs might simply indicate provincial production or a less expensive range. Any connection with Byzantine iconoclasm is unlikely as Egyptian and Syrian theologians were generally unsympathetic to Constantinople, especially after the unpopular appointment of Cyrus (630–40) as Byzantine patriarch in Egypt (Carroll 1988). In similar vein it cannot be assumed that the presence of classical motifs means the fragment predates AD 392, when the Byzantine Emperor banned all pagan rituals and performance, nor that Sasanian motifs in the pattern necessarily prove manufacture during the brief Persian occupation of Egypt (619–27/8).

The ground colour of the tunics varies considerably from bleached cream through to red-orange. This vibrant colour may relate to Islamic sumptuary regulations, defined in the reign of al-Mutawakkil (847–61), which required non-Muslims to wear honey-coloured garments in public. In this context it is interesting that the Arabs referred to Byzantines in the early years as the *Banu al-Asfar* (*banu*: clan, people; *asfar*: safflower red or yellow).

The typical weave for the tunics and associated hangings was plain weave with a s-spun warp but examples survive of 'loop-pile', in which the main or supplementary weft has been pulled up to form loops. (Velvet is produced by warp loops.) This technique is found in a range of fabrics, from fine lightweight work to heavy-duty coverings. Perhaps the medieval Arabic word *mukhmal* (meaning 'velvety') used to describe wiping napkins referred to this.

It is thought a vertical loom, up to 3 m in width, possibly warp-weighted, was generally used in Egypt. If so, perhaps the dovetail tapestry weave was deliberately employed instead of slit weave because it added no extra strain on the vertical warp, and this may explain why cotton and silk warps are never extensively found in early Islamic Egyptian textiles: neither would have withstood heavy up/down beating and the pull of the warp-weights. Archaeological work at the early seventh-century Monastery of Epiphanius, Luxor, revealed evidence of treadle pit-looms, but the suggestion that certain woollen fragments from fifth-century Egypt were made on a drawloom is contested in some quarters.

Coptic woollen tunic, 8th–9th century. Recent dye analyses reveal that the deep red-orange colour of this tunic and some other related fragments was produced by weld and madder dyes. (Manchester, T.8358)

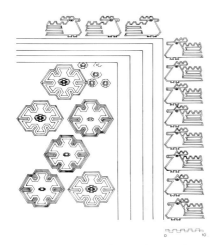

Pattern diagram of one of several carpet fragments, *c.* 10th century, found at Qasr Ibrim, Upper Egypt. The undyed cream wool warp is z-spun, two-ply s-twist, and the undyed weft is also z-spun. The z-spun wool pile in five colours is formed by the so-called 'Spanish' knot. Largest piece 38 × 90 cm. (London, EA T.29)

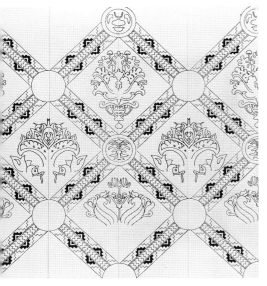

Pattern reconstruction by Ellen Levine of a silk twill, late 8th century, possibly of Syrian manufacture. Some silks with similar motifs or compositions have been assigned an Iranian provenance. (Cleveland, 51.91)

As far as is known, the Islamic conquest resulted in neither major resettlement nor conversion of the weavers. However, it cannot be said that their craft was respected. An early ninth-century Christian patriarch recorded the desperate plight of the linen-weavers of Coptic Tinnis in the Nile Delta (Serjeant 1972, p. 138):

> Although our earning is not sufficient for the bread of our mouths we are taxed for tribute and pay five [gold] dinars a head in taxes. They beat us, imprison us, and compel us to give our sons and daughters as securities. For every dinar they have to work two years as slaves.

Despite the hardship, business evidently flourished because by the eleventh century there were 50,000 weavers in Tinnis alone (Lombard 1978).

Tribute from the eastern lands

Carpets and other (floor?) coverings were accepted as tribute in the early Islamic period. During the reign of al-Mamun (813–17), for instance, sixty thick coverings (*fursh*, perhaps felts) from Tabaristan, twenty carpets (*bisat*) from Armenia, and 120 from Tunisia were dispatched with other textiles and cash to Baghdad. Their excellent quality and pleasing appearance are praised but not described in the texts, and the few fragments found as emerging from various Silk Road sites are too small for any reconstruction of their overall patterns. One piece, from around the late third to fourth century AD, has seven colours making up the long wool pile, twisted around single warp threads, the so-called 'Spanish knot'.

Cut looped pile was used in sixth-century Iran as shown in cream (undyed) wool remains excavated at Shahr-i Qumis (Kawami 1991). It is unlikely that this technique produced the most renowned Sasanian carpet, seized from the Ctesiphon royal audience hall in 21 AH/AD 642 and subsequently cut up and dispersed. Known as the Spring of [Shah] Khusrau, it depicted a garden with plants and water channels, decorated with pearls as well as gold and silver (? thread). Possible evidence of Umayyad carpet design is a floor mosaic at the Khirbat al-Mafjar complex, Jordan, built probably in the 740s: a tasselled fringe edges a semicircular composition of a leafy tree sheltering a couple of grazing antelopes on one side and witnessing a lion attack on the other.

Recently scientific analysis has yielded a calibrated dating of AD 795–1052 (Crowfoot, forthcoming) for fragments of a wool carpet found with tenth-century textiles in a Coptic burial context during the Qasr Ibrim excavations, Upper Egypt. A row of robotic-like birds guards a natural-coloured field scattered with large, flattened rosette forms.

Tribute from the northern and eastern regions was also paid in silk. The multiplicity of terms used in the early Islamic period reveals the rich variety of patterns, colourings, qualities and types of silks available, but the precise meanings are far from clear. A popular silk, *dibaj*, produced in various weights, is known from a late twelfth-century description as being (*EI*[1], 'Dibadj', slightly amended):

> . . . beautifully dyed. The [pattern] designs on which are neatly arranged, the silk fine and the structure compact, the colour shining, the weight heavy and which had remained free from the traces of fire during the process of smoothing (*fi jandaratihi*). The poorest quality is that which possesses the opposite qualities.

Perhaps it was a generic term for any highly patterned silk twill.

The 'Marwan' silk compound twill, mid-8th century, North Africa. One main and two pattern warp (z-twist), and pattern weft (no discernible twist) in four colours, it has a yellow split-stem-stitch inscription detailing the place of production as Ifriqiya, and the Umayyad Caliph Marwan. (London, 1314–1888 and T.13–1960)

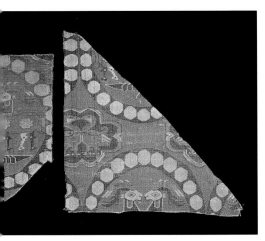

Two pieces of a silk compound weave thought to be 8th century, Tang, found in Dunhuang, Tarim Basin, with the 'pearl' roundel pattern inhabited by confronting gazelles. (London, OA MAS 862 a and b)

Judging from extant pieces generally classified as Iranian, or Syrian and occasionally Egyptian, three pattern compositions dominated in this early period. One consists of a simple repetitive device, perhaps a quatrefoil or heart-shaped motif. Another is based on a lozenge grid, sometimes containing stylised palmette forms. But of the hundred or so weft-faced silks (and a few toothed tapestry-woven wool examples) classified as Sasanian and post-conquest Persian, c. AD 600–800, over half are patterned with 'pearl' beaded roundels often framing a single or paired animal or bird form, arranged in rows sometimes with stylised floral interstices. The animal or bird is frequently shown with a 'flying scarf' around its neck, thought to indicate royal ownership. The early Arabic term al-Khusrawani ('of the [Shah] Khusrau') perhaps described this composition, but the medieval Persian parand and parniyan specifically meant silks decorated with pearl roundels, woven in eastern Turkistan (Chirvani 1991).

The roundel pattern was associated with court dress throughout Asia for many years, as seen decorating royal garments on the Sasanian Taq-i Bustan bas-reliefs, Kirmanshah; on the seventh-century Afrasiab murals (Uzbekistan); and within a Tang painting recording a 641 Imperial audience of a Tibetan envoy. It had wide currency in the Islamic world. Besides featuring on the so-called Marwan silk it appears on kingly garments depicted in an Umayyad wall-painting at Qusayr ʿAmra, and later on murals from the ʿAbbasid Samarra palace complex, Iraq, before passing into early Islamic metalwork, church wall decoration at Ani (eastern Turkey), and textiles of Byzantium and Islamic Iberia.

The silk robe (Hermitage Museum, St Petersburg) excavated in the Caucasus, a region known for dibaj weaving, proves such fabrics were indeed used for garments, and its assigned dating c. 750 to 850 is supported by inscriptions on the related Marwan II textiles mentioned above and in the next chapter. On some silks extra linear elements are shown on animal haunches and bird wings, and links or 'jewelled clasps' appear to join the pearl roundels. As such details feature in the seventh-century Afrasiab murals, it suggests manufacture around this time (Bier 1978). Also it is thought the grouping of the binding warp in threes in some fragments indicates late Sasanian production (*E. Iran.*, 'Abrisam'). However, the most secure dating evidence is found with similar weft-faced, compound twill silks with roundels found in sealed Chinese tombs in the Tarim Basin region, from AD 653 to 663 (Meister 1970, Riboud 1977).

If it is difficult to date these silks precisely, identifying their provenance is more problematic. One piece in the Victoria and Albert Museum, London, has been reassigned at least four times since the 1940s. Such silks were made throughout Asia from China to Byzantium for centuries, and although a 1930s study (Ackermann repr. 1964) confidently designated fragments to some seven Iranian weaving centres, classification continues to be based on stylistic details and colouring rather than on detailed technical and structural analyses.

Occasionally the textile itself carries the information required. One dark blue twill silk from a Belgian church reliquary has an ink inscription in a seventh-century hand, identifying it as Zandaniji work (Shepherd and Henning 1957), and indeed medieval Zandana, near Bukhara, was famous for its cottons and patterned silks for over three centuries. With a pattern clearly based on the 'pearl' roundel composition, enclosing confronting horned 'rams' either side of a stylised tree, this large fragment has several distinctive technical features perhaps exclusive to Zandana production.

Other early Islamic textiles were known by their place of manufacture. The district of al-ʿAttabi in ʿAbbasid Baghdad lent its name to the fabric ʿattabi, and in turn to the English words tabby (plain) weave and tabby cat. It was probably a silk taffeta, striped like a zebra according to one text, or to another with subtle ripple markings like a damascene sword, which suggests a moiré appearance. It was in such demand that similar fabrics were soon produced elsewhere in the Islamic empire but no examples seem to have survived.

Individuals, such as the ʿAbbasid caliph al-Mutawakkil (d. 861), also gave their name to fabrics (Masʿudi 1984, p. 234):

> Everyone wished to imitate his dress, so lengths of this [Mutawakkili]
> material fetched high prices and the technique of producing it was
> perfected . . . A few pieces are still to be found . . . a kind of *mulhama*
> cloth, very beautiful, finely woven and of a very good colour.

But what was *mulham*? Al-Mutarrizi in the mid-twelfth century defined it as a fabric with a silk warp and wefts of another yarn. This had led modern historians to identify plain-weave fragments with silk-floss warp and cotton weft as *mulham*, although al-Mutarrizi did not specify cotton, and other silk mixtures have survived.

From the Geniza documents of medieval merchants (Goitein 1967, vol. 1; Stillman 1972) alone we learn there were twelve kinds of silks all differently priced, and Serjeant (1972) in his preliminary study collected some 160 terms. Pattern terminology is just as rich and confusing. There were at least four different (but in what way?) striped fabrics such as *habar*, *makhtut ʿalayha*, *muzannar* and *jari al-qalam*. Materials decorated with circles and spots like copper or gold coins, the eyes of wild birds and animals, were extremely popular, judging just by the abundance of names found in the literature.

It was a period when metallic lustred ceramics and glass were fashionable in Islamic society. As possessing gold utensils ran counter to ᶜulama advice and rendered the owner liable to tax (Cooper 1973), the various gold-decorated textiles (for example, *mudhahhab*, *mufassal*, *mawzun*) could have been attractive alternatives for the wealthy to enjoy in a booming economy.

One famous Egyptian fabric called *Abu Qalamun*, but also known as *bu qalamun*, *buqalimun* and *qalamun*, was said to have had a particularly dazzling appearance 'treasured by all the kings of the earth' (Ibn Zawlaq writing *c*. 1000 in Serjeant 1972, p. 145). The eleventh-century traveller Nasir-i Khusrau likened its sheen to lustred ceramics, and earlier writers had compared it to the 'fire' of opals, or iridescent plumage (Baker 1991). Certain surviving dress-weight silk fragments do indeed have such a shimmering quality.

There is another possibility. Perhaps *Abu Qalamun* was, as Maqdisi (tenth century; Serjeant 1972) stated, byssus or sea-wool. Off the shoreline of southern Spain and North Africa the mollusc *Pinna marina* was harvested for its fine, silk-like 'beard' which was then woven into dress fabric worth 100 gold dinars a garment in the mid-tenth century, or even ten times that by the closing years of the century, about three months' salary for a doctor. ᶜUmari witnessed divers at Safaqus, south of Tunis (Serjeant 1972, p. 197):

> . . . bring[ing] out tubers like onions with a kind of neck which has hairs on the upper part. These tubers like onions, burst, and let forth hairs (threads) which are combed and become like wool. They spin it and make a weft of it so as to pass a warp of silk through it. They make checked (*mukhattam*) stuff or stuff without checks.

However, if the modern reader is confused by the plethora of terms, medieval Islamic society was not. A late tenth-century commentator noted that 'people used to compete with each other in trafficking in these garments; they would seek to acquire in trade the various types of fabrics and would describe to each other the different varieties of them' (al-Thaᶜalibi in Bosworth 1968, p. 97). The attire of a tenth-century Baghdad man of culture included over twenty types of textiles, products of specific weaving centres across the empire, from Lower Egypt, southern Arabia and Iran to the eastern borders. Along with his garments he would carefully select his *mandil* (kerchief) from Yemen, Egypt, Iraq or Iran, to be worn in the belt or held in the hand. Used for wiping, it was made of silk or linen, sometimes with a velvety texture. The most expensive Egyptian ones were 'like the inner membrane of an egg' and 'softer than the zephyr', costing as much as a complete garment. Although often white, the *mandil* could be coloured and embellished with gold borders, fringes, embroidery or painted inscriptions (Rosenthal 1971, p. 93):

> I am the *mandil* of a lover who never stopped
> Drying with me his eyes of their tears.
>
> Then he gave me as a present to a girl he loves
> Who wipes with me the wine from his lips.

Although *adab* (etiquette) literature was scornful of brightly coloured attire, commercial documents reveal that the public's appetite for colour was insatiable. Exact fabric shades were specified, such as 'pistachio green', 'Egyptian onion purple' and 'African thigh black'.

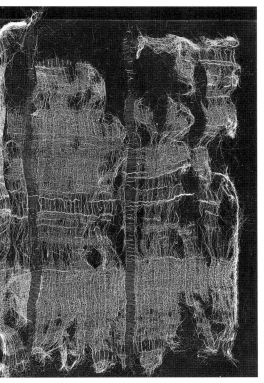

Plain-weave fabric, assigned to 11th century. Possibly byssus and silk fabrics have similar fine quality. The stripes are formed by a brown metal (? tarnished silver) carried on an s-twist silk core; the warp and weft have no discernible twist and cannot be visually identified as silk. 28.6 × 13.9 cm. (London, 8230–1863)

Fragment of a silk weft-faced compound twill, probably 6th–8th century. Over the last forty years the provenance of this piece has been reassigned four times. The main and binding warp are z-twist, while the weft has no discernible twist. It has been argued that early Central Asian silks are distinguished by the use of floss, gummed silk for the paired warp, but that by the 7th to 8th century warp groupings of three to four z-twisted threads are found. (London, 8579–1863)

RIGHT Silk edgings of a Buddhist sutra wrapper, dated to 8th century, from Dunhuang, Tarim Basin. These edgings and some other silks share certain technical features which might distinguish Zandaniji work: similar pattern composition; loom width measurement with a distinctive selvage-fringe; fugitive dye-colouring; a warp grouping of three to four z-twist silk; and a weft of floss silk. (London, OA MAS 858)

RIGHT Silk compound twill fragment, found in a 1258 context in the Church of St Sernin, Toulouse, but generally dated to 12th-century Iberia. The ground is dark blue with main warp in beige silk and seven pattern weft in various colours. The Kufic inscription below the peacock forms reads 'Perfect blessings'. (Paris, CL 12869)

Islamic Iberia

Despite its geographical isolation, the court at Córdoba was eager to learn of the latest fashions and tastes, through such ninth-century visitors as the ᶜAbbasid court singer Ziryab and a century later *émigré* Egyptian textile craftsmen. The so-called Veil of Hisham (*c.* 976–1013) was obviously inspired by contemporary Egyptian courtly textiles, whereas another fragment of similar date, with a peacock roundel pattern worked in silk and gold-thread tapestry weave, now in Madrid's Instituto de Valencia de Don Juan, has a distinct Sasanian flavour. Perhaps predating both items, a piece of silk lampas in the Victoria and Albert Museum, London, has an ᶜAbbasid flavour (p. 61) in its pattern.

Occasionally there was a deliberate intention to deceive the customer. One early twelfth-century example proudly carries, in each of the small pattern medallions, the legend 'This is one of the things made in Baghdad', but the spelling and calligraphy betray its Iberian origin. Such deceptions were common and constant: fourteenth-century *hisba* regulations (Ibn al-Hajj in Serjeant 1972, n. 56, p. 46) still warned the textile merchant that:

> It is incumbent on him when he has pieces of cloth derived from a district the cloth of which is much sought after by the public, not to sell the cloth of another district as the manufacture of the first, even though the two districts are close to each other . . .

The beauty and quality of Iberian textiles resulted in their use as Christian ecclesiastical vestments, burial and reliquary wrappings in Spain and elsewhere, a tradition which has assisted modern scholars over the problem of dating. In the Salamanca Cathedral archives two silk fragments, patterned with eagles and possessing a diasper structure similar to the Boston piece (pp. 10–11), were attached to documents of 1183 and 1199. Probably contemporary is another highly patterned reliquary silk known as the Cope of King Robert, from Toulouse. Bands of different-coloured wefts lend horizontal emphases to the composition of stylised trees and confronting peacocks, whose tails form a pointed arch above their heads; above and below runs a simple Kufic inscription calling for 'perfect blessings'.

The Buyid controversy

In any survey of medieval Islamic textiles the thorny issue of the so-called Buyid controversy has to be addressed. A number of silk fragments, reportedly from a burial area close to Tehran, came on to the market from the late 1920s onwards. It was believed that with one or two exceptions they dated from the period when the ᶜAbbasid caliphate was controlled by the Shiᶜi Buyid family (932–1055). Everything seemed to suggest a flourishing industry in medieval northern Iran, manufacturing burial silks with Shiᶜi inscriptions, sometimes specially woven to unusual shapes. Following technical analyses of pieces in the Abegg Stiftung collection, Berne (Lemberg 1973, Vial 1973, Hoffenk-de Graaff 1973a), and subsequent lengthy (and increasingly acrimonious) debates over the findings, an extended dating to *c.* 1220 was generally accepted (Shepherd 1975).

None of the fragments resembles the tenth-century 'Shroud of St Josse' with its high colouring and striking composition of towering elephants, framed by Sasanian 'hearts' and a Bactrian camel train, with a cockerel in each corner. Instead most of these silks, whatever their weave, have very subdued colour-

Silk compound plain weave, c. 1027–1210, confirmed by scientific analysis. The main warp is z-twist tan silk, while the tan ground and green pattern weft have no discernible twist. The inscription is pseudo-Kufic and is unreadable. 23.5 × 22.8 cm. (Cleveland, 39.506)

OVERLEAF Detail of the 'Shroud of St Josse', mid-10th century, eastern Iran, and possibly brought to France after the First Crusade (1096–9). Displaying great technical skill, this compound twill has a warp of z-twist silk, while the seven pattern weft of silk has no discernible twist. The elephant motif, bordered on the left with a camel train, measures 30 × 30 cm; and the total loom width was probably 127 cm. Although this detail implies a strict symmetry, three pattern reconstructions have been suggested. (Paris, AO 7502)

ing, sometimes darkened by a post-weave tannic dyebath. Some patterns relate to medieval Islamic Iberian and Byzantine silks as found in the Bamberg medieval reliquary collection, and to the Lyons silk of Anatolian Seljuq Sultan Kay Qubad I or II (1219–37 or 1249–57 respectively). They consist of large roundels containing single or paired figures, or feature great heraldic birds, such as the Ganymede piece in Cleveland Museum of Art with its two-headed eagles, sheltering a human form between their spread wings and gripping small quadrupeds in their talons. A few are decorated with elegant foliated Kufic calligraphy superimposed on graceful arabesques. Others have a densely packed arrangement of stylised foliage, surrounding small medallions containing seated figures, or a series of large rhomboidal diamonds set against a plain ground. There are pieces of clothing also, but the cut of these is atypical and highly questionable.

A number of fragments from the Cleveland Museum of Art have been subjected to sophisticated AMS Carbon-14 testing (Indictor n.d.) and the stylistic content of the textile inscriptions published in detail. The findings starkly reveal the perils of dating by design motif and composition. Of the twenty pieces tested only four including one from the Textile Museum, Washington, DC, may be confidently dated c. 1023–1260. Two were later production of the Timurid/Safavid period, that is, pre-1650. The remaining fourteen must be considered twentieth-century fakes.

ويحل القفص والجبال والقبس والبالة انها لضغت علي بالة فاضاعت بقص من زها

فنشد مذرجها فلما دانت وقف بالرقعة درهما وقطعة وقلت لها ان رغبن في المشوف المعلم

واثرت الي الدرهم فوحي بالسر المهم وان ابن ان نرجو فخذي القطعة وابر زن

فانت الي استخلاص البدر بالنجم والابلج الهم وقالت دع جدا لك وباع عا بد لك فاسقط

طلع الشيخ وبلدته والشعر وناج بردته فقالت ان الشيخ من اهل نروح وهو الذي وشن

3

EARLY ISLAMIC PERIOD II
TEXTILES AT COURT

In spearheading the revolt against the Sunni Umayyad regime the ᶜAbbasid family proclaimed its close relationship to the family of the Prophet and ᶜAli, and drew on Shiᶜi support largely from the eastern provinces. Although the ᶜAbbasid rulers then quickly disassociated themselves from the Shiᶜi movement, it continued its missionary work. It divided into two main groupings, each supporting the succession of divinely guided spiritual leaders (Imams), one (the *Ismaᶜiliya*, or 'Seveners') recognising the unbroken line of seven Imams, and the other, of later importance in Iran (the *Ithna ᶜAshari*: literally 'Twelvers'), believing this line continued through five more generations. Drawing on Ismaᶜili support in North Africa, ᶜUbaydallah, a Shiᶜi claiming direct descent from Fatima, the Prophet's daughter and wife of ᶜAli, established himself in AD 910 as the Mahdi (Righteously Guided), the spiritual and political leader in the region of Tunisia. To stress this ancestry he and his successors took 'Fatima' as their dynastic name and included the titles of Imam and Mahdi on honorific inscriptions. Their influence spread with the success of their military campaigns and by early AD 969 the fourth Fatimid ruler, al-Muᶜizz, was in control of Egypt and building his capital al-Qahira, 'The Victorious', or as it is now known, Cairo.

At its zenith around 990 Fatimid sovereignty was recognised across North Africa, in Syria, the Hijaz and Yemen, but the ambition to oust the ᶜAbbasid regime in Baghdad was never realised. From 1060 control of the Levant had passed to various hereditary governorships nominally loyal to Baghdad, not Cairo. The Crusaders picked off the incumbents one by one until Salah al-Din (Saladin), *wazir* or first minister to the Fatimid court from 1169, united local Muslim chiefs and governors against the invaders. Three years later he ordered the Fatimid Imam-Caliph's name to be omitted from the *khutba* (public homily given in mosques on Fridays) and replaced by that of the ᶜAbbasid ruler. This formally marked the end of Fatimid rule and Shiᶜism as the state doctrine; in its place was set the Ayyubid dynasty – 'Ayyub' (Job) being the family name of Salah al-Din – which was to last until 1249, and the primacy of Sunni doctrine was re-established.

In the ᶜAbbasid period court ceremonial became increasingly more elaborate. Influential officials like Nizam al-Mulk (d. 1092), the famous Seljuk *wazir*, advised that the regime's authority and prosperity should be displayed in sumptuous court dress and furnishings. It was advice heeded at the highest levels for many centuries throughout the Islamic world. Yet at the same time there was an intellectual nostalgia for the simplicity and purity of spirit perceived as characterising the Rashidun period. Medieval commentators praised the austere dress and low-keyed ceremonial attributed to the Rashidun caliphs as sure signs of their piety, connecting the ostentatious lifestyle of former Umayyad rulers such as Hisham (724–43) and his nephew Walid II (743–4) with hedonism and general ineptness. The contradiction was never resolved in intellectual circles.

It is unclear whether the Umayyad caliphate initiated the practice of adopting a dynastic colour, as did the ᶜAbbasid and Fatimid regimes. The Umayyad rulers did don white for the Friday prayer and public processions, but various coloured robes were worn for audiences. Hisham received guests clad in red like a Sasanian shah, despite a *hadith* that it was Satan's colour. His nephew held audience wearing yellow and gold jewellery, both matters of censure. As their ᶜAbbasid critics knew from their own times, yellow clothing was for female entertainers and non-Muslims; it was best avoided except for private festivities.

From their first uprising black became so identified with the ᶜAbbasids that they were known in Byzantium and China as the 'black-robed ones'. Caliph al-Mansur (754–75) is traditionally credited with introducing black for the ceremonial dress of high-ranking court officials and the ᶜulama '. . . as a sign of mourning for the martyrs of their family [i.e. of ᶜAli] . . . and as a sign of reproach directed against the Umayyads who had killed them' (Ibn Khaldun, vol. 2, pp. 50–1). Neglect or refusal to wear it at the twice-weekly audience was tantamount to open rejection of ᶜAbbasid authority. Even when ᶜAbbasid political power ended in 1258, Sunni theologians and jurists continued to wear black on formal occasions, thus acknowledging the theological leadership of the ᶜAbbasid caliphate in exile. Honorific garments, royal flags and official document cases were black and usually of silk. The dye used is not named, but as a late tenth-century court chamberlain recalled how a perspiring official had to wipe the colour from his turban cloth off his face, it was clearly fugitive (Salem 1977).

In emphatic contrast the Shiᶜi Fatimid regime chose white for its dynastic colour and honorific robes. For the three major Ramadan processions the Fatimid ruler dressed in white silk decorated with gold thread, as the earthly incarnation of the Divine Intellect, the Divine Luminosity, untarnishable and pure. Thus to mark the official end to Fatimid control in North Africa the Zirid regime (972–1148) ordered all white fabric to be dyed and Fatimid *tiraz* to be removed. The importance of that latter step is described below (p. 53).

Flags and parasols

By the tenth century flags were items of caliphal insignia on and off the battlefield. The Prophet had ridden into combat under various coloured flags, including black and white, some hurriedly made from garments and horse-

'Listening to the theologian', *Maqamat al-Hariri*, 1237, probably Iraq. Something of the colour and richness of medieval Islamic dress fabrics is conveyed in this miniature. The men's garments show the placing of *tiraz* bands on the 'dropped' shoulder-sleeve seam, while small gold squares on their turban cloths suggest the fashionable positioning for the so-called 'factory-marks'. (Paris, Arabe 5847, f. 58v)

trappings (Hinds 1971). Tradition has it that one of these, now known as the *sancak-i şerif* (that is, the Prophet's standard), passed into Ottoman hands in the early sixteenth century and thence into the Topkapi Saray, Istanbul.

The most important Fatimid military banners (*ᶜalam*) were known as the 'Two Standards of Praise [to God]', made of white silk decorated with gold, some two cubits long (about 40 cm) and a cubit and a half wide. Behind them and flanked by two lances with gold crescent-moon finials, hung with seven pennants of red and yellow, was carried a narrow banner or striped silk bearing the words 'Victory is from God' and 'Conquest is near!' (al-Qalqashandi in Hamblin 1985, p. 154). Among the ceremonial flags were two featuring red and yellow lions (one of ᶜAli's epithets), with their mouths so cut that in the breeze they looked as if they were roaring. No Fatimid textile fragment has been identified as a banner, but from Burgos in Spain an Almohad flag of the gonfalon type is thought to date from the first half of the thirteenth century. Its field is dominated by a central multipointed star guarded by bands of Quranic verse (*sura* 61, vv. 10–12), in exuberant Maghribi Naskhi script, referring to struggle and the reward of Paradise.

Just as important was the Fatimid caliphal parasol (*mizalla*), about 75 cm high, formed of twelve panels, with a circumference of some 250 cm (twelve cubits). Its colour matched the caliphal robes worn on the occasion. Used only outside the palace compound and always returned via the Fatimid royal tombs, it seems to have symbolised the royal house in the sense of both building and lineage (Sanders 1984).

Lowering the curtain

From Umayyad times, concomitant with developing court ceremonial, the caliph withdrew increasingly from public gaze. At audiences it became the practice for the court chamberlain, as his title *hajib* denoted, to raise an ornate curtain dramatically revealing the caliph seated in splendour and to lower it at the end of the proceedings. This use of the *hijab* (curtain, veil) was probably borrowed from Sasanian or possibly Byzantine court ritual. We have no descriptions of Umayyad court *hijab* but those of the ᶜAbbasid court stunned the Byzantine envoys in 917, glittering with gold thread and patterned with birds and animals, along with the tens of thousands of other palace textiles and carpets decorating the palace corridors and rooms.

In Fatimid Cairo caliphal seclusion was understood to reflect the ruler's close spiritual relationship with the Divine. Even on such public days as the three Friday prayers during Ramadan the caliph proclaimed the *khutba* from the mosque *minbar* (a stepped rostrum) concealed behind plain white curtains. The *mihrab* (niche indicating the direction of Mecca), too, was curtained, carrying red silk Quranic inscriptions (*suras* 1 (Fatiha), 62 and 63). At other times, as for the reception of the Byzantine Emperor Basil II (976–1025), the Fatimid *hijab* carried gold thread signifying the brilliance and luminosity of the caliphate.

Palace curtains from fourteenth-/fifteenth-century Nasrid Iberia have survived; that of the Cleveland Museum of Art is of red satin, resembling an ornate wooden door, with 'panels' of Naskhi script announcing 'Dominion belongs to Allah alone' and a 'cornice' of merlons guarding the Nasrid dynastic motto 'There is no conqueror but Allah'.

The idea of conducting official business and receiving guests in curtained and draped surroundings quickly percolated through Islamic society. Early thirteenth-century Syrian artists depicted governors and the ᶜulama at work with a *hijab* ostentatiously drawn back, and medieval trousseau lists (Stillman 1972) carefully detailed curtains. About 200 cm or less in width, they were hung at windows, in doorways and on the walls of the *salamlik* or reception rooms. A well-known source of domestic furnishing fabric was Bahnasa, some 300 kilometres south of Cairo and famous for its linen, but North African silks were also popular. Tabaristan was known for heavyweight hangings, which when drenched with water and rose oil cooled and perfumed the atmosphere – an idea introduced into the western ᶜAbbasid provinces, it was said, by Caliph al-Mansur (754–75).

Coverings for cushions, pillows, multi-unit sofas (*martaba*) and various beds were other important elements in medieval furnishings. In wealthy households the *martaba*, the main feature of the reception room, was covered with silk from Byzantium, costing thirty to forty dinars (a doctor's monthly salary), or from Tabaristan, at about half the price. Jurists and theologians sat at their deliberations with large bolsters or cushions (*misnad*) with distinctive pointed corners placed behind them, and even in private households cushions were allocated to guests according to their status (Sadan 1976). Mid-thirteenth-century bridegrooms were expected to present a range of cushions in the trousseau, although in the eleventh century these had been provided by the brides. Given the opportunity newly-weds declined those decorated with birds, preferring a wide range of monochrome colours embellished with gold fringes, tassels and striped borders. Another passing eleventh-century fad was to have the bridal-bed canopy in an emerald-green fine linen (*sharb*), rather than white, sky blue, pomegranate red or yellow.

Tiraz and its function

The significance of omitting the ruler's name in the *khutba* has been noted at the beginning of this chapter. It proclaimed the rejection of the existing political authority, when coupled to withdrawal of coinage from circulation and removal of official honorific textile inscriptions (*tiraz*). The importance of *tiraz* and its courtly connection were described by administrator and philosopher Ibn Khaldun (d. 1406) (vol. 2, p. 65, slightly amended):

> It is part of royal and governmental pomp and dynastic custom to have the names of rulers or their peculiar marks [ᶜalamat] put on [rasama] on the silk . . . The writing is brought out by weaving a gold thread or some other colored thread of a color different from that of the fabric itself into it. [Its execution] depends upon the skill of the weavers in designing and weaving it. Royal fabrics are embellished with such a *tiraz*, in order to increase the prestige of . . . those whom the ruler distinguishes by bestowing on them his own garment when he wants to honor them or appoint them to one of the offices of the dynasty.

Originally from the Persian *tarazidan* ('to embroider'), the Arabic word *tiraz* was extended in time to describe dress, robe of honour and even aspects of ceramic architectural revetment. The introduction of such a system is traditionally attributed to the Umayyad caliph ᶜAbd al-Malik (685–705), probably based on Sasanian or Byzantine models (Day 1952, Stillman 1972). The earliest-known Islamic *tiraz* workshop was set up by Hisham (724–43), but soon all the major textile centres boasted them. They were broadly divided into

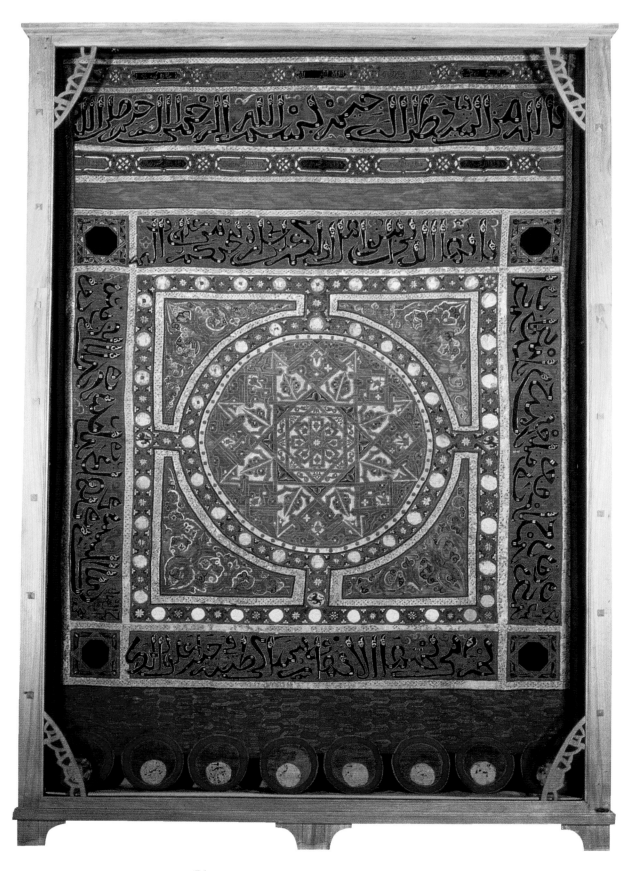

LEFT The Almohad flag known as 'Las Navas de Tolosa', first half of 13th century, Iberia. Tapestry-woven silk with gold thread. The deep bands framing the central star carry Quranic inscriptions (*sura* 61, vv. 10–12). The closed crescent motifs on the tabbed fly possibly represent the imprint of horseshoes, symbolising the victorious battles and conquests of early Islam. 3.3 × 2.2 m. (Burgos)

Linen and wool slit-tapestry woven fragment, 9th century, Egypt. The heaviness of this piece suggests a furnishing fabric, perhaps made in Bahnasa, a centre famous for such work. The linen warp is s-spun, z-plied, while the linen and wool weft is also s-spun. The inscription reads 'In the name of Allah, blessing from Allah on its owner. Of what was made in the tiraz of . . .'. 80 × 83.2 cm. (Cleveland, 59.48)

Fatimid *tiraz*, probably last quarter of 10th century/first quarter of 11th century, found serving as a burial shroud in the Qasr Ibrim excavations, Upper Egypt. Made of undyed linen, the warp and weft are both s-spun with a tapestry-woven inscription in red silk (no discernible twist) which reads 'In the name of Allah, the Merciful, the Compassionate . . .'. The scale and style of this monumental Kufic (the ascenders measure 7 cm) are similar to *tiraz* made for the ͨAbbasid caliph al-Mutiͨ (946–74).
(London, EA 1990.1–27.4410)

two types of establishment: the *khassa* ('exclusive') which produced textiles from clothing to tents and furnishings solely for the court; and the ͨ*amma* ('public') whose products were also available for public purchase. Both were controlled by government officials, because of the court connection and the security required for the bullion used as metal thread: *tiraz* on one military robe could cost 500 gold dinars, and in 1122 over 14,000 robes were needed at just one court ceremony. Orders with an estimate of costs were drawn up by the Royal Wardrobe and despatched to the *tiraz* master (*sahib al-tiraz*) who was responsible for the weavers and other staff, the payment of their wages, the equipment and inspection of the work. The finished fabrics were checked both at the workshop and in the palace. If the court officials considered the work fell short of the estimated cost, the master was directed to recover the amount from the craftsmen. However, if the quality exceeded that estimated, no further money was forthcoming.

In the ͨAbbasid empire the *tiraz* comptroller was frequently also head of the government postal/espionage service and the mints. In Fatimid territories the chief of *tiraz* workshops was entitled, when on official duty, to use several items of royal insignia, such as the parasol (*mizalla*), and three kinds of dress usually exclusive to the ruler, including the *badana* (costly seamless clothing). For some years it was customary for his name to be included in the *tiraz* legend so we know a certain al-Shafiͨ remained in charge of Fatimid *tiraz* for over twenty-five years, from 910–11 to 937–8 (298–326 AH).

Tens of thousands of *tiraz* fragments have survived, and generally their inscriptions are taken as sole proof of authenticity. Most are scraps divorced from the original piece because earlier in the twentieth century, when collectors' interest focused upon epigraphy, extraneous fabric was often removed. With it went evidence of loom width, original usage and exact positioning of the *tiraz* ornament. Some pieces decorated with monumental calligraphy and at least a metre in width could have been hangings as mentioned in the texts. At least three linen *tiraz*, found during archaeological excavations at Qasr Ibrim, Upper Egypt, ended up serving as burial shrouds. The fringes and width of some Yemeni *tiraz* suggest use as shawls, turban cloths or sashes,

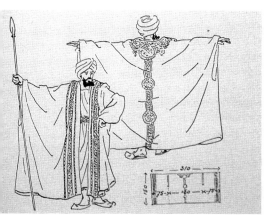

The 'Veil of St Anne', 1096 or 1097, on the order of the Fatimid ruler, al-Mustaᶜli. Probably brought to France as booty after the first Crusade, its dimensions suggest that this particular Egyptian *tiraz* fabric was intended to be worn in the style of the ᶜaba cloak. 3.1 × 1.5 m. (Apt, Vaucluse)

and just occasionally the inscription itself specifies the function, as does the Samuel b. Musa ᶜimama (turban cloth) fragment, now in the Islamic Art Museum, Cairo.

In thirteenth-century Arab painting turbans are often shown with decorated ends and a small gold square ornament among the folds. Similar couched or painted 'squares' have survived, usually designated as 'factory marks' by modern textile historians. Also depicted are three kinds of gold 'armbands' on robes: plain, with inscriptions, or with floral motifs; while two distinct types current around 1285 are mentioned in the literature: the *tiraz mudhahhaba* (gold *tiraz*) worn on the underrobe; and the *tiraz zarkash* (?highly patterned silk) for the outer robe, worn exclusively by the élite palace bodyguard of the Egyptian Mamluk regime (1250–1517). After the mid-fourteenth century *tiraz* 'armbands' appear less frequently in paintings, perhaps relating to the 1293 Mongol ban on woven inscriptions on non-court silks (Mayer 1952, n. 1, p. 34; Serjeant 1972, p. 68). Instead Persian manuscript painters portray courtly robes with *tiraz* 'between the shoulders' (al-ᶜUmari, d. 1349, in Quatremère 1838) as decorative panels, in the style of later Chinese 'mandarin' squares.

Perhaps the most famous *tiraz* is the so-called Veil of St Anne from the Cathedral of Apt, Vaucluse, France. It is a length (310 × 150 cm) of bleached plain-weave linen with three parallel bands of tapestry-woven decoration of red, green and blue silk floss with some gold thread; these give the name of the Fatimid caliph al-Mustaᶜli (1094–1101), a date either 489 or 490 AH (1096 or 1097) and the place of production as Damietta, in the Nile Delta region, famed for its superior undyed linen manufacture. The patterning of bands is in the Coptic tradition, while the figural representations in roundels reappear in later Islamic Iberian work. Probably this length was intended as an honorific (*khilᶜa*) garment of the first or second grade given its rich ornament: the two ends would have been folded into the centre and sewn along one selvage so forming the shoulder seam of the classic ᶜaba garment, with the *tiraz* bands running down the front edges and centre back.

Tiraz patterning

The typical pre-eleventh-century *tiraz* is bleached or natural plain-weave linen or cotton, with a line of embroidered or woven calligraphy beginning with *bismillah* ('In the name of Allah'), then giving the ruler's name and titles, a salutary phrase, the place of manufacture and the date. The inscription may stand alone in stark simplicity, or alongside narrow band(s) of abstract forms or stylised animal or bird motifs contained in cartouches. There are, however, many variations, and indeed two of the earliest-known *tiraz* have a very different composition.

The so-called Marwan silk with its aligned rows of 'Sasanian pearl' roundels (p. 39) is indeed a *tiraz*. Its embroidered Kufic legend in split-stem-stitch names the place of production as Ifriqiya, a region outside Umayyad control during the caliphate of Marwan I (684–5), so the Marwan given as Commander of the Faithful (a caliphal title) in the inscription was presumably Marwan II (744–50). The second fragment in the Textile Museum, Washington, DC (inv. no. 73.524), also refers to Marwan but this has a very different structure, of wool worked in a fine-toothed tapestry weave with z-spun weft and z-plied warp. These weave details suggest it was made in the eastern Islamic lands (Kühnel and Bellinger 1952).

A much coarser piece is the Samuel b. Musa turban cloth, now in the Islamic Art Museum, Cairo (inv. no. 10846, also given as 10864), made of plain-weave linen with a tapestry-woven Kufic inscription and Coptic-styled band of flattened circles separating cartouches holding single bird forms. Fayyum (south of Cairo) is given as the place of manufacture along with a date which may be read as 88 AH or 188 AH (AD 707 or 804).

The difference in quality should not suggest the importance of *tiraz* was shortlived; the Egyptian workshops were still operating in 1309. However, it was the Fatimid regime more than any other which employed *tiraz* to proclaim its political and religious ethos.

RIGHT Section of a *tiraz* ordered by the Fatimid caliph, al-Zahir (1021–36). The bleached linen warp and weft are both s-spun, with the long inscription emphasising the caliph's ancestry tapestry-woven in blue silk of no discernible twist.
(Toronto, 970.364.2B)

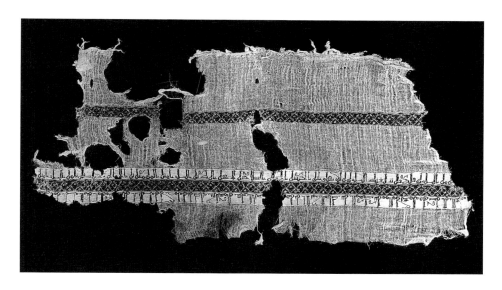

Fatimid *tiraz*

A fine example of the overt political and religious message on Fatimid *tiraz* is now in the Royal Ontario Museum, Canada. The Fatimid ruler al-Zahir (1021–36) had the inscription stress his filial relationship to the self-professed 'divine' al-Hakim (996–1021) and his 'pure ancestors', a phrase which in Shiʿi Islam meant the Prophet and ʿAli (Golombek and Gervers 1977, p. 108):

> [In the name of Allah] . . . the Merciful, the Compassionate. There is no God but Allah. Assistance from Allah and speedy victory to the Servant of Allah [Muhammad] and his friend ʿAli Abi-l Hasan, the Imam al-Zahir li-iʿzaz-din-illah, Commander of the Faithful, son of the Imam al-Hakim bi-amr-illah, Commander of the Faithful. Allah's Benedictions and His Mercy and His Blessings upon them both and their pure ancestors, the Imams, the Guides, the Mahdis. From what was ordered to be made in the public factory of Damietta in the year 412 [1021–2].

Tapestry-woven *tiraz* fragment attached to a fine checked cream and blue linen, probably second half of 12th century, Egypt. The *tiraz* (30 × 17 cm max.) has a s-spun linen warp with the weft in three colours of silk, no discernible twist; the tapestry weave is worked in both slit and dovetail techniques. The inscription band of 'good fortune and prosperity' is 2.5 cm deep, and the zone of interlacing and stylised bird forms is 4.5 cm deep. The plain-weave linen has z-spun warp and s-spun weft.
(London, OA 1901.3–14.52)

Such specific and lengthy inscriptions were superseded in the mid-eleventh century by short, general legends calling for 'Victory to Allah', 'Good fortune', or some such; similar sentiments decorated Fatimid military flags and banners. The vagueness of the legends may reflect the loss of caliphal authority to the military in this period (Britton 1938, p. 21), or perhaps identifies ʿamma ('public') workshop production. Whatever the case, they were rendered more insignificant in time as the decorative edging bands came to dominate the composition in size and complexity.

After al-Hakim's reign (996–1021), the cursive Naskhi script was increasingly employed in preference to stately Kufic, but no uniformity in the lettering of either is found. Proportions are not always subtle, nor is the hand elegant and rhythmic. On some examples the ascenders are only 0.7 cm in height, while on others they are over 8 cm. Such 'monumental' Kufic was favoured by both al-Mu'izz (ruled in Cairo 969–75) and al-Hakim, echoing *tiraz* made in Egypt for the 'Abbasid ruler al-Muti' (946–74).

There were other changes, which suggest alterations in working practices. Until around 940 both s- and z-spun linen warp and weft were used in Egyptian *tiraz*; thereafter z-spun yarns are rarely found (Kühnel and Bellinger 1952, Golombek and Gervers 1977). From the second quarter of the tenth century there was a vogue for tapestry-woven *tiraz* bands in wool and silk. Before then, and again towards the end of Fatimid rule, inscriptions were typically embroidered in silk, back-stitch on earlier pieces and chain-stitch sometimes on loosely woven stuffs. The more cursive calligraphic styles favoured in the later period were easier to achieve by embroidery than by weaving, but the decorative stitching carefully imitated the surface appearance of weave.

'Abbasid *tiraz*

The *tiraz* from the eastern Islamic lands are generally on unbleached cotton, sometimes glazed, or silk-cotton mixtures in fine weft-faced plain weave. The cotton, and the embroidery silk if it has a twist, is z-spun. But examples of linen and of silk have survived: in these both warp and weft are z-spun. At least one 'Abbasid silk *tiraz* has a tapestry-woven inscription, but most are embroidered in chain-stitch, with blanket- and back-stitch for minor details. A number have the inscriptions painted or stamped in gold. The few examples so far published open with the usual *bismillah* benediction, followed by the ruler's name and that of the *wazir* (frequently the comptroller) if the piece is early tenth century or earlier, and finish with the place and date of manufacture.

It may be that 'Abbasid *tiraz* were woven separately as bands and then sewn on to cloth as depicted in a 1229 frontispiece (Tokapi Saray Museum, inv. no. A III 2127), and some fragments do show signs of sewing. No *tiraz* on a black ground, the 'Abbasid colour, appears to have survived but in any event the commissioning of *tiraz* was not a caliphal prerogative. The three words on a Dumbarton Oaks, Washington, DC (inv. no. 30.2) piece of z-spun diamond-twill linen (did the medieval *mu'ayyan* 'bird's eye' fabric look like this?) are enough to link it with a tenth-century Buyid or Samanid ruler, while another silk fragment in the Textile Museum, Washington, DC (inv. no. 3.116) names a Buyid ruler, describing him as 'the light of the community and the refuge of the nation'. A very striking non-caliphal *tiraz* is the large silk hanging known as the Shroud of St Josse (pp. 46–7).

Yemeni *tiraz*

The early Islamic Yemeni ikats are also *tiraz* pieces, typically of plain-weave cotton with z-spun warp and weft. It is the tie-dyed ('asb) warp, but sometimes the weft also, which produces the overall pattern of small lozenge forms. According to its inscription, the earliest-known fragment was produced in San'a during 270 AH/AD 883–4, and manufacture in this region continued for at least 100 years. The legends are either painted in gold or embroidered in cream-white cotton thread, close to the edging fringe. A second grouping of Yemeni *tiraz* has been identified which possesses yellow s-spun silk in the warp; some examples are ikat but at least one, now at Dumbarton Oaks, Washington, DC (inv. no. 33.42), was pattern-woven (Glidden and Thompson 1989).

Tiraz from Islamic Iberia

The pattern and motifs of the early Iberian *tiraz* correspond to those employed by the Baghdad and Cairo courts. The so-called Veil of Hisham could have been made in Egypt, so similar is it in fabric (linen), decorative technique (tapestry weave in silk and gold thread) and pattern arrangement (a band of octagonal shapes containing zoomorphic forms) between the inscription naming the Córdoban ruler Hisham II (976–1009; 1010–13). A fragment of Iberian silk lampas (Victoria and Albert Museum) naming al-Rahman (probably ʿAbd al-Rahman III, 912–61) owes much to ʿAbbasid decorative repertoire with its lozenge grid containing pairs of addorsed animals and confronting birds.

An eleventh-century silk made into a chasuble for the Quintanaortuna church, near Burgos in Spain, develops the theme of connecting roundels containing heraldic quadrupeds. Its inscription probably refers to ʿAli, the

Detail from the 'St Thomas à Becket' cope, 1116, Almería (southern Iberia), as given in its Kufic inscription. The blue silk twill is reportedly covered with laid and couched work in gold thread. (Fermo)

Detail of linen plain weave with tapestry-woven decoration in six silk colours and gold thread, naming the Iberian Umayyad caliph Hisham II (976–1009; 1010–13). The 'Veil of Hisham' was found in 1853 wrapping a Christian relic. (Madrid, 292)

Almoravid ruler of North Africa and Iberia from 1106 to 1142 (Shepherd 1957). Further afield in central Italy, at the Cathedral of Fermo, a magnificent ecclesiastical garment, said to have belonged to St Thomas à Becket, is of blue silk twill smothered in couched gold thread. Amid the large medallions and eight-pointed stars, both inhabited with birds, quadrupeds and human beings, the Kufic inscription names the Iberian textile centre of Almería and gives the date 510 AH/AD 1116–17 (Storm-Rice 1959). Like the Quintanaortuna chasuble the silk has two sets of z-spun warp, while the weft has no discernible twist; the gold thread is reportedly gilt animal substrata wound round a silk core.

The *tiraz* of the Almohad dynasty (c. 1147–1238) assumed a more independent character in its patterning, while the legends became increasingly general. As the fourteenth-century Ibn Khaldun explained (vol. 2, p. 66), the early Almohad rulers declined to patronise the *tiraz* workshops:

. . . because they had been taught . . . the ways of religion and simplicity. They were too austere to wear garments of silk or gold. The office [of *tiraz* inspector], therefore, had no place in their dynasty. Their descendants in the later [years] of the dynasty, however, re-established it in part, but it was not nearly as splendid [as before].

Perhaps this reticence also extended to figural representation because, although some tapestry-woven and lampas fabrics are decorated with occasional human figures in the style of late eleventh-century Fatimid work, geometrical motifs proliferate.

The Nasrid rulers (1230–1492) developed the geometrical emphasis, employing assertive colours to complement strong two-dimensional patterns of interlaced geometric shapes arranged on a diagonal grid. Occasional horizontal bands of various widths break up the endless repetition of stars juxtaposed with rosettes. Another group of Nasrid textiles is characterised by an arrangement of narrow alternate stripes of Andalusian *thuluth* calligraphy and stylised palmette-leaf motifs. Similar pattern stripes decorate certain fourteenth-century silks from Central Asia, but without the animated Andalusian script. Both compositions have parallels in contemporary architectural tile and plaster decoration, as seen in the Alhambra complex, Granada, so perhaps these textiles were designed as hangings and furnishing fabrics for Nasrid palaces.

OPPOSITE Silk lampas, 14th century, Iberia. The formal geometric interlaced patterning on these silks often relates to contemporary painted stucco decoration. (Lyons, 29686)

4

MAMLUK TEXTILES

Shortly before the regime lost control of Egypt (1250) and then its Syrian territories one of the last Ayyubid sultans, al-Salih (d.1249), pursued an extensive programme of purchasing young men in the belief that military training, conversion to Islam and manumission would instill in these *mamluks* ('owned') total loyalty to the ruler. Similar systems had underpinned other regimes in the Islamic world, and the Ottoman bureaucracy and army were also to be largely manned in this way. In Egypt and Syria it was to provide the rulers for the next 250 years.

For convenience the Mamluk sultanate is divided into two periods: the Bahri (1250–1382) and the Burji (1382–1517). Established by al-Salih, the Bahriyya *mamluk* regiment, barracked near Cairo on the Nile (Bahr al-Nil), largely originated from the Turkic-speaking Central Asia region. This faction controlled state affairs from about 1276 and then over the years lost power and influence to the Burjiyya regiment (*burj*: [Cairo] citadel), formed in 1279 with Circassians, whose authority lasted until 1517. Both groups determined the selection of the sultan, who then had to walk a political tightrope, rewarding his proposers yet exerting enough personal control to stay on the throne. Few succeeded for any length of time.

Despite this in its heyday Mamluk authority was recognised from the Libyan desert to the Euphrates, from Arabia and the Sudan (Nubia) in the south to south-eastern Anatolia in the north. The Mongol advance into the Levant region had been halted in 1260 by the able *mamluk* commander Baybars, who as sultan installed an ᶜAbbasid as caliph in Cairo, according

Silk lampas, 13th–14th century. The warp has slight z-twist; the (?silver) gold metal z-wrapped on a silk core and the distinctive warp 'bundle' at the selvages suggest Middle Eastern manufacture. Similarly patterned silks but with different structural features were probably made further east. (London, 1269–1864)

OPPOSITE Detail of silk tapestry-woven panel, *c.* last quarter of 14th century, found at Qasr Ibrim, Upper Egypt. Probably originally in white, gold, black and pale blue silk on z-twisted warp of white silk, this panel decorated the woollen cloak in which Bishop Timotheos, who died after 1372, was buried. 27 × 107 cm. (London, EA 1990.1–27.439)

Silk damask, early 14th century. The yellow colour, now faded, and the small medallion forms, variously reading 'Glory to our master', 'the sultan the king', 'al-Nasir', 'the suppressor of heresy', 'Muhammad ibn Qalawun', 'may [Allah] prolong his sovereignty', all suggest special court use in the interrupted reign of al-Nasir Muhammad b. Qalawun (1293–1341). While most Mamluk textile patterns have a strong symmetrical quality, this example belongs to a group featuring more fluid, asymmetrical designs influenced perhaps by Chinese Yuan silk imports. (Cairo, 3899)

him honour but no power. Military success continued. The Crusaders surrendered their last outpost in 1291. Peace was concluded with the Mongols in 1323, and in 1401 Timur Leng (Tamerlane) was forced to abandon his territorial ambitions in Syria. However, the emerging Ottoman state and the warring Turkoman tribal confederations in the east proved more serious.

There were also internal problems with devastating outbreaks of plague from 1348, low Nile floods and consequent famine. Economic revival was suffocated by excessive taxation. The Portuguese 'discovery' of the Cape route to the east Indies provided a welcome answer to foreign merchants seeking to escape the heavy customs dues on the Red Sea/Cairo/eastern Mediterranean route and the rapacity of Mamluk officials. But it was the refusal of the élite Mamluk regiments to accept training in firearms and artillery which brought about the end of the state. In 1517 the musket-bearing soldiers of the Ottoman Empire entered Cairo, and Mamluk lands became Ottoman provinces.

Colour and Mamluk society

The dynastic colour of the Mamluk regime was yellow, as under their former masters, the Ayyubid sultans. It was used for the royal parasol, standard and pennants, and for some battledress. Only during the last fortnight of May

was white worn by the Burji sultans to mark the beginning of summer. The presence of the ᶜAbbasid caliph in Cairo meant that black was seen at court but there it was limited to his attire and to the investiture robe he gave each new sultan. Black silk with white, gold or black embroidery now became the customary colour for the Kaᶜba *kiswa* sent by the Egyptian sultan annually to Mecca, except during Barsbay's reign (1422–37) when red silk was used. Generally speaking red was best avoided, although it was used for some military uniforms. It was the required dress colour for both Samaritans and prostitutes. One wonders into which category the Mamluk owner of the red silk face veil uncovered in the Qasr Ibrim (Upper Egypt) excavations fell.

It had been the loudly voiced criticisms from a North African official visiting the court which prompted the re-issue of certain sumptuary regulations in 1301 concerning *dhimmi*s living under Mamluk protection. In the capital Cairo, Alexandria and Damascus Jewish and Christian men appearing in public were expected to wear yellow or blue turbans respectively and their womenfolk like-coloured wraps. Blue was also worn for ecclesiastical garments. The Coptic Bishop Timotheos, who died some time after his consecration in 1372, was buried at Qasr Ibrim, Upper Egypt (Crowfoot 1977), in a blue-black woollen cowled cloak with silk facings and a cotton lining; a tapestry-woven panel in four silk colours decorated the shoulders and back. His multipanelled shirt and trousers were made respectively of z-spun linen and cotton. Also of interest is his *mandil* (kerchief) of fine-quality linen with patterned twill bands in silk: despite its simple appearance its making required a complex loom arrangement.

Colour regulations also applied to Muslims. Since early ᶜAbbasid times green had been popularly associated with descendants of the Prophet's family, especially those espousing the cause of ᶜAli, but in 1371–2 this was formally recognised. A Mamluk edict required both male and female descendants to wear some green fabric on their outdoor clothing so due respect could be paid to them.

The convention that a regime's authority and prestige were reflected in ostentatious display was upheld by the Mamluk sultanate. There was the occasional sultan like Barquq (1382–9; 1390–9) who declined to wear silk in accordance with Sunni guidelines, but it was he who, weary of seeing the white robes of the ᶜulama, ordered them to don more colourful clothing to complement the rich attire worn at court. By all accounts the parades and audiences of the Mamluk sultans were as magnificent as those of the ᶜAbbasid and Fatimid regimes and more gaudy. A number of Bahri sultans were praised for raising standards in dress, insisting their army commanders wear satin tunics and patterned silk *kalawta*s (head-coverings). Vast amounts were spent on court garments. The *sirwal* (trousers) of one amir's wife in 1341 were valued at 10,000 gold dinars, and a festive robe worn by one of Sultan Barsbay's ladies cost 30,000 dinars, which outraged the ᶜulama. Even allowing for exaggeration the amounts are staggering, and it is frustrating that no further descriptions of such items are given.

More is known about the honorific garments, presented as *khilᶜa* by the sultan, the caliph and occasionally by high-ranking officials. These came in a glorious range of hues, monochrome or striped, with the type of fabric (usually silk but for the ᶜulama wool), its precise colouring and cut, fur trimming and extent of gold embroidery corresponding to the rank and post of the recipient. A top amir could expect two garments, one of yellow satin and the other of red, lined with squirrel and beaver and decorated with gold embroidery, a gold *kalawta* with a cotton and silk turban cloth, colourfully embellished, as well as a jewelled belt and sword and a royal horse. Such presentations marked every major change in career, as well as the grand court events. At the 1309 investiture of Sultan Baybars II, for instance, more than 1,200 honorific robes were distributed.

After the closure of the royal textile workshops around 1341, *khilᶜa* textiles were made and for a short time sold openly in one of the Cairene bazaars. Similarly *tiraz* incorporating the name of the sultan or leading amirs were

Detail from a linen fragment, 13th–14th century, Egypt. The dense embroidery in back-stitch provides a dramatic contrast for the elegant Naskhi inscription, which reads 'happiness and eternal prosperity'. The warp and weft are z-spun, while the embroidery silk has no discernible twist. (Geneva, JFB I-68)

manufactured in ordinary workshops, according to Ibn Khaldun (d. 1406). Few examples patterned in the Fatimid/Ayyubid *tiraz* tradition seem to have survived, and perhaps only high-ranking fief-holding *mamluks* were permitted *tiraz* (Mayer 1952). There are fragments with short, even abbreviated sultanic titles but within pattern compositions far removed from earlier models, which raises the question whether these would have been recognised in Mamluk times as *tiraz*. Instead the courtly device now most associated with the Mamluk regime is the blazon.

The amiral blazon

The personal devices (*rank*, 'colour') of the *mamluk* amirs were essentially related to their duties at court. In the Bahri period the motif was simple and stylised, generally contained within a circle: two polo sticks denoted the Chief Polo Master, a goblet for the Cupbearer, a napkin lozenge the Master of the Robes, and so on. The Burji *mamluks* preferred composite devices which could include up to six motifs. The same combination could be used by more than one amir and retained if the *mamluk* was invested as sultan, although after 1341 it became customary for the sultan's titles to be incorporated in a cartouche form. It could also be employed by members of the family, both male and female.

Such *rank*s were displayed on building exteriors, metalwork, glass and ceramics. In theory they had to be removed immediately after the death or dismissal of the office-holder (Ibn Sasra, vol. 1), and certainly it would have been possible to unpick the blazon appliqué on a number of surviving Mamluk textiles. One such is a horse/mule head-trapping, now in the Textile Museum, Washington, DC, made of yellow woollen cloth with an applied composite device framed in blue, of a goblet, with a napkin placed above and below. Some fragments, embroidered and applied, were made to function as flags or pennants, judging from their 'tabbed fly' markings.

At times it is unclear whether a motif within the pattern is signifying a blazon. A deep closed crescent form could be the *rank* of the Master Groom or the family of a high chancery official, as well as the house of Sultan Qalawun (1280–90), whose descendants ruled until 1390. And the presence of a repeat disc form (as in an ogival lattice composition) could identify the silk as made for the Royal Taster whose circular blazon symbolised a table top.

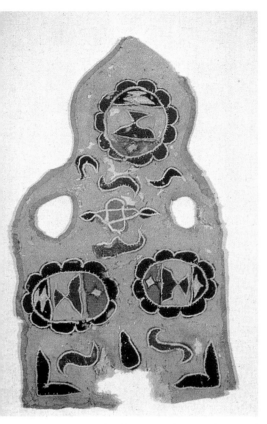

ABOVE Appliqué work, a pack-animal head-piece, probably 15th century. The ground and appliqués are plain weave with warp and weft both z-spun wool, and the motifs outlined with z-spun cotton couching. The composite blazon includes devices originally associated with the Master of the Robes (napkin lozenge) and the Cup-bearer (goblet). 48 × 26.5 cm (max.). (Washington, DC, 73.693)

OPPOSITE ABOVE Silk plain-weave triple cloth, 14th century, Egypt or Syria. Both warp and weft have a slight z-twist. The deep closed crescent motif could denote a Mamluk blazon. 11 × 16.7 cm. (Cleveland, 83.121)

OPPOSITE BELOW Detail of silk, plain and fancy weave, 13th–14th century, Egypt or Syria. Earlier in the twentieth century such dress-weight striped silks were classified as Ayyubid (1171–1249) due to the absence of any figural representation. Recently a more flexible terminal-date has been adopted in many quarters. (Cleveland, 19.28)

In the early Mamluk period the important Syrian manufacturing centres were Aleppo, famous for cotton-growing and dyeing, as well as marketing Indian textiles; Damascus for cotton-, linen- and silk-weaving; and Baalbek whose fine cottons were much in demand in Cairo. In Egypt the textile towns of the Nile Delta had largely recovered from Ayyubid evacuation and demolition in anticipation of Crusader attack (1192 and 1229).

Perhaps this rebuilding occasioned a minor revolution in the weaving sheds, because at some time tapestry-weaving in Egypt was largely abandoned for drawloom weaving. Alternatively it could be that this change was prompted by craftspeople fleeing the Mongol advance and settling in Mamluk territory. The visit of Sultan al-Ashraf Sha'ban (1363–76) to a drawloom workshop was clearly a novel experience (al-Nuwayri in Marzouk 1965, p. 161):

> He [the sultan] raised his head up to see the top of the looms where the 'draw-boys' raised up and lowered the top threads. He observed how the motifs of birds, geometric designs and other patterns were produced by these threads that went up and came down till each of the birds and other motifs were completed.

Patterned silk-weaving was now equated with glass-blowing and goldsmithing, crafts which Ibn Khaldun (d. 1406) and no doubt other high-ranking administrators considered distinguished highly sophisticated societies. Perhaps mindful of the skill and time required to set up the drawloom pattern lashes, guild rules of the late Mamluk period specified that apprentices served four, not the usual three, stages of training.

Pattern design

The development and chronology of Mamluk textile design have yet to be clearly defined, and recent detailed analyses of a few Mamluk silks (Wardwell 1989a) reveal the need to isolate Mamluk production before attempting to chart pattern chronology. That is easier said than done as there was a lively cross-trade in textiles between Europe, China and Mamluk lands. However, it could be that silks incorporating gold or silver thread wrapped round a silk core and a distinctive selvage of bundled warps are products of Mamluk Egyptian and Syrian looms, whereas those with metal carried on a cotton core or animal substrate were very probably made outside Mamluk territories to the east.

Ayyubid and Mamluk painting is of no great help (with a caveat that few manuscripts have been published in their entirety). In a British Library manuscript, *Maqamat* of al-Hariri, c. 1300 (inv. no. Add. 22114), some robes are decorated with a 'squared' motif which could relate to a group of double- and triple-cloth silks, patterned with small squares, each struggling to contain a stylised bird, quadruped or plant form. Another pattern motif, of a square with each right corner extended into a triangle, found in the same work and in another copy (British Library, inv. no. Or. 9718 c. 1275–1300), connects with an (Indian ?) stamped resist cotton in the Kelsey Museum, University of Michigan (Barnes 1993, inv. no. 94117a/b).

There was clearly a vogue for stripes, judging from surviving silks. One two-coloured double-cloth piece has wide bands, alternately containing calligraphy or dense patterning with animated rosettes, in the manner of contemporary metalwork decoration. Its inscription refers probably to a certain Yemeni sultan who died in 1321, but there is no suggestion that it was made

there. Also datable to the fourteenth century or later by the style of its (?excise) stamp, an excavated length of dress-weight silk, now in the Islamic Art Museum, Cairo (inv. no. 23099), is decorated with broad and narrow stripes, sometimes inhabited with running hounds, again as on Mamluk metalwork. The stamp names the town of Asyut (Assiut), but it may be a tax stamp rather than loom-shop identification. From the same Jabal ᶜAdda excavation in Upper Egypt is a Mamluk garment, whose colourful stripes carry stylised arabesque elements. It shares a distinct construction detail with a small coat in the Victoria and Albert Museum, London, classified as Ayyubid from its narrow vertical stripes in madder, indigo, black and cream.

As in Almohad and Nasrid Iberian silks geometric motifs featured in Mamluk textile pattern but instead of the Iberian formality of the diagonal grid here the stars, circles and rosettes appear to rotate on their own axes, constrained from spinning across the fabric by plaited ties. Some examples have less frenetic designs with the geometric form accompanied by birds, animal and fish forms, shown flying, running or swimming over the surface.

71

White linen plain-weave fragment with z-spun warp and weft and stamped design in perhaps tannin. Its pattern closely resembles a piece in Cairo, which has been dated to the late 15th century.
(Oxford, Newberry 1990.441)

As on fourteenth-century metalwork and enamelled glass, chinoiserie motifs such as the *qilin* lion, phoenix, lotus and peony appear, and at times the total composition closely resembles certain Chinese Yuan silks. It is tempting to date this vogue for 'chinoiserie' to the reign of Kitbugha (1295–7) and the following three decades, when Mongol Oirati influence was strong in court circles. Not only did a number of *mamluks* originate from this region, but at the turn of the century 10,000 Oirat families settled in Mamluk Syria. Modern historians also draw attention to the recorded gift of 700 silks sent by the Mongolian khan to the Mamluk sultan to mark the 1323 peace treaty. Indeed, several 'chinoiserie' silks classified as Mamluk include metal thread on animal substrate, suggesting manufacture elsewhere, though not necessarily Mongolian (Wardwell 1989a). Wherever produced, these elements gracefully complement the sweeping curves of the Arabic calligraphy, the designs being usually worked in only two or three colours in addition to the field. Several dyes on Mamluk silks have faded considerably; could this be associated with the reported shortage of Mamluk alum supplies (p. 28)?

Another pattern grouping is assigned to around the mid-fourteenth/mid-fifteenth century because of depictions in contemporary Italian paintings. The highly decorative composition of ovoid or tear-drop medallions, embellished with sophisticated foliate surrounds, is rendered in lampas weave. The inclusion of brief royal legends in cartouches, in the style of a blazon, also suggests post-1341 production.

Closely associated in technical structure to this group, but markedly different in patterning, is another series of dress-weight silks assigned to the Burji period. In some pieces the arrangement of diamond or square forms is

Silk lampas (reversed), 14th century. The main blue and binding tan warp are both z-twist, while the two weft in brown and tan have no discernible twist. A favourite decorative motif on mid-14th-century Mamluk metalwork and also glass, fish had connotations of wealth (through maritime trade). 15 × 16.7 cm. (Cleveland, 83.120)

impassively inert, while in others an uneasy visual tension is created by elaborately plumed half-palmette leaves framing static central forms, here more complex in character. The typical colouring of a dull indigo satin field and acid yellow or green tabby or twill patterning also sets these silks apart.

Embroidery

A cheap alternative to woven patterning was embroidered work. There was a thriving bazaar industry, with the client choosing designs, colours and stitching techniques from samplers of work. One sampler in the Newberry collection, Ashmolean Museum, Oxford, has a totally haphazard arrangement of small motifs, such as stylised fish and birds among incomplete decor-

LEFT Silk lampas, probably late 14th century. Although sharply different in both colouring and patterning from other Mamluk silks, this group of bichrome silks with a deep blue, dull satin ground possess a very similar technical structure. 22.9 × 25.7 cm. (Chicago, 1983.746)

ABOVE Linen sampler, probably Egypt. The fabric is plain weave with both warp and weft z-spun with the embroidery worked in pattern darning, in four colours of floss silk. Similar narrow banding patterns are occasionally seen decorating garments in certain mid-14th-century Florentine paintings. 41.5 × 26.5 cm (max.). (Oxford, 1984.479)

ative bands of various widths, often infilled with whirling rosettes formed of s or z triangles. The floss silk, usually indigo blue or dark brown, is employed either for the motif or conversely for the ground, leaving the motif in 'relief'. Mamluk linen 'shirts' made up of a series of cut panels often have seams embellished with this work, and garment bands depicted in mid-fourteenth-century Florentine paintings sometimes incorporate similar detail.

As in some Fatimid *tiraz*, the manner and visual appearance of Mamluk embroidery in floss silk often imitate the surface quality of weave. If required, the work was made fully reversible with double running-stitch, but other techniques such as pattern darning, couching, split-stem and counted close herring-bone (the reverse showing horizontal lines) were used for pieces to be viewed from one face only.

Not all Mamluk embroidery was on a small scale: the Brooklyn Museum, New York, has in its collection part of a large ogival medallion shape in linen, criss-crossed with indigo-blue silk embroidery to form foliated compartments. Its generous size suggests use as a tent panel or awning section.

Textile printing in the Mamluk period

Earlier in the twentieth century many fragments of printed cottons were acquired in Egypt by collectors. They were said to have been found in the ruins of Fatimid Fustat, now a Cairo suburb, but Pfister (1936, 1938) argued that certain parallels with fourteenth- to fifteenth-century Gujarati architectural decoration suggested most of these 'Fustat' pieces were imports from north-west India, excluding a few with unmistakable Mamluk designs. Subsequently this hypothesis has been presumed as proven; even 'spotted' and 'daisy' scatter patterns, which have a universal distribution, have been unhesitatingly assigned to India (Gittinger 1982, Eastwood 1990). However, new work (Barnes 1990, 1993) on the Newberry collection of printed fragments (Ashmolean Museum, Oxford) which suggests other sources of supply encourages fresh appraisal.

We know that cotton cultivation was widespread in the tenth-century Islamic world, from the eastern provinces to North Africa and Iberia, including Egypt and Syria. Tenth-century Yemeni ikat cotton-weaving survives (p. 60), and contemporary textual references suggest the wax-resist technique was practised. Wooden blocks (Ettinghausen 1977), now in the Metropolitan Museum of Art, New York, have been identified as textile printing blocks of the Fatimid period; certainly at least one 'Fustat' print motif echoes certain Fatimid rock-crystal decoration. Medieval Iraqi, Iranian and Yemeni cottons have z-spun cotton warp and weft so this feature is not exclusive to Indian production. Nor can it be argued that indigo-dyeing on linen and cotton was then an exclusive preserve of South and South-East Asian workers, although the difficult technique of madder-dyeing on these fabrics perhaps was at that time.

A number of printed fragments were clearly inspired by Mamluk silks. Apart from the whirling geometric and calligraphic compositions mentioned above, there is a striking example with two pieces now in the Islamic Art Museum, Cairo. A linen fragment (inv. no. 14816), variously described as stamped with silver or resist-printed, has a dense pattern of lobed squares containing a roundel of a pair of addorsed birds, alongside broken octagons inhabited by hares and hounds. It mirrors exactly the woven design on a

Knitted fragment in stocking-stitch on four needles, Egypt. Two-plied (s-twist) of z-spun cotton in white, light and dark blue. At present all such work is considered to be Fatimid, 11th–12th century. 30 × 31 cm. (Geneva, JFB M-117)

yellow and faded purple (elsewhere incorrectly identified as green) silk tunic found during the Jabal ᶜAdda archaeological excavations. The alternating 'building blocks' pattern filled with stylised motifs, seen on some Mamluk fourteenth-century silks, has a resemblance to certain printed cottons classified as Indian from Qusayr al-Qadim, Upper Egypt, abandoned in that century, and again among printed fragments in the Newberry collection, Ashmolean Museum, Oxford.

Given the use of cotton yarn with a z-spin, and presumably influenced by Pfister's theory concerning the origins of the 'Fustat' printed cottons, Bellinger (1954) proposed Indian manufacture for certain knitted socks in the Textile Museum, Washington, DC. Recently, however, knitting with similar pattern motifs organised in horizontal bands, sometimes including a foliated Kufic or pseudo-Kufic inscription, has been classed as Egyptian work, dating from the end of the eleventh or early twelfth century. A favourite colour scheme was obviously one or two shades of blue alongside the white cotton, but several examples considered to be a century or so earlier employed over five colours in intricate patterning, produced in stocking-stitch as were the others. Apart from the socks, intriguingly worked from the top of the toe instead of the edge of the ankle, there are other tubular items with no heel shaping. Their function is unclear. Perhaps they were belts or, as has been suggested, baby leg-warmers; another possibility is that they were spindle-holders.

Detail from a silk tunic coat excavated at Jabbal ʿAdda, Upper Egypt. The complex pattern of inhabited lobed squares and broken octagons is repeated on a printed linen fragment. The coat lining carries an excise or workshop stamp, akin to chancel seal imprints of the end of the 15th/early 16th century, although the silk is considered to be late 14th century or earlier. (Cairo, 23903)

The years of decline

The year 741 AH/AD 1340–1 is seen by historians, medieval and modern alike, as a watershed for the Mamluk textile industry. For the first time the supervisor of the Alexandrian royal textile workshop was appointed by a government official, not by the sultan; this suggests a withdrawaʾ of royal patronage. Shortly after, its closure was announced, quickly followed by that of Cairo.

Worse was yet to come. By 1348 plague was sweeping through Egypt from Syria, causing the death of approximately one-third of the population; outbreaks continued through the century. Production dropped, but because demand had fallen dramatically prices remained stable until the 1390s, when those of wool, linen and cotton rose three to ten times. By 1405 prices had stabilised but the damage had been done. In 1394 there had been some 14,000 silk looms in Alexandria but by 1434 only 800 were still in operation. Despite probable exaggeration, the figures reveal that the Egyptian textile industry had suffered severely, and the textile centres of Syria, such as Aleppo, Hama, Baalbek and the Damascus region, had been further devastated by Timurid military action.

Heavy import/transit dues and frontier closure between Syria and Iraq discouraged trade and investment. The main Syrian toll station of Qatya saw its annual custom revenues fall sharply (Lapidus 1967) from around 330,000 gold dinars in 1326 to a meagre 8,000 in the 1490s, and by 1438 ships calling at Bulaq, Cairo's major port, had halved in number. The abolition of certain taxes on raw cotton, Syrian linen and linen bleaching came too late to stimulate workshop production. Just as the élite companies of Mamluk soldiery ignored the potential of firearms, so the Mamluk textile manufacturer failed to utilise new water-power technology being developed in southern Europe.

With lower production costs high-quality Venetian and Florentine fabrics, already highly prized in Burji Mamluk society, could be sold at lower prices. In the closing years of the regime harsh economic measures were reintroduced to offset the Portuguese blockade of the Red Sea. These caused such hardship that a commentator recorded bitterly that each day of Qansuh al-Ghawri's reign (1501–16) was like 1,000 years to the common people.

Mamluk carpets

While the Mamluk textile industry was battered by heavy taxation and stiff competition from European exports, one sector prospered, that of carpet-

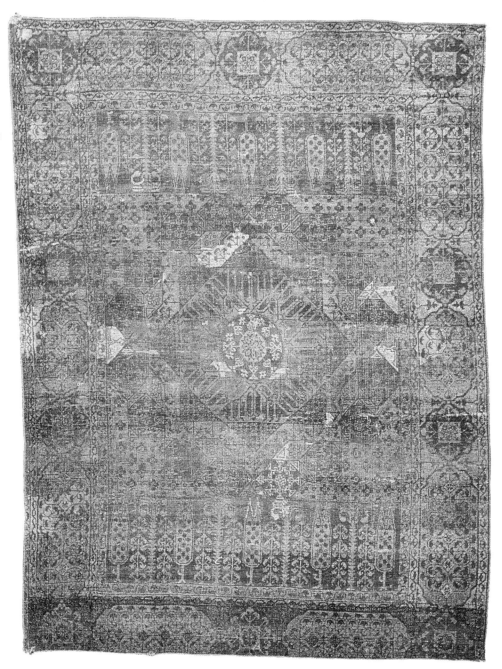

Carpet, with warp, weft and pile of wool, c. 1500. The composition of a central squared field edged with deep bands of cartouches broadly resembles the layout of late Mamluk manuscript frontispieces, while the stylised plant motifs including papyrus and palm-trees and their placing are distant echoes of Pharaonic Egypt. The warp is s-spun wool, four-plied (z-twist) with the weft and pile s-spun wool, asymmetrical knotting. 1.88 × 1.34 m. (Washington, DC, R16.1.3)

weaving. Despite fragments recently unearthed from archaeological sites in Egypt (p. 38), there is no documentary evidence suggesting that *knotted* pile carpet-weaving was undertaken in Egypt before the third quarter of the fifteenth century. Then seemingly out of nowhere well-crafted, knotted pile carpets of sophisticated colouring and design rolled out in the last years of Mamluk rule. One theory is that production was somehow related to waves of migrants fleeing political turmoil in western Iran and settling in Mamluk territory.

Certainly the colouring and patterning of these rugs are far removed from those of Mamluk textiles. Instead of relying on a few tones like dark blues, salmon pinks and apple greens, the carpets explode in a firework display of vibrant colour. The field is usually cherry-red wool, with the motifs in bright leaf green, powder blue, with touches of yellow and white. As the individual design elements are not separated from the field by a dark (out)line of single knots, the observer is presented with conflicting retinal images. The composition typically centres on a large star or octagonal shape, containing and surrounded by a myriad of small, stylised pattern motifs of rosettes, spiky papyrus and lotus plants in a Pharaonic manner, stiff cypresses and palm trees. With deep borders and broad cartouches top and bottom the formal spatial arrangement echoes that found in Mamluk illuminated manuscript frontispieces.

The size, high technical quality and complex composition all suggest these carpets were commissioned for religious and palatial interiors. A couple even include amiral blazons within the design which could associate them with the reign of Qait Bay (1468–96) and his successors. Cairene production continued for many decades years after the Ottoman conquest in 1517, still employing the characteristic composition and colouring, as shown by the Palazzo Pitti carpet woven in the second half of that century (King and Sylvester 1983).

Silks from Timurid Central Asia

Until recently only one piece (now in the Dom-und Diözesanmuseum, Vienna) could be securely dated as an early fourteenth-century Central Asian silk. Used as a burial garment for the Hapsburg Archduke Rudolf (d. 1365), it was originally a *tiraz* fabric of the il-Khanid ruler of Iran, Abu Saʿid, a descendant of Chingiz (Genghis) Khan, and thus made some time during his rule, between 1319 and 1335. A wide band decorated with diamond and polylobed medallions flanked by peacocks is edged with a narrow stripe inhabited with running animal motifs, either side of the inscription band. Its essential pattern-stripe arrangement recalls contemporary Islamic Iberian textile design and is broadly echoed in an early Ottoman fragment (Ettinghausen 1959). A number of other silks, such as the Regensburg Treasury fragments, datable to the mid- to late fourteenth century, possess similar compositions but with more overt 'chinoiserie' motifs (Wardwell 1989b).

Textiles were an important feature of Timurid economy and trade. Genoese and Venetian merchants worked from Kunya-Urgench, south of the Aral Sea, and Tabriz with large amounts of Iranian produced silk passing through Sultaniya. The Timurid capital Samarkand was itself a famous silk-weaving centre, attracting dealers in Chinese stuffs and housing Syrian and Iranian artisans, captured on military campaigns. But as for actual fabrics so prolifically displayed in Timurid manuscript painting little survived, scarcely surprising perhaps given the destruction wreaked by Timur Leng's armies. A few fragments have been identified as Timurid (as in Lowry and Lentz 1989), as these share certain iconographic details with Central Asian metalwork and bookbinding.

However, assigning a provenance and date purely on design details is speculative, as shown by the recent AMS Carbon-14 tests (Indictor n.d.) on some 'Buyid' fabrics mentioned above (p. 45). Indeed, those very analyses revealed that two Cleveland Museum of Art 'Buyid' fragments (inv. nos 68.221 and 50.64) were probably manufactured in the late Timurid period: their dense composition of roundels and diamond forms inhabited by confronting birds and beasts, separated by short inscription bands, had led scholars to presume they were some 200 years earlier in date. Several other late medieval silks are thought to have been woven in Central Asia, and these share common technical features (Wardwell 1987, 1989a, 1989b) which possibly distinguish production of the Khwarizm region, west of Bukhara: a lampas twill structure – not found in contemporary Chinese textiles – of silk warp; and z-spun cotton for both ground weft and metallic thread core, the metallic thread itself being silvered or gilded animal substrate.

Part of the burial outfit of Hapsburg Archduke Rudolf (d. 1365). Silk lampas with both the paired main and binding warp z-twist, with the weft including gilded silver and gold z-wrapped on s-twist silk core. The inscription reads 'Glory to our lord the most great sultan, the exalted ruler ᶜAla al-Dunya . . . al-Din [A]bu Saᶜid Bahadur Khan, may Allah perpetuate his rule', a formula employed by the il-Khanid Abu Saᶜid from 1319 to 1335. (Vienna)

OVERLEAF Detail of silk and cotton mixture, lampas weave, late 14th century, with (?gilded-) silver animal substrata z-wrapped on z-plied cotton core. The paired main warp is z-twist silk, while the ground weft is z-spun cotton; the selvage is formed of two bundles of warp around which the weft threads turn. The structure of this and other associated fabrics, along with the use of gilded leather, strongly suggest Central Asian manufacture. (Nurnberg, Gew 488)

5

OTTOMAN OPULENCE

During the late thirteenth century the Turkic family of Osman (Italian: Ottoman) embarked on an expansionist policy from its base in north-western Anatolia. This *gazi* (frontier warrior) ethos was to remain pivotal to the Ottoman sultanate for the next 400 years. In no time Byzantine authority outside Constantinople had been limited to a landstrip around Prusa (Turkish: Bursa) and to Trebizond (Trabzon) on the Black Sea. Tribute and taxes from captured territories poured into the treasury, their raw and manufactured materials fuelled a fast-growing economy, and their peoples provided cheap labour. Under Hanafi Sunni law one-fifth of these prisoners of war became the property of the sultan and alongside purchased slaves entered the Imperial household or joined the crack Janissary regiments, after receiving training, instruction in Islam and manumission.

In 1326 Bursa became the Ottoman capital for forty years, until it was recognised that Edirne (Adrianople) was strategically better placed for the numerous military campaigns into eastern Europe. The sultanate barely survived Timur Leng's attacks from the east, but his death in 1405 allowed it respite to rebuild and consolidate its authority.

The capture of Constantinople in 1453 by Sultan Mehmed II (d. 1481) heralded a new wave of military activity in the west (the Balkans and Hungary) and the east (Syria and Egypt, Iraq and Iran). Renamed Istanbul, the city became the third and last Ottoman capital, with an intellectual, artistic and cultural life befitting a major political power. Jews and Christians fleeing

Detail of Ottoman embroidery, 17th century or earlier, on linen. The *kum iğnesi*, or 'sand' stitch, may be simple pattern darning in floss silk but its extreme fineness, working over and under single fabric threads, is remarkable. (London, T.99–1923)

persecution or turmoil in Europe were welcomed in their thousands by Mehmed II, keen to use their skills and expertise. The reign of Suleyman the Lawgiver or, as he was known in Europe, the Magnificent (1520–66) was seen as a golden age, with a court and ceremonial eclipsing those of many Renaissance rulers. The reign of Ahmed III (1703–30) was also a time of great artistic and cultural outpouring, known as the 'Tulip Period', despite a continual battle to preserve territorial frontiers from major European offensives after 1655. However, the cost of maintaining control over such a vast region and diverse peoples was staggering in manpower, equipment and revenue: the administrative system was creaking dangerously under the strain. At its zenith the Ottoman sultanate ruled over 25 million people in thirty-two provinces, from the southern Mediterranean seaboard into the Sudan and western Arabian peninsula, from Vienna to Tabriz.

The importance of Bursa

As the first Ottoman capital and an established trade centre, Bursa quickly became the main entrepôt for textiles from Iran, Egypt and Syria. All silk passing through Ottoman territory had to be weighed on the city's official scales and tax paid according to the weight and quality (of cocoons, thread or fabric) and the origin of the merchant, Europeans generally paying 25 per cent or so more than Ottoman subjects. Such transit dues brought in 120,000 gold ducats in 1487, a significant contribution to the treasury, but fell dramatically the next century owing to trade embargoes on Persian silk. Another levy on probably locally produced fabrics was the *damga resmi*, or stamp-duty, assessed by the *muhtesib* (market inspector). Tax evasion was rife, so his duties involved checking bale seals, weights and storage facilities. As in Mamluk lands, illegal mixing of different yarns was a constant problem (Anderson 1989, p. 162); another practice, dealt with in a late eighteenth-century English-Turkish commercial phrase-book (Ebied and Young 1980), was saturating silk bales before weighing.

Bursa was a silk-weaving centre in its own right, already in 1483. By 1504 over ninety different types of luxurious textiles were manufactured on its 1,000 looms, and it was supplying the court with sumptuous cushion velvets and other furnishing fabrics. Fourteen years later just one order for the palace required 750 bolts of satins and patterned silks to be made and dispatched, and although some evidence (Tezcan and Delibaş 1986) suggests that after 1550 palace workshops took over most production, Imperial orders were still being placed with Bursa. With mulberry-tree planting and silkworm rearing in the locale beginning in earnest from the late 1580s, Bursa's trading monopoly in silk was virtually complete. Other towns, like Bilecik nearby, manufactured luxury textiles but none shared its reputation. However, during the seventeenth century the port of Izmir (Smyrna) became the centre for European dealing, with Bursa losing its exclusive right to the official scales. Naturally this affected the city's economy, but more serious was the loss of Bursa's population (and thus skilled workers) by one-third in the final years of the century, presumably caused by the plague which also swept Izmir.

Ottoman guilds

In Bursa, as elsewhere in Ottoman territory, the textile guilds were responsible for ensuring that government regulations were obeyed, and in the early sixteenth century these concentrated on quality control, as in 1502 when 1,000 weavers in Bursa were cautioned for poor work and official anxiety expressed over reduced warp thread density, loose weave, short width and inferior dyes. The warning about dyes if nothing else must have been heeded because unlike Mamluk and Safavid work there is little sign of fading on Ottoman silks and velvets. A century later bad workmanship was still causing some anxiety, but official concern had turned to questions of price and profit: in 1603/4, for instance, the Bursa silk-merchants' guild was persuaded to agree to raw-silk importers getting increased profit. In return the guild officers could press the central administration to take action against unfair practice, even if it was a local problem, as shown by the Bursa weavers' demand in 1564 to control the illegal mixing of filaments by local silk-twisters.

Each Ottoman guild had its patron 'saint': Adam and Idris (Enoch) for the tailors, Seth for the button and *gömlek* (shirt) makers and wool staplers (White 1845, vol. 3). The silk-workers took Eyub (Job) as theirs, as it was said the worms which had so plagued him had been transformed into silkworms. Typically the guild consisted of masters (*üstad*s), journeymen (*kalfa*s) and apprentices (*çirak*s), but the Bursa textile guilds did not acknowledge the *kalfa* category; instead the apprentice had to serve for a minimum of two years in a workshop after training before getting a licence (Gerber 1988). During the sixteenth century the main source of labour was purchased prisoners of war who were manumitted after training or fulfilling contracted quotas, in one case eighty lengths of flowered gold velvet (*muzehhab güllü kadife*) (Gerber 1988, Rogers 1986b). With the scaling down of Ottoman military operations the price of such slaves rose steeply, so the masters turned to hiring weavers on a weekly basis and using outworkers, male and female, for reeling, spinning, dyeing, bleaching, fabric burnishing, and so on.

Archival records (Gerber 1988), suggest the Bursa weaving shops each housed generally fewer than ten looms, requiring perhaps twenty workers, far fewer than the twenty to sixty looms previously estimated (Çizakça 1980). Inventories list the looms as inexpensive pieces of equipment, presumably assessed on their scrap value.

Designs and motifs

Far from selecting a dynastic colour the Ottoman court of the sixteenth and seventeenth centuries revelled in the whole range, from the vibrant to the delicate and sombre. The richer tones are generally found as ground colour in Ottoman silks where small amounts of metal thread embellish brightly coloured motifs which appear to float on the surface. Conversely, pastel shades used in context with simple forms are often found when the field is silver or gold thread, so enhancing the two-dimensional effect.

The colouring and patterning of the earliest-known Ottoman fragment naming Sultan Bayezid (probably Bayezid I (1389–1402) – the second Ottoman ruler of that name ruled 1481–1512) are broadly similar to fourteenth-century striped silks of Islamic Iberia and Central Asia. Perhaps this is linked to the early fifteenth-century 'Romantic Turk' movement, when court poetry and literature emphasised the Turkic tribal ancestry of the Ottoman house (Wittek 1936).

Studies earlier this century assumed that a clear chronology of pattern development could be charted. Unfortunately, things are rarely that simple.

Silk voided and cut velvet with twill details, variously dated to end of 15th/second quarter of 16th century. Main warp is given as z-plied, and the main weft z-twist, with gilded silver s-wrapped around s-twisted silk core. Such velvets with *hayati* blossoms and *rumi* leaf patterning are generally classified as Ottoman, although other provenances have been suggested. (Krefeld, 00976)

Detail of a cut, unvoided velvet garment, said to have belonged to Sultan Mehmed II (d. 1481). If the *çintemani* motif was a royal device, perhaps it symbolised the three titles of Chief, Warrior and Emperor used by certain Ottoman sultans and their proclaimed mastery of two seas and two continents. (Istanbul, 13/6-2/3228)

Ignorant of the Bayezid silk's existence at that stage, scholars thought simple, bold pattern repeats of, say, a disc or carnation fan characterised early production, and were then transformed into discrete geometric compositions. They considered that floral motifs were later introduced alongside or within star or diamond shapes, or, conversely, temporarily replaced by two stylistic elements favoured in manuscript illumination, metal and ceramic surface decoration – the *rumi* (arabesque scroll and split-leaf palmette) and *hayati* (characterised by the Chinese cloud and 'lotus' motifs). After this, ogival lattice compositions became fashionable, perhaps occasioned by the 1517 conquest of Mamluk territory. By the last quarter of the century floral elements had grown ever more intricate, according to this argument, with early seventeenth-century pattern characterised by meander stems moving in parallel, with blossoms and leaves 'blown' in alternating directions. The uneven tension of static floral motifs with elongated profiles and nervous, spindly stems in later work was considered an accurate reflection of Ottoman artistic (and military) decline.

Such neat theories do not survive rigorous inspection. The underlying problem is the difficulty of dating the silks and velvets accurately. Pictorial and textile evidence suggest some patterns were concurrent and remained in production for a long time. A few pieces, like the chasuble of Metropolitan Anthony of Moscow (1572–81) with a lattice design, may be assigned *terminus ante quem* dates. Many of the thousands of garments and textiles in the Topkapi Saray Museum, Istanbul, have labels naming royal owners, but these are known to be often unreliable.

One motif had a particularly long life. Known now as *çintemani* (Sanskrit: *chintamani*), it is formed of three closed crescents, arranged in pyramidic fashion, underlined by two thick wavy 'tiger-stripe' lines: at times the two

elements appear separately which may or may not imply the total device. Ottoman archival documents mention a textile pattern called *pelenk*, but there is some debate (Öz 1950, Denny 1972, Tezcan and Delibaş 1986) whether it relates to this motif. Nevertheless, a 1680 lexicon (Meninski) defines *pelenk* as relating to both leopard- and tiger-skin markings (that is, spotted and striped).

The closed crescent form itself was not new: it had featured in Mamluk textile patterns and on Iberian/North African flags where perhaps it alluded to heroic horsemanship and battle exploits of the Prophet's uncle, spreading the message of Islam. Further eastwards, in Central Asia, three circles arranged as an inverted triangle had been the blazon of Timur Leng, while in Persian manuscript painting the mythical hero Rustam is shown in a tiger-striped tunic, signifying bravery and masculine strength. Whether any of these associations were consciously adopted is arguable, but the *çintemani* design, in part or in totality, features repeatedly on Ottoman palace artefacts: the sultan's throne, tiled panels in the royal harem and treasury buildings, court garments and carpets, royal horse-trappings, and so on. As Goodwin (1971) notes, it has been interpreted as depicting the sun, moon and Venus rising over the Milky Way; moons over forks of lightning; the Three Truths (Knowledge, Law and the Way); and linked to Buddhist symbolism. If this motif was indeed a royal device, perhaps it symbolised the three titles (Khan, Gazi and Caesar) used by Mehmed II the Conqueror and his successors, and their proclaimed mastery over two seas and two continents.

A similar query regarding symbolism arises over the floral motifs, used so extensively on Ottoman textiles now in public and private collections, reflecting the Ottoman passion for gardens – or perhaps just the taste of nineteenth- and twentieth-century collectors. Singly, combined and frequently overlaid one with another, the peony, lotus, pomegranate, prunus, carnation or dianthus, rose and bluebell, and of course the tulip are shown framed in sweeping *saz* (water reed) plumes and acanthus leaves. In Ottoman mystical poetry of the period (Schimmel 1976) certain plants were imbued with meaning. The *çinar* tree (Oriental Sycamore) with its open five-pointed leaves was described as leading the garden in prayer alongside cypresses, evergreen, stalwart and deep-rooted in the Muslim faith. The petals of the rose represented the Muslim community gathered about the Prophet, while the blood-red tulip symbolised those willing to die for the faith. However, there is no evidence that this symbolism was transferred to secular textiles, any more than on to contemporary pottery.

Indeed, the parallel use of motifs and compositions on Ottoman ceramics and textiles prompts the question who designed these patterns? The general high level of design, often a masterly combination of excitement and constraint, of movement and arrest, argues that the work was not independently initiated in each small local workshop. Its diffusion across various media suggests that cartoons were prepared by court artists and sent to the workshops, where the warp masters tied up the drawlooms and organised the pattern lashes. Certainly the Bursa archives so far published make no mention of a pattern-designers' guild, but neither has any palace record of drawings being dispatched been found as yet.

With the vast quantities of Iranian silk passing through Bursa and later Izmir it is not surprising that much Ottoman textile terminology derives from

LEFT Silk lampas, mid-16th century. The floral and leaf details closely resemble court manuscript illumination of the 1560s, although the garment label (naming Sultan Bayezid II (1481–1512) suggests an earlier dating. Possibly this sophisticated work was characteristic of *heftrenk* production; it was produced in at least two colourways. Pattern repeat of 2.5 m. (Istanbul, 13/37)

RIGHT Silk lampas with a meander composition, 16th century. Four-pattern weft with (?silver-) gold carried on a silk core. As few Ottoman velvet and silk examples of the meander composition are known, it suggests this was a less favoured design than the ogival lattice. Few structural analyses of Ottoman silks have been published, but it seems typically the silk warp and weft were z-twist. (Lyons, 29420)

Persian. However, apart from a group of patterned silks in which isolated floral sprays are arranged in offset rows, it seems that contemporary Persian textile design had little influence. Ottoman composition generally has a less pronounced illusion of depth and omits any figural representation. Indeed, there is such a noticeable absence of human, animal, bird and insect motifs in Ottoman fabrics that when such elements are incorporated one questions the textile's provenance. It was the court's adherence to the Hanafi law which proscribed such motifs, or so the explanation runs; however, there are figural motifs on Ottoman ceramics and on textiles of contemporary Mogul India, also Hanafi in persuasion.

Contemporary Italian patterned fabrics had a greater impact on Ottoman textile design. As early as Mehmed II's reign (1451–81) over 110,000 ducats were spent by the court on purchasing luxury fabrics from the Italian states. A number of Imperial robes were tailored from these sixteenth-century velvets and silks and others are patterned with Italian-styled motifs. In turn Ottoman textiles influenced the designs of Lucca and Florentine work which borrowed the ogee lattice and meandering stems, as well as certain floral motifs, such as the carnation, pomegranate and tulip. The cross-fertilisation was such that with our present knowledge it is difficult to assign a provenance, one way or the other, with any confidence. Reath's work (1927) into the structural differences between Ottoman and Italian luxury textiles was after all no more than a preliminary study.

In contrast to earlier times patterns employing calligraphy were limited to textiles with a religious or related function, such as the Ka'ba *kiswa* cover, military flags, tomb covers and later prayer-rugs. Contemporary European paintings depicting naval and land battle scenes show a wide range of Ottoman flag and banner designs, and every corps had its standard. Examples typically feature alongside the *shahada* and verses from Victory *sura* 48, the legendary double-bladed sword, the *dhul faqar*, said to have been given to 'Ali by the Prophet after the Battle of Badr AD 624. The six-pointed Seal of Solomon, or an eight-pointed star, and roundels of *thuluth* calligraphy naming the four Rashidun caliphs complete the composition.

Flags shown in paintings are sometimes contained in fabric sheaths decorated with chevrons and writing. Perhaps this association of fighting for the faith led to similar designs being used for Ottoman cenotaph covers. Often on green or red silk lampas, which to a mid-eighteenth-century traveller (Thompson 1744, vol. 2) respectively denoted the deceased was a descendant of the Prophet or a Janissary, the elegant *thuluth* inscriptions in white generally include the *shahada* and *sura* 2, v. 144, which refers to praying: 'We see the turning of your face [for guidance] to the heavens . . . .

Fabrics

The exact meanings of many Ottoman textile terms have been lost. The word *çatma* is thought by some scholars to refer to voided velvet and by others to a fabric with metallic thread. The characteristics of *selimiye* and *seraser* are ill-defined, although it is now generally accepted that both were silks or silk-cotton mixtures with gold or silver thread in the weft, along with the fabric *kemha* (Persian: *kimkha(b)*, 'kincob'); however, the 1680 Meninski lexicon states that the latter was a highly flowered silk damask. It is possible that *serenk* (Persian: 'three colours') was a silk without metallic thread woven with yellow and two or more colours and that *heftrenk* (Persian: 'seven colours') was a sophisticated lampas weave incorporating many different-coloured pattern wefts, as seen in two royal robes in the Topkapi Saray, probably mid-sixteenth century in date. Woven patterns of such complexity were obviously costly to produce, but records show that by 1640 *heftrenk* was cheaper to buy than *atlas*, usually defined as monochrome satin. It is inconceivable that a patterned silk cost less than a plain silk, so perhaps the term had wider meaning in later years.

One of the most expensive silks was *seraser*, on account of the quantity of precious metal used in the weave. A fur-trimmed garment of this fabric could be worth three times more than a choice male slave. In a vain attempt to control the flow of bullion from state coffers the sultan in 1566 ordered that the number of *seraser* looms be reduced to 100, and as a result over 200 Istanbul looms ceased operating. A decade later Bursa *seraser* looms were similarly affected. Certain velvets were also costly, like *kadife-i çatma-i ala*, thought to have a variegated pattern with metal thread, worth around 3,400 silver *akçe* a length, and *kadife du-hav* (? cut and uncut velvet) which was about a third less (Rogers 1986b). Such high prices would have precluded many purchasers, and sumptuary regulations would have acted as a further constraint.

Sumptuary legislation

The Ottoman administration and *ulema* (Arabic: *ᶜulama*) held that the display of wealth in excess of one's social standing would inevitably lead to discontent and rebellion unless curbed. Thus believing that social unrest would be defused at a stroke, Murad IV (1623–40) ordered everyone to resume wearing attire associated with his/her class, profession and status. Public disquiet over growing affluence of non-Muslim communities in Ottoman territory prompted regulations stipulating the wearing of inexpensive linings and certain styles of clothing, head-covering and footwear to emphasise the lower social position of these communities (Galanté 1931, Faroqhi 1984). As leaf-green was now firmly associated with certain important Muslim leaders, non-Muslims, whether European or Ottoman subjects, were punished severely if seen wearing it.

Theoretically ostentatious and luxury fabrics permitted only to those with status and wealth (Mustafa ᶜAli in Tietze 1982, pp. 580-1, slightly amended):

Heavy silk cloth and brocades, spectacular rare [*seraser*], velvet, and [*kemha*] after the latest fashion have to be reserved to the kings and their princes. Cloths of lesser quality, satin [*atlas*], [*kemha*], and shot silk, are appropriate for vezirs, *begs* [commanders] and *beglerbegs* [governors]. Materials which are inferior to these in appearance and in a way more popularly in demand befit the middle classes . . .

Whether the official rulings had a more lasting impact in Ottoman times than in earlier periods is questionable. A Turkish proverb runs: 'The prohibition of the ruler lasts three days.' However, in court circles it was a different story.

Textiles at court

Social and professional identification through dress was perhaps most apparent in the Ottoman *hil'at* (Arabic: *khilᶜa*) system. Apart from the usual presentations on the installation of the sultan, and promotions and dismissals from

RIGHT Cenotaph cover of silk lampas, 18th century, possibly belonging to a Janissary. The circles and pendant forms contain pious invocations; one narrow chevron carries a Quranic verse (*sura* 2, v. 144), with the *shahada* ('There is no god but Allah, and Muhammad is His prophet') decorating the broad band. (Washington, DC, 1.84)

ABOVE Ottoman silk flag captured by Polish forces at Vienna in 1683, featuring the double-bladed sword, *dhul faqar*, given by Prophet Muhammad to ᶜAli after the Battle of Badr, 624. (Krakow, 3981)

OPPOSITE The Ottoman textile term *seraser* perhaps applied to fabrics of this kind. A similar fragment of compound plain weave has a main warp of s-two-plied silk and a binding warp of floss silk, possibly gummed; five weft, two of which are silver and also (?silver-) gold s-wrapped around a z-twist silk core. The label on this garment names Mehmed II (d. 1481) as the owner, but the pattern suggests at least a 16th-century date, when a number of Ottoman princes were so named including Sultan Mehmed III (1595–1603). (Istanbul, 13/9)

Cushion silk velvet with red and green pile, and silver on a silk core. Such cushion silks and velvets featuring a large floral motif, often 'inlaid' with other blossoms, repeated two or three times in offset rows between a lappet border top and bottom, are generally dated to the 16th century. On completing the composition the weaver did not cut the finished piece from the loom but inserted a wooden baton and immediately began on another piece. 128 × 64 cm. (London, 86–1878)

LEFT Ottoman caftans with such patternings in different fabric qualities were presented as hil'at (Arabic: khil'a) to foreign envoys and members of their entourages, according to rank, in the 17th and 18th centuries. (Istanbul, 13/866)

OVERLEAF Detail showing fabric crowd barriers, from a miniature painting of the royal parade celebrating the 1596 capture of Eğri (Erlau, Hungary) by the forces of Mehmed III, Shah-name of Nisari, 1598. (Istanbul, H. 1609, f. 68B–69A)

office and so on, the major distribution of court hil'at was at the annual Bayram celebration after Ramadan. Made by 105 tailors in five Istanbul workshops during the seventeenth century, hil'at robes were graded in at least four classes, ranging from 'plain' to 'most excellent'. As before, the quality, quantity and cut depended on the office and rank of the recipient: thus chief pages in the treasury in the early eighteenth century merited three gold and three satin caftans at Bayram, but the underlings received only three damask ones. The special kapaniçe robe, a prerogative of the sultan, was presented to vassal princes of Wallachia and Moldavia, whereas European envoys received only caftans for many years, as described by Dr John Covel (1893, p. 196) of the English entourage in the 1670s:

> The stuff is of white silk, flower'd with great branches, some times half moones (and the like), yellow or tawny, all with very great weales; and, according to the dignity of the persons, they are of cloth, of silver, or gold, or with more or less gold and silver wrought in the silk. There were give[n] 16 amongst us. I sold mine for 6½ dollrs. My Ld.'s was worth 25 or 30 . . .

A sizeable portion of state expenditure went on hil'at; in 1690–1 it was over 6 million silver akçe, almost half that spent on clothing the Janissaries, then some 55,000 strong (Mantran 1962). This was apart from the tens of thousands of garments needed for the royal household, of which a fraction, some 2,500 items, survive in the Topkapi Saray Museum, Istanbul.

To see the court assembled was a spectacular event: even the cosmopolitan Hapsburg envoy, Busbecq, the man responsible for taking the Turkish tulip bulb to the Low Countries, was lost for words (1694, p. 96): 'I am not able to describe the Gaudiness of the Show: in one word, 'twas the most glorious one I ever saw in all my life.' The rich variety in head-dresses, from the small truncated 'cone' turbans of low-ranking ulema to the majestic plumed caps of the Janissary veterans, was matched by the glitter of the ceremonial dress. It was customary for bolts of silks to be spread before the royal mounts and the crowds to be contained behind textile barriers stretching for miles, as John Sanderson saw in 1596 (1931, p. 60): '. . . the people, his subjects, Turks, Jewes, and Christians, held at length great peces of cloth of gould, velvett, sattin, and dammaske of all sorts and colloures . . . .'

The court's appetite for textiles appears to have been insatiable. Just one order from Selim I (1512–20) to Bursa in 1518 detailed 750 lengths of fabrics to be immediately dispatched to the palace. Fifty years later, over a month, one weaving master in the court workshops had to supply 103 pieces of seraser, serenk, kemha, velvet, çatma and other fabrics; additional materials were to be provided by outside suppliers.

Drapes and hangings, cushions and floor covers were needed in quantity. One royal wedding procession in the mid-seventeenth century included 240 mules loaded with such furnishing fabrics (Baudier 1652). The small audience chamber of the sultan alone had twelve window hangings and twenty bolsters and cushions on the throne-bed – and there were some 300 rooms in the harem section. With the caveat that published technical detail is sparse there is little to distinguish the furnishing fabrics from dress silks and velvets except weight. Similar patternings and colourings are found in both until the eighteenth century, when carpet compositions, such as 'medallion' designs, influenced cushion velvet patterns.

Embroidery and printing

According to a 1680–1 court record, in the small royal audience chamber at the Topkapi Palace alone were some sixty embroidered items. As official pay registers of 1526 include five *zerduz* (gold embroidery) masters, originally from Tabriz, Bosnia, Hungary and Georgia, such work was probably produced on site. Gold thread and jewels embellished the bolsters, cushions and drapes for the great throne-bed, while there were window and wall hangings of gold-worked crimson satin and floor coverings couched in gold thread. The richness of this work was such that, disposing of such items in the mid-nineteenth century, the Royal Mint retrieved over 900 kg of gold and 88,000 kg of silver from the metallic threads (Tezcan and Delibaş 1986). On sixteenth- to seventeenth-century work, generally on heavier materials like velvet and sometimes leather, the metal thread was deliberately worked to create textural and surface patterns in the manner of metal repoussé work. A few coloured silks were introduced to highlight certain details. Both motif and surface details were taken from court manuscript illumination, clearly seen in an album page of Murad III (1574–95) (Codex Mixtus 313 fol. 17v, in the National Österreichische Nationalbibliothek, Vienna).

Several centres in the Ottoman European, western and eastern Anatolian regions were renowned for their embroidery. Purchases could be made in the bazaar but not always of the quality desired. One royal order for seven bedspreads, each measuring over 3 m, was turned down by a team of ten women outworkers who admitted they could not achieve the fineness of work required, which suggests that 'sand' stitch (*kum iğnesi*) was specified in the order (Celal 1939).

The embroidered area was sometimes small in size, perhaps slipper tops, a sash, a headband. There were wrappers for turbans, garments and towels; as a mid-nineteenth-century observer noted (White 1845, vol. 1, p. 104):

> No object, great or small, is conveyed from one person to another; no
> present is made – even fees to medical men – unless folded in a
> handkerchief, embroidered cloth or piece of gauze. The more rich the
> [fabric] envelope the higher the compliment to the receiver.

Door and window hangings and coverings known now as 'quilt covers' in the West were worked either before or after lengths were seamed together. Before stitching began the pattern was often pounced on to the reverse of the cotton or linen.

In some cases the relationship to contemporary ceramic and textile designs is noticeable. For large-scale work, as in Ottoman tile panels, the colours number usually only three or four, on a white, blue or red ground; however, there are examples with ten or more shades. On more intimately sized items the handful of colours tend to be pastel in tone, such as pinks, light blues and soft greens. Black silk was often used for outlines, but it has since largely disintegrated because the mordant proved corrosive. Metallic thread is sparingly used for highlights, sometimes as 'frost', that is, 'stretched' round the silk core whose colour augments the other floss or z-spun silks used in the work.

From the few printed Ottoman fabrics identified (Pfister 1938, Spuhler 1988) it seems luxury silks inspired several patterns. One in the Newberry collection, Ashmolean Museum, Oxford, has fat stylised 'pine-cones' separated by small rosettes and open 'carnation' heads, with a border of flowering plants

Detail of printed and inked linen, 16th–17th century. Plain weave with z-spun warp and weft. The stamped design of 'pine-cones', open carnation fans and small rosettes is edged with a 10.6-cm band of sprays of carnations and tulips alternating with flowering bushes. 20.8 × 38.5 cm. (Oxford, 1990.467)

and cypress trees, somewhat in the manner of a *seraser* fabric thought to be seventeenth century (p. 95). Originally on a white or cream ground most of the design is now marked in a dark grey, with touches of red in two shades, one a pigment.

Textiles and the Ottoman army

Once a year ten *arşin* (approximately 7 m) of broadcloth along with similar lengths of cotton for shirting and turbans were given to every Janissary, and their regiments formed but one section of the army. Then there was the navy to be supplied: just one Imperial shipyard order in 1565/6 required 5,000 sailcloths and 4,000 cotton lengths. To meet demand cotton cultivation in south-east Anatolia was increased, and sales to Europe banned.

The styles and colours of Ottoman military uniform were numerous, but perhaps for the modern reader one of the most intriguing items is the talismanic shirt, worn for protection. Some were roughly worked but a few, associated with the royal household, are finely decorated garments. In these the fabric is completely covered with Quranic verses, pious invocations and 'magic' squares containing auspicious numbers and alphabetical letters (each possessing a set numerical value) in coloured inks and gold and silver stamping. Both the cutting to shape and decorating would have been executed at auspicious times, as advised by the Royal Astronomer.

The Janissaries also had to be supplied with their distinctive white felt head-dress, produced by a guild of ten workshops. Legend had it that its 'folded sleeve' appearance commemorated the blessing given by the Sufi dervish mystic Haci Bektaş '[who] rent off a long Sleeve, which he wore

101

continually on his Right Arm, and putting it upon the Head of one of the Soldiers, cried out prophetically . . .' (Hill 1710, p. 19).

The military also had to be provided with shelter on campaigns. In 1683 25,000 tents were pitched before the gates of Vienna to accommodate members of the royal household, officers, men and stores. The making, repair and storage of such campaign tents were the responsibilities of the *Mehter-i Hayme Cemaati*, first set up with thirty-seven craftspersons by Sultan Mehmed II in 1478; by 1650 it employed 2,000 men. The Ottoman sultans were not innovative in employing tents in this manner. The Fatimid caliphs relied on tents for certain ceremonies: one took 150 men nine years to make at the cost of 30,000 gold coins (Serjeant 1972), and one of the royal Burji Mamluk tents needed 300 men to erect it. Of the magnificent examples used by Timur Leng in Samarkand as court reception rooms only pictorial representations in Timurid manuscripts remain.

We are more fortunate with Ottoman tents, as a number have survived in collections in Istanbul, Vienna, Budapest, Krakow and Stockholm, and reportedly there are fifty examples in the Hermitage Museum, St Petersburg. The size and appearance of the felt or broadcloth campaign tent depended on its specific function and occupants. Those housing high-ranking officials or the sultan himself could have numerous apartments and were always richly patterned inside and out. The Polish king, Jan Sobieski, wrote to his queen about those he seized at Vienna: '. . . it is impossible for me to convey to you the refinement and luxury which reigned in the vizier's tents: they contained baths, small gardens, fountains, fish-ponds and even a parrot' (Mansel 1988, p. 35).

To lend some privacy the 'royal' tents were surrounded by fabric fences and hangings, themselves often gaily decorated: '. . . in imitation of flowers and arabesques, and stitched with gold thread and coloured silks . . .' (White 1845, vol. 3, p. 50). The broadcloth or felt motifs, applied or inlaid, are

Lotto carpet, probably late 16th century. Although the Venetian artist Lorenzo Lotto often included such rugs in his work, they feature in Italian paintings as early as 1516 and clearly were fashionable in Dutch mercantile households well into the 1660s. (Washington, DC, R34.18.4)

RIGHT Ottoman cotton tent with a pitched roof, three side curtains and canopy, taken by Polish forces at the 1621 Battle of Chocim on the Dniester. The (?excise) stamp on the lining has been read as AH 1007/AD 1598–9. (Krakow)

LEFT Royal Ottoman talismanic shirt, second quarter of 16th century. To protect the wearer the linen surface is covered with pious invocations, talismanic symbols and Quranic verses including *sura*s 18, 36–46 and 48. Suleyman the Magnificent wore a small skull-cap so decorated underneath his turban. (Istanbul, 13/1150)

arranged in architectural and landscape conceits. Stylised floral compositions are framed by two-dimensional arches, while window openings are completed by 'grilles' of silver thread embroidery. In some court tents embroidered landscape panoramas decorate the top portion of the tent 'walls'.

The main Ottoman suppliers of woollen cloth were the Balkan workshops of Salonika and Plodiv, which struggled to clothe the ever-expanding Ottoman army. Despite an Imperial programme of workshop expansion in 1703, the fixed state prices for wool cloth proved ruinous. Merchants realised it was more profitable to export the raw wool and buy the cheaper European woollen cloths. Not that all the imported stuffs were cheap: a fashionable gentleman of early eighteenth-century Istanbul would have proudly sported an outer robe of 'Londra' (English cloth) over his caftan of Persian gold-patterned silk. However, the real prize was the domestically produced fabric, mohair.

Mohair

If Bursa was synonymous with silk, Ankara (European: Angora) was renowned for its fine goat-hair and the moiré mohair cloth made from it. Ambassador Busbecq noted in his letters of 1555 (Forster 1968, p. 50):

> The pieces which have received the marks of the very broad 'waves' in continuous lines are considered the best and choicest. If the 'waves' are smaller and of varying lengths and run into one another . . . this is counted as a defect . . .

Dernschwaum, his travelling companion, described and illustrated its manufacture in detail, how the yarn was greased, woven, soaped and washed, and boiled in tall copper cauldrons for a day (French 1972, pp. 242–3):

> As soon as it is taken out of the cauldron, they put the boiled chamlet, all 70 pieces, under a press and squeeze the water completely out. . . . From these boilings and pressings come the water (marks) on their own. . . . At the presses they have 7 men pulling on one thick baulk. If they are skilled, one man could, with effort, turn it, in the way they press wine at Vienna. Their chamlet presses, however, have two spindles: the press-beam is 3½ Viennese els long, the spindles are short and thick.

The city and the neighbouring region also produced grosgrain, a silk and mohair mixture with a corded appearance to the tabby weave. Such was one seventeenth-century English admiral's liking for 'grogram' that it eventually resulted in the British sailors' rum ration being called 'grog' (Anderson 1989, p. 164).

Rugs and carpets

Wool was also in demand for carpet-making. For the court weavers (*Cemaat-i Kalicebafan-i Hassa*: the Society of Imperial Rugmakers) it is likely that design cartoons were prepared within the palace. The similarity to contemporary luxury textiles in composition and motif is striking, particularly in the case of the so-called Cairene rugs. Sharing a similar technical structure to earlier Mamluk carpets, these were probably made in Ottoman Cairo or in Istanbul, for in 1585 Murad III ordered a number of Cairene weavers to the capital. Apart from the palace workshops there were carpet-makers in Istanbul, Kütayha, Uşak and nearby Güre, the latter definitely making rugs to Imperial order and design in 1553. However, although records list certain designs to specific centres (Rogers 1986a), it has not proved possible to identify either pattern or production.

As the term 'rug' suggests here, some examples are small in size. Prayer-rugs with their wide borders and inner arched frame sometimes supported with 'columns' are typically 70 cm by 50 cm. Demand for these was such that in 1610 the *ulema* strongly advised against including overt Muslim designs (for example, the Ka'ba, Quranic inscriptions), as the rugs were sold to un-believers (Faroqhi 1984, Raby 1986). Others, like the so-called 'Medallion' and 'Star Uşak' carpets styled in the manner of contemporary book-binding decoration, are much larger. The field colour preferred for these high-quality 'court' rugs is a deep red or blue, rich fertile ground for the realistic and imaginary blossom motifs worked in six to nine colours.

At first glance these luxury pieces have little in common with late eighteenth- to nineteenth-century carpets, known in the West by such names as 'Ghiordes' and 'Ladik'. The spatial consideration, the linear rendering of motif and the colouring look so different, but closer inspection reveals that many of the stylised motifs were originally derived from 'court' rugs.

A less extensive palette is employed for carpets best known through the paintings of Holbein and Lotto, whose names now identify these two pattern types. Only a handful of dyes, such as powder blue, yellow and green, are used in the repetitive geometrical elements placed 'into' the scarlet red ground. The primary colours together with the complex intensity of the motifs would normally produce conflicting retinal images for the observer, but a single line of deep-brown knots serving as an outline substantially reduces the impact. The patterns have no immediate link with other media in the Ottoman world, the closest parallel being seen in Central Asian saddle-covers and floor coverings as depicted in certain thirteenth-century Chinese paintings.

6

SAFAVID
SPLENDOUR

Within fifty years of Timur Leng's death in 1405 two Turkoman tribal confederations, called the Qara- and Aq-Qoyunlu (Black and White Sheep respectively), were fighting for political dominance in Iran. In the ensuing turmoil people increasingly looked to the Safavid family in the Ardabil region for leadership, spiritual and political. Supported by other Turkomans and by the Sufi dervish order (thus the dynastic name Safavid), the young Isma'il seized Tabriz and the title shah in 1501, and within the decade most of Iran had come under the Safavid banner of *Ithna 'Ashari* ('Twelvers') Shi'ism. This territorial expansion and the emphatic Shi'i stance of Isma'il and his descendants brought the dynasty into conflict with the Sunni Uzbek rulers in Afghanistan and the Sunni Ottoman sultanate.

Despite continuous warfare on the Ottoman frontier which led to the Safavid capital moving from Tabriz, to Qazvin (1548) and finally Isfahan (1596), the long reign (1524–76) of Isma'il's son, Tahmasp, saw the economy revive. State monopolies on certain raw materials including silk brought merchants from East and West to the court, eager to obtain preferential treatment for their trading concerns, for this was the age of the great East India companies. It was to the Safavid court at Tabriz that the Indian Mogul Emperor Humayun (d. 1556) fled in 1544. This sojourn had important repercussions on the development of Mogul art and design, including textile and carpet patterns.

Silk lampas with satin ground and twill details, now much faded, with metal thread, end of 16th/early 17th century. The name of Ghiyas appears on the camel-howdah of this free interpretation of an episode in the Layla and Majnun romance, with the love-crazed Majnun seeking solace among wild animals. Another silk lampas, also with Ghiyas's name, elsewhere, has a less fluid composition of the same scene.
73 × 69 cm. (Copenhagen, B21/1931)

Within court circles the cultural impact of Persia and Georgia was increasingly felt as the shah worked to curb the turbulent political and military influence of the *qizilbash*, certain Turkoman chieftains, responsible for the early Safavid territorial expansion. In their place Persians were promoted to government offices and later, in the reign of Shah ᶜAbbas I (1587–1629), men from the Caucasus and Georgia were bought in to form a new military élite, the *ghulaman-i khass*. Despite frequent urban uprisings, political confidence rose with the retaking of lands lost to Ottoman forces, paralleled with the flowering of the arts under royal patronage and a flourishing export trade in textiles.

However, major problems concerning delegation of power and state finance remained largely unaddressed, while in the last decade of the seventeenth century official religious persecution alienated the Armenian and Georgian Christian, Hindu, Jewish and Zoroastrian communities in Iran and the Sunni Muslims of Afghanistan. When rebellions broke out in the north-west provinces and the eastern regions, the regime found it had few friends. After appalling losses the capital Isfahan surrendered to Sunni Afghan tribal forces. Russian forces moved into the Caspian region, while the Ottomans took control of the Caucasus. Trade came to a virtual standstill during 1722–5. What remained of Safavid authority was in the hands of the military Afshar commander, Nadir Khan, and in 1736 he assumed the title of shah. Despite military successes, his unremitting campaigning brought the country to its knees. His assassination in 1747 resulted in political fragmentation, but within a decade two powerful families had emerged: the Zand in control of the southern regions, and in Persian Azerbaijan the Qajar family, formerly of the Safavid *qizilbash*.

The court and the guilds

The luxury fabrics of Iran had long been admired by merchants and travellers like Marco Polo. The patterned silks and satins of Yazd were of such quality that they were sent as diplomatic gifts to the Ottoman sultan by Yaᶜqub, the leader of the Aq-Qoyunlu Turkomans (1478–90) (Woods 1976). From the outset the Safavid regime was an active patron of the industry, and centres like Qum, Savah and Tabriz in the north and Kashan and Isfahan in the south quickly grew in importance. Some textile regions never quite regained their fifteenth-century reputation, such as Hormuz and Khurasan, but the velvets of Khurasan could still rival Genoese work in the third quarter of the sixteenth century.

Weaving and dyeing shops were established by Shah Ismaᶜil, and sericulture promoted. However, hostilities with the Ottoman sultanate led to economic embargoes which hindered the export trade. ᶜAbbas I, who had learnt to weave in his youth, moved to improve matters, if only to finance his military reorganisation. The lands of the troublesome *qizilbash* were seized and transferred to royal ownership, and in 1598 the major silk-producing regions of the southern Caspian came under Safavid control. Caravanserais were constructed and roads built to facilitate the transportation of goods. A royal monopoly on silk trading was established, as a 1603 East India Company report recorded (Ferrier 1986, p. 457):

> . . . the ould Emperor Shaw Abbas [I] by his commands prohibited all
> men what nation soever to buy any silks unless from his hands, and to

the ende all should be collected and brought into his Magazenes, hee sent his owne servants with ready Money to all places where silks grewe to buy from the Countrey people. . . .

The shah took one-third of the silk 'crop' and set minimum prices on the rest. Private trading was discouraged by imposing on each load a tax of 12 *tuman*s (over 919 g silver) on non-government silk, destined for export, and an import tax of 4 *tuman*s on silk brought in for processing (Steensgaard 1975). The expertise of Armenian merchants in the domestic and export silk markets was harnessed by the state as their families were moved *en masse* to both the Caspian area and Isfahan. To minimise the impact of embargoes the overland silk caravans were rerouted through Astrakhan to Europe to bypass Ottoman Bursa, so cutting road tolls which added 400 per cent to the original price (Anderson 1989), and a Persian diplomatic mission set sail to Lisbon in 1603 with 200 bales of silk to show the viability of shipping silk.

The virtual royal monopoly on silk continued until 1629 when uprisings of Caspian silk-'growers' forced the shah to abolish the arrangement. At a time when the total population was about 8 million, some 3 million living a nomadic life, more people were employed in silk-weaving than in any other craft, with over 1,000 looms in one quarter of Kashan alone. The majority of textile workshops were privately owned but there were royal weaving shops. Weavers worked to set loom widths and patterns, but special orders were undertaken by negotiation; the uniquely patterned gold and silver stuffs ordered by the King of Siam in 1713 required extra loom equipment and a year's work (Floor 1987, p. 22).

Textile workers were protected to a degree against the galloping inflation of the last Safavid years by the guild system, which allowed prices to be adjusted every month, with an annual major review. In seventeenth- to eighteenth-century Isfahan (Keyvani 1982) eight of the thirty-three major guilds, excluding those of tailors and haberdashers, were actively associated with textiles: these were gold-pattern weavers (*zaribafan*), each employing twenty to thirty workers, and *gulabatun*- and *naqda-duzan* (gold and silver thread embroiderers); the drapers who dealt in shawls, tents and woollen stuffs; textile dyers; fabric printers; cotton and wool weavers; tent- and saddle-makers; braid sellers; and makers of prayer-rugs and rush mats. Each guild had its own parade flag, *ᶜalam*, and distinctive standard finial, and frequently its own argot. To the surprise of Chardin (1711, vol. 2), the mid-seventeenth-century French traveller and craftsman, there was no journeyman status in the Safavid textile guilds as such but rather a *muzdar* or hired worker category.

The Kashan and Isfahan guilds provided certain garments to the court free of charge, but an important source of supply was the royal ateliers (*buyutat-i saltanati* or *karkhana*s), housed within palace grounds and also set up in provincial capitals, which made luxury textiles for court use and for export at a profit. With a yearly budget of about 14 per cent of total state expenditure these ateliers from Shah ᶜAbbas's time were in the charge of two court officials and individually controlled by a workshop master and supervisor, the latter responsible for selecting the textile pattern (Keyvani 1982). The craftsmen themselves were not exclusively Persian by birth and Muslim by faith; some were foreigners, occasionally prisoners of war. As government employees perhaps numbering 5,000, they received board and lodging, clothing, unemployment and sickness benefit, with a triennial salary review and bonus

Various banners carried in guild parades in late 19th-century Tehran. The central lozenge-shaped flag with cotton ribbon ties and mirrors was that of the potters' guild.

system. Their title *darbasta* ('tied') implies royal craftsmen were not allowed to undertake outside work; indeed, there was no link between the *karkhana* masters and those of the urban guilds. However, during the second half of the seventeenth century the system began to break down with the bazaar undertaking certain processing. By the end of the century the royal dyehouses and certain silk workshops ceased production. From then on the weaving of gold- and silver-patterned silks, velvets and carpets and all dyeing were undertaken by private concerns, with the palace providing the raw materials.

The importance of silk

By the beginning of the seventeenth century silk was the main trading commodity in Iran. From commercial and diplomatic documents it has been calculated that the total production of silk around 1618 was about 1.3 million kg weight, of which a third was retained for domestic use in the weaving of textiles and carpets. Some twenty-five years later the silk crop had increased 50 per cent, peaking at over 2.7 million in 1670. There were four qualities of silk filaments, the most expensive being *shaᶜrbaf* and the cheapest Shirvani raw silk, reeled from the broken cocoon, known as Ardass in England (after a town in Georgia). Contemporary records contain fascinating information but often raise more questions than they answer. There are the usual problems regarding terminology, and European transliterations, past and present, often cause added confusion, with writers sometimes unaware of the difference between, for instance, *shaᶜrbaf* (filament) and *zarbaft* (luxury fabric), and *darai* ('of the Emperor Darius'; red or 'variegated' silk) with *du-ru* and *du-ruya* (double-sided) and *du-rangi* (two-coloured).

A 1618 East India Company report (Ferrier 1976) mentions that Yazd and Kashan velvets 'of all colours and prices' were available for purchase but infuriatingly omits any technical or design description which might assist in distinguishing the manufacture of each city. In the twentieth century Ackerman (repr. 1964) eagerly designated surviving silks and velvets to various Safavid manufacturing centres but not on any scientific basis. From European sources it is clear that aside from velvet-weaving the Yazd and Kashan workshops produced satins which resembled Italian Lucca work in some manner and damasks. Taffetas could be watermarked or given a lustrous sheen, but apparently plain-weave 'shot silk' was not in production. As this simply involves weft of one colour silk and warp of another shade, presumably it was not fashionable. Although Western records state that the usual width was 26 in (66 cm) and length 6¾ yd (6.17 m), surviving silks and especially velvets are somewhat wider. We are told that sixteen lengths of pure silk taffeta cost the price of one of 'double and a half pile' velvet, scarcely surprising given the extra silk required for the velvet pile warp and the specialist weaving involved. The Persian 'sugared' velvets did not sell well on the English market. Were these decorated with large patterns (Ferrier 1976), or was this the name for those velvets 'encrusted' with 'purl' or 'bright check' gold thread highlights?

Even the costly rich-patterned *zarbaft* silk was available in some 100 (unspecified) varieties, and foreign merchants could choose between lengths woven in Isfahan, Kashan and Khurasan. For Chardin (1711, vol. 1, p. 215) there was no doubt – the best textiles came from Kashan:

All the wealth and livelihood of Kashan comes in the main from fabrics

Detail of a silk waist-sash, probably from Safavid Iran, 16th–17th century. Not only did the fashion for wearing such decorative sashes spread to eastern Europe and Mogul India, but so did their manufacture. (Cambridge, T.48–1912)

of silk, and gold and silver brocade. There is no other place in Persia where more satin, velvet, taffeta, tabby-weave, damask, floral silks and silks [woven] with gold or silver is made than in this city and its surrounds.

Kashan was also famous for the production of silk for waist-sashes measuring about 4 or 5 m in length and some 60 cm in width. According to reports, the patterns were so designed that when folded and rolled the waist-sash appeared to be two separate fabrics, one striped and the other essentially floral. Isolated motifs of flowering plants typically decorate both sash ends, while the rest of the fabric is patterned with narrow horizontal stripes carrying waves of floral elements or rows of leaf forms. In the most luxurious examples the ground is gold or silver thread with seven or more pattern silk wefts, with two or three shades of each colour. Across Asia to eastern Europe such sashes were highly prized, and when demand exceeded Persian production in the eighteenth century Armenians organised manufacture in Istanbul, Russia and Poland.

Detail from a miniature painting in the *Khamsa* of Nizami, *c.* 1501–10, Tabriz, showing the Shah Isma͑il *taj* both with and without the addition of a turban cloth. As with dervish headgear, the shape and detail of the *taj* had religious significance. (Istanbul, H. 762)

Textiles at court

In the manner of earlier Islamic dynasties the Safavid regime adopted a dynastic colour, worn in a distinctive form of red headgear, as introduced by Haydar, then leader of the Shi͑i Safavids, shortly before his death in 1488. The *taj-i Haydar* ('crown of Haydar') and the type introduced by Shah Isma͑il, '. . . made with twelve foldings, in form much like the Bottles used in *Languedoc* and *Provence*, which have great and flat Bellies, and very long and narrow necks' (Olearius 1669, p. 235), quickly led to the Safavid supporters being called the *qizilbash* (redheads). The twelve *tark*s, or padded sections, which rapidly decreased in width from the rim edge to end in a tall finial, symbolised the wearer's allegiance to the Shi͑i doctrine of the twelve Imams, while the baton-like finial perhaps represented *axis-mundi*, the spiritual leadership of the Imamate. The materials used in its construction have been variously described, but a damaged example, discovered in 1970s' archaeological work at Ribat-i Sharaf (Kiani 1981) and incorrectly identified as a purse, proves that early sixteenth-century *taj*s were made of cotton padding covered with red silk, perhaps dyed with madder extensively grown in the Ardabil region. Around this a white or coloured turban cloth was wound.

Occasionally the shah also wore red garments, but rather than having a dynastic significance the colour indicated his mood (George Manwaring in Ross 1933, p. 221):

> The King's disposition is noted by his apparel which he wears that day; for that day which he weareth black, he is commonly melancholy and civil; if he wears white or green, yellow or any other light colour, he is commonly merry; but when he weareth red, then all the court is afraid of him, for he will be sure to kill somebody that day.

This association of summary execution and the wearing of red continued into the mid-nineteenth century, and various sumptuary regulations requiring Jews to include it in their dress reflected the negative symbolism. Black, the colour of mourning and revenge (see p. 50), was worn by all the court during Ramadan and Muharram, months of special significance for Shi'is, and at other times of great sorrow. After his defeat by the Ottoman army at Chaldiran in 1514, Shah Isma'il donned black and ordered all military flags to be dyed that colour and emblazoned with the word *al-qisas* 'revenge' (Savory 1980). In contrast to Ottoman society green was not held in high regard, and indeed this provided important ammunition for eighteenth-century Afghan leaders seeking Meccan theological approval for their rebellion (Krusinski 1728, vol. 1).

Besides the *taj* early Safavid court artists depicted certain high-ranking court officials wearing robes with elaborate decoration around the neck. Known as the 'cloud-collar' in modern parlance because of its similarity to Chinese Ming (1368–1644) collar ornament, it had a long history in the region, according to the pictorial evidence. A superb example, now in the Museum of Oriental Art, Moscow, is embroidered with gold thread and coloured silk. Its motifs, medallion forms and their positioning, but not lobed shaping, are echoed in the embroidered panels and bands on a dark green velvet robe, said to have been the gift of Shah Muhammad Khudabanda (1578–88) to the Ottoman sultan in 1583, now in the Topkapi Saray Museum.

As with its Ottoman neighbour the Safavid court luxuriated in textiles. Shah Tahmasp reportedly changed his robes up to fifty times daily, and on his death in 1576 over 30,000 garments, excluding turban cloths, and 200 ass-loads of silk were found in the royal wardrobes. Acquisition on this scale was not rare: the linens, cottons and silks accumulated by Shah Husayn (1694–1722) were sufficient to clothe an army of 100,000 men. Every seven years the royal wardrobe, the responsibility of the *sahib-jam* of *rikab-khana* (Master of the Wardrobe), was emptied and the contents burnt to retrieve gold and silver from the metallic threads. Thus the last Safavid wardrobe dispersal yielded bullion for the Zand regime to raise a force of 25,000 men.

Nau Rauz, the Persian New Year celebrated at the March equinox, was marked with royal gifts of textiles to the court and the customary presentation of *khalat* (Arabic: *khil'a*) was followed. The exact procedure for ordering the honorific garments and the quality of metal thread (see p. 26) are known from the court administration manual *Tadhkirat al-Mulk*, written *c.* 1725. The shah's decision to award *khalat* was recorded by the vizier, then passed to the superintendent who collected the fabric from the workshops. For garments actual cutting of the fabric was carried out in the royal *Qaychachi-khana* (tailoring department) at an auspicious hour, as advised by the Court Astronomer. Cloth of gold was reserved for the highest officials, the lower ranks receiving satins and other quality silks, moiré taffetas or perhaps only cottons. One delegation from Holstein in 1637 was presented with robes, turban cloths and over 200 lengths of fifteen assorted silks, including satins and damasks (Du Mans 1890). Even in 1746 when the economy was in total chaos, the annual distribution of court *khalat* was 12,000 garments.

Colour and pattern

As Richard Hakluyt (1903) reminded an English merchant in 1579, 'in Persia they have great colouring of silks', and East India Company documents some fifty years later listed some of the shades that Persians were eager to buy, such as various reds and gallants ('flame'), popinjay (parrot green), straw,

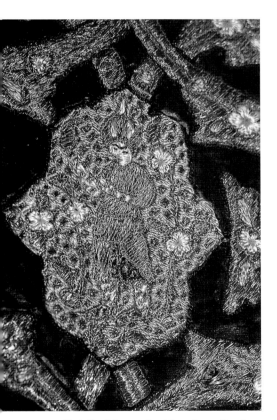

Detail of the embroidered appliqué decoration on a dark green velvet robe, recorded as sent to the Ottoman sultan by Safavid Shah Muhammad Khudabanda in 1583.
(Istanbul, 13/2088)

RIGHT Portrait of Sir Robert Shirley, 1622, by Van Dyck, in his *khalat* robes as Safavid envoy to the court of St James, London. By this date the Shah Ismaᶜil *taj* had been replaced in court circles by a large turban. (Petworth)

ABOVE Silk plain-weave warp ikat with brocaded pattern, 17th century. The warp has a slight z-twist; the main and one pattern weft have no discernible twist, while the metal is s-wrapped on an s-twist silk core. 45.5 × 28.5 cm. (Washington, DC, 3.103A)

OPPOSITE Silk compound twill of irises and poppies, end of 17th/early 18th century. Both the main and binding warp are z-twist, while the weft in three colours have no discernible twist, with both (?silver) gold and silver s-wrapped on s-twist silk core. 103 × 28 cm. (Lyons, 30157)

hare, pink, orange, peach, lavender and ash. Although many Safavid silks have faded (unlike Ottoman fabrics), it is still clear that bright colours with strong dark outlines were indeed features of sixteenth-century manufacture, and in later years a more pastel palette of salmon pink, pale green and pale blue was preferred with outlines in less strident tones. A new colour also came into vogue in the early seventeenth century – *nafti*, named after Baku oil; however, no example appears to have survived.

To incorporate these colours into lampas weave up to ten supplementary wefts (not all continuous) were employed, and Chardin (1711, vol. 2) mentioned seeing as many as thirty shuttles in operation with looms manned by six weavers. A typical Safavid lampas, with a satin ground and twill binding, has a width of 68 cm. This is slightly wider than measurements given in East Indian Company records, as is the average velvet width (72 cm). The Safavid velvet may have only two or three colours in the pile warp, but the most elaborate examples employ eight or so, with or without the addition of brocaded gold or silver thread, as foil or thread, and occasionally 'purl'. The pile warp does not necessarily travel the total loom length; the weaver could introduce and discontinue different colours as the pattern required. Thus the reverse of a Persian velvet in this period often has a patchwork appearance despite its tight, organised weave, so different from Ottoman work in both respects. Safavid velvet pile is usually formed of paired warps, the increased density creating an exquisite, sensuous softness. In some examples the pile is solid, uniformly covering the whole surface; in others it is voided to reveal the satin foundation. In itself this provided a lustrous smooth surface, but, as Sonday (1987) has noted, the Safavid weaver often added supplementary wefts of metal thread. This use of the voided surface is found in Indian Mogul velvets but not widely seen in Ottoman work apart from some velvets classified as early Ottoman where just the pattern outlines or motifs are voided or 'recessed'.

However, it is the inclusion of human and animal motifs that immediately distinguishes Safavid dress-weight silks, velvets and carpets from Ottoman textiles. The reader must decide if the usual explanation that Ithna ᶜAshari Shiᶜism permitted such representation whereas Ottoman Hanafi Sunni convention condemned it is adequate. The seventeenth-century traveller Pietro Della Valle (1663) thought such figural textiles were woven in Kashan, but another European (Du Mans 1890) identified them as Isfahani work. What is in no doubt is the close resemblance to contemporary manuscript painting. The proportions, poses and details of these human, animal and bird forms used by the court artists are faithfully transported on to these luxury fabrics, occasionally placed on a monochrome ground devoid of context but generally arranged within a landscape setting.

It is interesting that, rather than proclaiming the Turkoman origins of the dynasty and its *qizilbash* supporters on these luxury fabrics, the Safavid designers turned for inspiration to Persian legends and literature, such as the *Shah-nama* and *Khamsa* of Nizami. In a typical silk double-cloth the vertical stripes carry cartoons depicting scenes from these well-known stories: the star-crossed lovers Layla and Majnun, Khusrau's sighting of Shirin, and Zukalya's failure to tempt Yusuf (biblical Joseph). Also fashionable were scenes depicting the hunt and pursuit (the dragon-slayer, the hunter, the rider leading a prisoner), and the subsequent feasting and relaxation, both favourite analogies in religious and philosophical poetry.

Small, simple repeats also feature in a group of velvets, assigned various dates. The lack of rhythm and movement in the motif arrangement, typically a row of seated figures or horsemen alternating with a line of trees, suggests bazaar, not court production.

In sophisticated silk and velvet patterns the repeat is designed to minimise vertical and horizontal emphases. Sometimes the motif is reversed in alternate units and rows, as in the so-called dragon-slayer silks. In others the motif is turned so that it appears to have four different 'faces'. The full pattern repeat may be over 2 m in length and may fill the full 72 cm loom width (Sonday 1987).

Several of these luxury fabrics carry a person's name somewhere within the pattern. A dozen or so names are thus recorded on a variety of weaves: that of ᶜAbdullah appears on a silk lampas, on a velvet and a double-cloth; likewise the signature of a certain Khwaja Ghiyas al-Din ᶜAli Yazdi. Fifty of Ghiyas's fabrics were among the 350 sent by Shah ᶜAbbas as a gift to the Mogul emperor Akbar (1556–1605). Another is Shafiᶜ, known to be the son of the famous court artist Riza ᶜAbbasi (d. 1635–6). This link and the close relationship to the style and manner of court manuscript and lacquer painting of the period suggest that the signature identifies the textile designer rather than the master weaver or the commissioning agent.

Reflecting the Safavid passion for gardens, flowers and plants are favourite motifs. Occasionally the flower heads are depicted as open blossoms carried on and falling over elegant, sweeping arabesque scrolls which are themselves arranged in a series of 'layers', but the usual design takes the form of an isolated spray repeated in offset rows. From delicate leaves at the base a thin stem curves up to a full, open head of perhaps a poppy, rose or iris. Often a tight bud and blossom shown in profile give balance to the asymmetrical composition, which sometimes includes birds and flying insects. With the silks the ground is often enhanced with metallic thread carried as a supplementary weft. Sometimes subtle diamond forms are produced by twill weave, but elsewhere the criss-crossing effect is produced by imprinted lines, ironed in as noted by Wills (1883, p. 191), resident in Iran in the third quarter of the nineteenth century:

> This he [the *utukash* or ironer] does by ironing a pattern . . . with the edges of his iron, generally a box-iron filled with charcoal; often, however, merely a heated rod. He irons upon a large jar, which he holds between his knees.

Related is a tight lattice pattern containing individual flowering plants, a composition exploited more freely in contemporary carpet design.

Afshar production

As mentioned earlier striking colours in patterned silks and velvets were replaced in the closing years of Safavid rule with quieter tones. The patterns themselves seem to change so little that modern textile and art historians have generally assigned fabrics as either Safavid or Qajar, but a small detail now permits a more precise dating.

A series of Persian figural silks, generally classified as seventeenth century, show the men wearing caps apparently with three points. This is the Afshar *kulah*, which actually had four points, said to have been devised by Nadir Shah himself shortly after his investiture in 1736. It was rumoured that the distinctive shape symbolised his control over Iran, Afghanistan, India and Turkistan, but it is now suggested that as the form of the Safavid *taj* had religious significance so this design alluded to Nadir Shah's introduction of Sunni Islam as state doctrine, with the four corners symbolising the four Rashidun caliphs (Diba 1987). Perhaps the 'classic' Safavid patterns were deliberately retained to give a veneer of legitimacy to the Afshar court. Despite

Both halves of an official Safavid velvet document case, dispatched to the Danish court at the end of the 17th century. The portrayal of both the falconer and the kneeling servant recalls the work of court artist Riza ᶜAbbasi. 68 × 16.5 cm. (Copenhagen, D 1227)

OPPOSITE Silk lampas with gold, early 17th century. Patterns based on a real or imaginary flowering plant, displaying full blossoms and buds carried on delicate stems, reflected the Safavid love of gardens. 64 × 40 cm. (Lyons, 27960)

RIGHT Detail of silk double cloth, 16th century. Plain weave, with staggered repeat of three cartoons: Yusuf and Zukayla, Khusrau on horseback and Shirin, and Layla and an emaciated Majnun. The inscription, freely translated, reads 'Sleep soundly and from our friendship glad tidings will arise.' 32 × 17.5 cm. (London, OA 1985.5–4.1)

RIGHT Silk compound plain weave with metal-thread ground, probably first quarter of 17th century. A similar piece featuring parrots was found in a Danish royal burial of 1627. 32 × 36 cm. (Copenhagen, 13/1991)

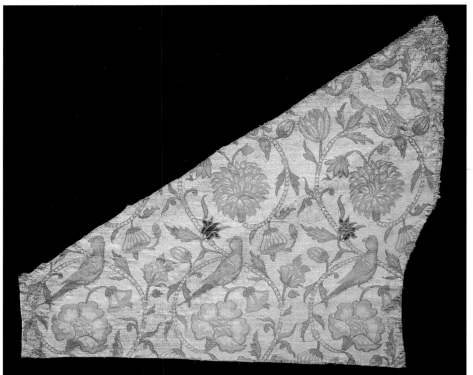

Central detail of silk, mid-18th century. One binding and four-pattern warp including silver carried on a silk core; and six weft including silver-gilt strip. In the early 20th century such fabrics were classified as 17th-century Safavid, although the characteristic headgear of the Afshar regime is clearly featured. (London, 313–1907)

holding the reins of power, Nadir himself waited some seven years before throwing off all pretence that he was acting for the Safavid family.

Carpets and *kilims*

During Shah Tahmasp's long reign (1524–76), if not before, royal carpet workshops were set up in Kirman, which according to observer Kaempfer (1977) produced fine wool carpets with animal motifs, in Isfahan in the royal gardens, Kashan, and possibly Tabriz and Yazd. By the 1720s Yazd court carpets were well known; high-quality work was also produced in the eastern provinces.

Many individual design elements incorporated into the composition of surviving sixteenth-century carpets and *kilims* are almost mirror images of those employed on luxury silks and velvets, and presumably design cartoons were prepared by court artists. As with Safavid textiles, there is no overt sign of Turkoman and Timurid patternings in the carpets. Even the Milan 'Hunting' carpet woven in 929 AH/AD 1522–3 (possibly 949 AH/AD 1542–3), shortly after the Timurid regime was finally ousted from eastern Iran, is in assertive Persian 'Safavid' style with hunters riding across a field of arabesques.

Working from cartoons, the weavers' contribution would have been limited to interpretation and making. At its best, as in the famous 'Ardabil' pair of carpets woven in 946/1539–40, the harmonious combination of composition, motif and colouring produced by fine workmanship and knowledge of material cannot be bettered, but at times the painstaking reproduction of an over-decorous pattern in carpets and silk *kilims* yields a less than satisfactory visual effect.

The Safavid colouring is unlike contemporary Ottoman work, but then this is to be expected with the different designs and the greater use of silk. The weavers were undoubtedly aware of the potential offered by the dramatic colour changes perceived by the observer viewing the silk pile in different lights. The fine silk filaments and the use of asymmetrical knotting allowed these intricate patterns to be faithfully worked; knot density could be high, around 55 per square centimetre.

In some carpets, the precursors of the 'Isfahani' and 'Herati' design groups, an illusion of depth is created by 'layers' of elegant arabesques, each carrying full flower heads, on a dark rich field. On 'Hunting' and 'Animal' carpets, so called because of the main motifs, the ground colour is generally a wine red. Conversely the two-dimensional design is emphasised by the heavy use of silver and gold alongside jewel-like tones in the 'Polonaise' rugs (a mistaken attribution arising from Polish heraldic devices on carpets displayed at the 1878 Paris Universal Exposition); records suggest that work of this kind was produced in Kashan. However, it is unwise to assign any one design group to a particular weaving centre. Beattie (1976) has shown that pieces closely related in pattern, motif and colouring have no similar warp/weft structure, while carpets sharing common technical features (such as coloured warp and selvage structures) may have markedly different patterns.

As only five of the surviving 1,500 to 2,000 Safavid carpets and rugs carry dates accepted as genuine, establishing a pattern chronology is problematic. And there is such a wide variety of compositions and motifs reflecting the courtly passion for gardens, hunting and feasting. What is clear is that Safavid court patronage raised the craft from pastoral and village work to a sophisticated, metropolitan art production, which was to inspire European nineteenth-century artists and designers such as Delacroix, Gauguin and William Morris.

OVERLEAF Safavid 'Hunting' carpet, with a
date in the central medallion which may be read
as AH 929/AD 1522–3 or AH 949/AD 1542–3. Silk
warp with cotton weft and wool pile of
asymmetrical knots (44 per sq.cm).
5.70 × 3.65 m. (Milan, d.t.1/154)

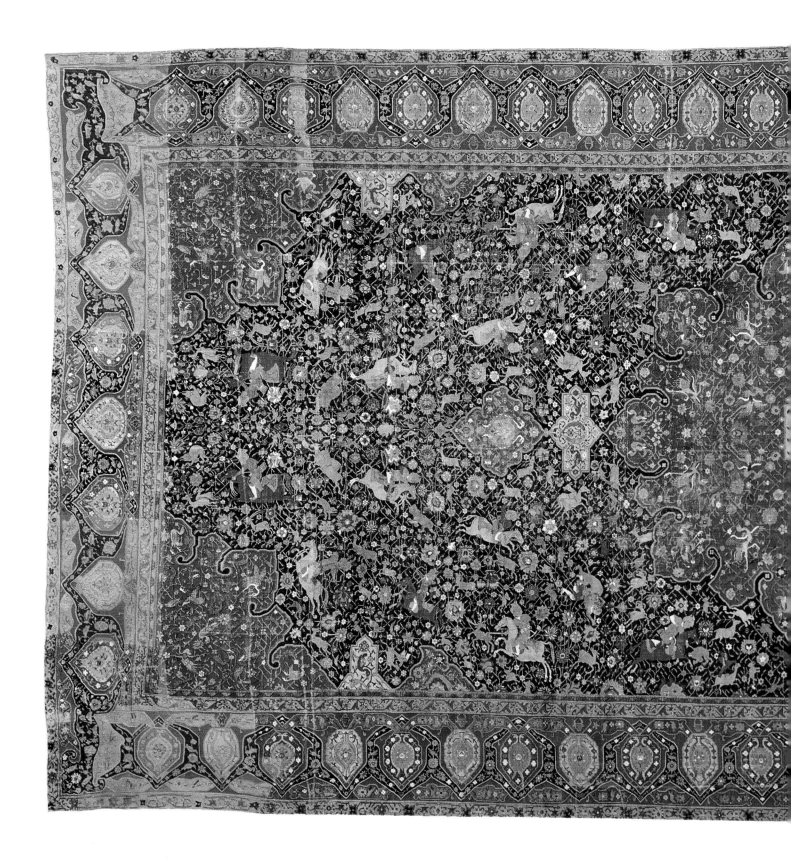

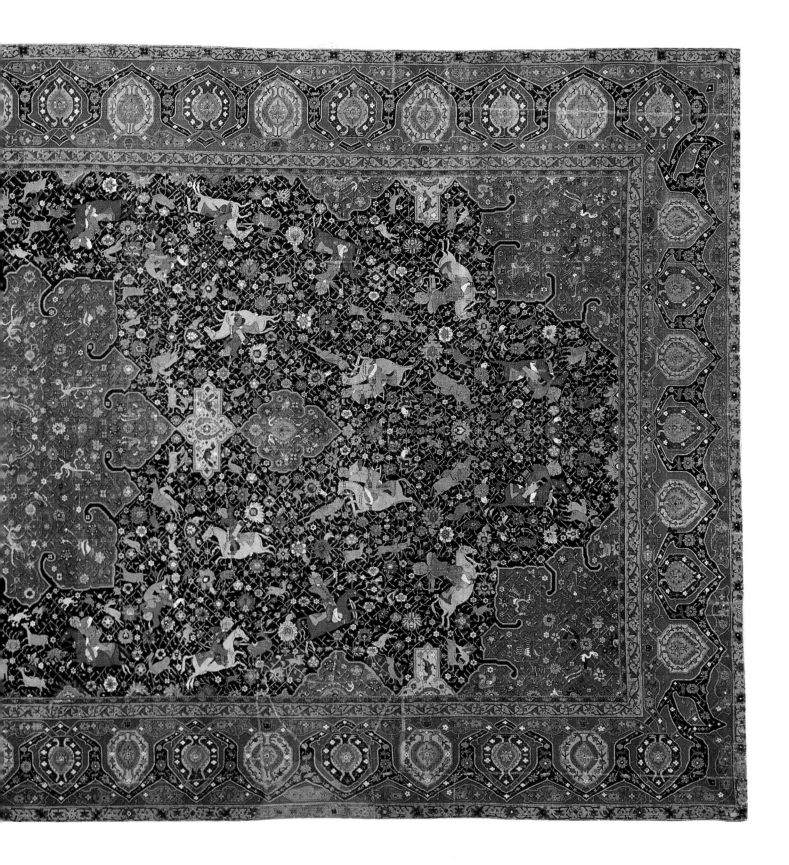

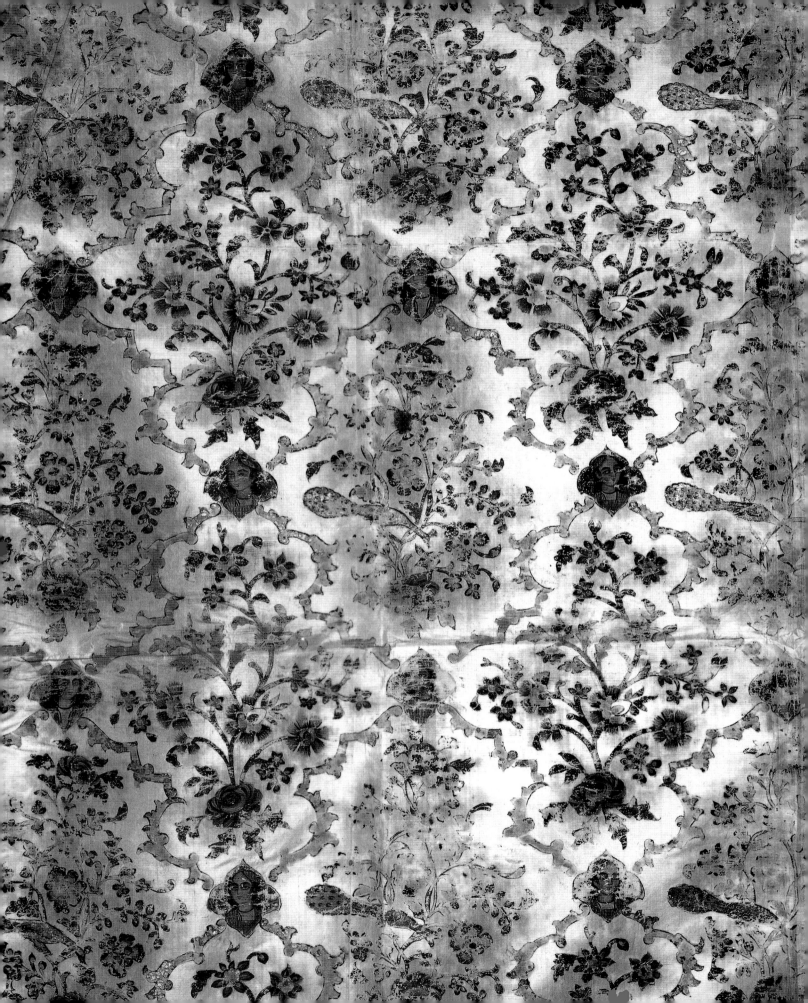

7

TEXTILES OF QAJAR IRAN

Establishing Tehran as its capital in 1786, the Qajar family brought Zand power to an end in the southern provinces of Iran in 1794 and swept up the remnants of Afshar rule in Khurasan. Administration was run on largely Safavid lines with long-standing problems regarding the economy and delegation of power still unresolved. The numerous Qajar princes were dispatched to the provinces as governors, where they squandered local revenues setting up glittering courts on the Tehran model and dreamed of outmanoeuvring their siblings to claim the throne. The Qajar regime achieved the territorial unity of Iran, but the establishment of internal peace and stability proved more illusory.

The Ottoman sultanate no longer posed a serious political threat, but both Russia and Britain had territorial ambitions in the region. Recognising this, Qajar princes and officials sought the support and protection of ambassadors, and increasingly the shah found himself unable to act at any level without regard to the European powers.

Internal dissension grew with demands for constitutional government. Real control, it was felt, issued not from the Gulistan Palace but from the Russian and British legations. Territorial losses in the Caucasus in 1828 prompted the Qajar shah to begin reorganising the army on European lines. With these and other reforms interest in Western styles was fired, fuelled by the influx of cheap textile goods from Europe and India. Domestic manufacture was

Silk plain weave with painted decoration, 19th century. The bird and floral motifs enclosed in lattice-work surmounted by small female faces are in the tradition of Qajar architectural decoration.
82.5 × 194.3 cm.
(Cleveland, 16.1483)

penalised by advantageous import arrangements, as set out in the 1828 Treaty of Turkomanchay. Under the Qajars government posts and trade concessions were sold to the highest bidder. Investment in manufacture and national infrastructure was negligible: only two serviceable roads existed in Iran, Qazvin-Tehran, and Qum-Tehran.

To the mid-nineteenth-century visitor the bazaars and markets of Qajar Iran seemed full of gloriously colourful fabrics (Grimaldi in Piemontese 1972, p. 299):

> . . . In addition to well-woven and finely coloured floor carpets, that are justly renowned everywhere, there were table cloths hand-made in masterly fashion, shawls of a Kashmir type, rich stuffs of silk and wool decorated with flowers and dazzling arabesques in very bright colours, cushions embroidered with silk gold and silver . . .

In fact by this time domestically produced textiles were already more difficult to find than some forty years earlier. In the first decades of Qajar control the auguries had been good. Sericulture was being resuscitated in the southern Caspian provinces after years of Afshar neglect: in 1744 Gilan's raw silk 'crop' was a mere 13 per cent of the 1670 harvest, but by 1820 production had tripled. Most of this was exported, with only one-fifth sent south for weaving to cities like Isfahan. The former Safavid capital was itself recovering from a devastating fifty years of war, famine and anarchy following the 1722 siege, and its depleted population of some 50,000 people was again making a name in textiles, weaving plain and 'coloured' coarse cottons and more importantly 'gold brocades, which are lately brought to great perfection' (Malcolm in Issawi 1971, p. 262). Shawls were woven in Kirman and Yazd, along with felt rugs, carpets and imitations of English damasks and velvets. European designs were also influencing much of the silk manufacture at Kashan. Rallying from a severe earthquake in 1779, the city 'the inhabitants of which are both ingenious and industrious' (ibid., p. 263) was known for its taffetas and silk-cotton mixtures. Tabriz and Mashhad were other important taffeta centres, but it was agreed the best-quality silk was woven at Resht.

Patterns and motifs

Following the Afshari example, early Qajar pattern-makers drew heavily on the compositions and motifs of sixteenth- to seventeenth-century textiles, as if to associate the new state directly with the renowned magnificence of the Safavid dynasty. So much so that many Persian silks of a certain quality were enthusiastically catalogued earlier in the twentieth century as Safavid, although the patterns sometimes featured figures sporting the special Qajar headgear, a tall lambskin *kulah*, or included 'full-blown' blossoms in the manner of courtly papier-mâché decoration and album painting of the early Qajar period (Diba 1987).

The typical Qajar floral repeat is small (10 cm or less) and stiffly symmetrical, arranged in rows, in vertical and occasionally diagonal stripes, or within a tight lattice. When featured as large technical repeats on a metal-thread ground, such work has usually been considered late Safavid production. A satin jacket in the Victoria and Albert Museum (inv. no. 954-1889) is patterned with a floral shrub motif surmounted with paired birds, clearly derived from late Safavid designs as represented in the same collection and in the David Collection, Copenhagen; the cut is, however, Qajar in style, so should the textile

Qajar oil-painting, first half of 19th century, illustrating the rich variety of fabric patterns employed in Qajar dress and furnishings.

OPPOSITE Silk lampas of paired birds and peacocks with plants, 18th century. Fabrics clearly inspired by such work were fashionable for Qajar garments in the mid-19th century. (Copenhagen, 38/1992)

be similarly assigned? There is at least one instance of earlier textiles being used in later garments, as in a crimson velvet *shatir*'s (court messenger/escort) coat (Khalili collection, London) with appliqués of Safavid silk.

But the motif really associated with the Qajar period is the *buta* ('flower') with its characteristic tear-drop form, variously described as a pine-cone, cypress tree, pear, palm (tree) crown, tear of Allah, the shah's aigrette, and so on. While derived directly from Kashmiri shawl designs, it had its origins in both Safavid and Mogul decorative repertoires. Developing from a recognisable plant form apparently bending in the breeze, the motif became increasingly stylised. The sense of movement disappeared as the mass of confusing ornamental detail increased. The outline took on a more assertive form, with the visual emphasis transferred from the (plant) base to the 'tendril tip'; the flowering plant became more like a sprouting bulb.

The compositional arrangements are echoes from the Safavid pattern repertoire but possess a greater formality, with consequent loss of rhythm and movement. This is confirmed in the weaving. The sophisticated and detailed

Silk tunic, plain weave with brocaded pattern of a floral spray. The surface floating weft, colour banding and the stiff formality of the motif are typical features of Qajar manufacture.
(London, T. 333.1920)

128

weaving of the Safavid period, which allowed minute colour changes within the motif, was not revived. Instead surface weft floats of different shaded silks often produced colour banding within the pattern unit. Sometimes the pattern was painted on the fabric surface, as in a yellow silk decorated with curvilinear lattice-work, filled with a flowering tree and peacock; small female faces are placed at the meeting points of the trellis.

Yet clearly some workshops were capable of undertaking the time-consuming manufacture of warp ikat silks. Polak (in Issawi 1971, p. 271) observed during his travels in the 1850s:

> In general, Persian silks are durable and lively in colour; by binding the skeins during dyeing, they produce delicately shaded, flaming designs; in brilliance and evenness of color, however, they do not measure up to European varieties.

Sadly Polak did not mention whether the patterning followed traditional (that is, Safavid) designs or echoed contemporaneous Central Asian work, which will be discussed briefly in the final section.

Silk lampas with silver thread, 18th century or later. The Safavid and Mogul 'flowering plant' motif has been so stylised that the *buta* resembles a sprouting bulb. 51.4 × 56 cm. (Cleveland, 15.660)

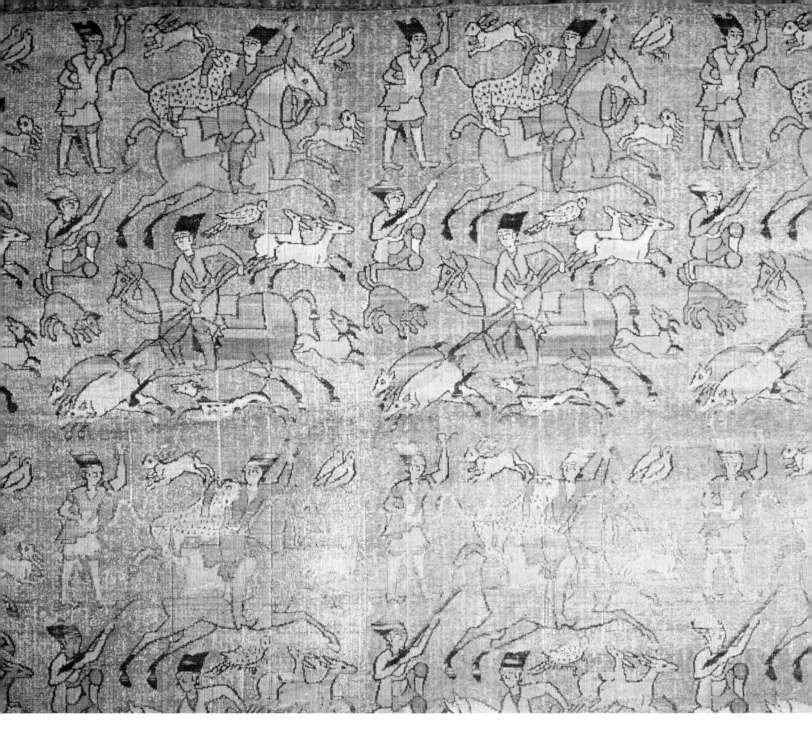

Silk lampas with gold thread, late 18th/early 19th century. Previously classified as 17th-century Kashan, such work featuring the black Qajar *kulah* headgear should be redated. (Lyons, 24392/79)

A new start

The flood of cheap imports into Iran caused a dramatic reduction for domestically woven textiles. By 1848 the British consul could report (Abbott in Issawi 1971, pp. 258–9):

> The manufactures of England have in a great measure superseded the use of Cotton and Silk fabrics of this country, owing to their cheapness, the superiority of the style and execution of the designs, and the greater variety of patterns . . . even the higher classes have often preferred European chintz to the more expensive silk dresses of their own country.

*Sha*ᶜ*rbaf* silk looms were reduced by almost two-thirds in a decade or so, and cotton print-works were only just surviving. Only the wealthy could afford home-produced woollen cloths, such as *tirma* (mohair) and *barak* (camel-hair),

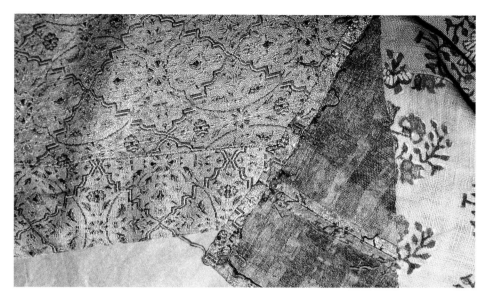

ABOVE RIGHT Detail of silk brocade jacket, showing reverse of silk and part of the printed cotton lining, early/mid-19th century. Such small repeat designs as on the silk and lining are seen in a number of variations on Qajar dress-weight fabrics. (London, 287–1884)

a coat of which was only slightly cheaper than a riding horse. Even so the gift of some Austrian broadcloth to an official would bring 'in return many valuable services' (Polak in Issawi 1971, p. 271).

The programme of state reform began with military reorganisation and re-equipment. The *sadr-i a^czam* (first minister) Mirza Taq-i Khan seized the opportunity this offered. During his short term in office (1848–51) as well as standardising weights and measures he placed orders for broadcloth for the new military uniforms with existing workshops in Mazandaran and Isfahan and with newly established ventures. Kashan was to supply greatcoats made out of silk-cotton mixtures. Factories were set up in Tehran (spinning) and nearby (calico-weaving), and Kashan (silk-weaving), with machinery and instructors brought in from England, Austria and Prussia, and textile craftsmen were sent to Moscow, St Petersburg and Istanbul to gain experience of factory work. Any textile enterprise could apply for assistance. One Tehrani woman was given finance and a five-year contract to make army epaulettes and aglets, previously supplied from Austria and the Ottoman Empire. But it was his promotion of Kirman shawl manufacture and printed cottons which earned Mirza Taq-i Khan special recognition.

Kirman shawls

In the first years of the Qajar dynasty it was the shawls of Kashmir that were highly prized and much sought after. In 1809 Fath ^cAli Shah (1797–1834) ordered their use to be limited to the royal family and leading court officials – in a fit of pique, it was rumoured, because the shah had been thwarted in purchasing some splendid examples. The official reason, however, was the shah's wish to promote the new shawl-weaving industry in Kirman (Brydges 1834, vol. 1), and indeed the ever-increasing amount of bullion leaving Iran to pay for both Kashmiri shawls and Indian printed cottons was causing grave concern in government circles. Barely had the Kirman weavers time to profit from this ruling before the Qajar regime slapped a special stamp-tax on their shawls, which brought in about half of the entire province's tax revenue (Seyf 1992).

Apart from Kirman, shawls were also manufactured in Mashhad and Yazd. As they were cheaper than their Kashmiri cousins, demand grew quickly as Mirza Taq-i Khan promoted the work to the extent that certain designs were known by one of his titles, 'Amiri' ('princely'). At one point in 1857 export had to be temporarily suspended, as supplies were so short. Their use in court circles is shown in Qajar portraits in which princes and officials wear the patterned fabric as honorific robes, garment linings and trimmings, sashes and turban cloths. As it was rare to use the cloth as actual shawls in the Indian fashion, few pieces were made as lengths.

The quality, patterning and colouring of the shawls were so closely based on Kashmir work that 'even experts were unable to differentiate between the Kirman woolen textile which was and still is known as Amiri cashmere, and that made in Kashmir' (Adamiyat in Issawi 1971, p. 294). However, critics argued that the Kirman red tended to be deeper and the motif bolder, with a greater emphasis on the *buta*. Fraser (1826, p. 369) noted that the field colour was black, blue, green, yellow, crimson or scarlet, although some had stripes. In all some seven design categories for Iranian shawls were recorded by Polak (Issawi 1971): *laki*, *lajavardi*, *butai*, *ahrami*, *shal-i gavazn*, *tirma* and *zangari*, but the pattern characteristics of each have not been isolated.

During the nineteenth century two techniques were introduced to save time and cut costs, for the 'traditional' cashmere twill-tapestry weave, itself said to have originated with Iranian and Central Asian weavers migrating to Kashmir in the second half of the fifteenth century, was both highly specialised and laborious work. An intricately patterned length could take over eighteen months to finish, assuming the rate of 2 cm a day was maintained. Husayn Quli Khan promoted the time-saving idea of carrying the weft across the back, and so doing lent his name to this type of silk shawl. Following later Kashmiri practice, embroidery was also used in the production of shawls, thus reducing manufacturing costs, and these *amli* cloths were very successful, we are told, because the Kirman workers employed more suitable 'stitching'.

The shawl-weavers worked over ten hours, six days a week, at vertical looms packed into dark, airless rooms. Child labour was preferred, as noted by various European travellers (Murdoch in Goldsmid 1876, vol. 1, pp. 186–7):

About sixty or seventy men and boys were seated in three rooms, working at looms placed horizontally before them. Each loom, worked by one man and two small boys, contained the fabric of one shawl . . . They sit so close together that their arms actually interlace, but, nevertheless, their nimble fingers work away with great rapidity. They make the shawls with the right side downwards, so that their eyes can be of very little use in guiding them, and they learn the patterns by heart. Extraordinary as it seems, these intricate patterns are learnt by heart and rote, not from painted pictures with long written explanations, but entirely from manuscript. The pattern of the shawl is composed in the same way that another man would compose a piece of poetry . . . We were informed that it would take a clever lad six months or more to learn a pattern, but that when once learnt it was never forgotten.

By the end of the century although the quality of yarn, design and colouring remained high, the standard of workmanship had dropped and with it the

Woollen Kirman shawl, twill weave, presented by Shah Nasir al-Din (1848–96) to the South Kensington (now the Victoria and Albert) Museum. Wool warp and weft in some ten colours with slight z-spin. (London, 884–1877)

Silk Kirman shawl with a corner turned back to show the reverse, third quarter of 19th century, purchased by Murdoch Smith as an example of Husayn Quli work. Both warp and weft of z-twisted silk. The 'loose supple' weave noted by Murdoch Smith was later criticised as a mark of poor quality. (London, 513–1874)

price. Kashmiri examples could fetch two or three times as much. The number of Kirman shawl-looms, given as 2,200 by Abbott (Amanat 1983), fell dramatically: only 120 remained in 1872, and those of Mashhad dropped to 300 (Goldsmid 1876, vol. 1). Business did revive in 1900 with some 3,000 looms in Kirman in operation with an annual output of £60,000 worth of goods.

Printed cottons

Textile printing was undertaken in Iran well before the Qajar period, and it is possible that an undated Persian document recording the initiation ritual for fabric-printers (Sarraf and Corbin 1973) relates to the Safavid period. A fascinating record, it details the questions to and the required responses of the initiate, according the technical processes and the equipment with religious symbolism of *Ithna ʿAshari* Shiʿism. However, it seems that Safavid printed cottons had only a limited market. One seventeenth-century French traveller

RIGHT Cotton printed hanging, second half of 19th century, plain weave with warp and weft z-spun, incorporating a number of printing techniques such as resist, mordant and dye woodblock stamping and hand-painting. (Washington, DC, 1980.8.5)

135

laid the blame on washing difficulties given the shortage of soap (a government monopoly until 1573) (Tavernier 1682, Keyvani 1982) but probably the royal levy of one-third of the cotton crop kept prices artificially high. Indian prints found eager customers even though Iranian cottons could be bought at less than half the price of taffeta. Indeed, it was his wish to control the steadily increasing bill for Indian chintz imports that led Shah ᶜAbbas I (Della Valle 1663) to promote cotton cultivation, and in the nineteenth century the Qajar regime resorted to similar tactics to the same end.

Fath ᶜAli Shah instituted rewards for Iranian designers and printers, and soon the quality of printing was on a par with imported work. For clothing and garment linings, the patterns were generally small 'wreathed and consecutive flowers in gay colours, sparsely thrown upon a ground, white, blue, red, fawn colour' (Fraser 1826, p. 362). These were set as isolated plants, or carried on interlacing arabesque scrolls densely covering the surface. Special designs with Quranic inscriptions were worked for use in burials, while for covers and hangings the composition was more open with a symmetrical or one-way design. An American diplomat, Benjamin, in Iran during 1882–3 was fascinated by the linings of his tent, the property of a former Qajar general (Benjamin 1887, pp. 269–70):

> Nothing could exceed the beauty of the intricate designs which completely covered the interior . . . Each panel had in the centre an agreeable representation of the conventional figure of a cypress, or tree of life. . . . Around this figure were wreaths of flowers, interwoven with birds-of-paradise, and at the base of the picture were grotesque elephants pursued by hunters brandishing scimitars. Over the junction of the panels were a pair of exquisitely comical lions of the most ferocious aspect, bearing naked swords in their right paws.

As he used the term 'kalemkar' (qalamkar: pen-work), it suggests these printed designs were drawn by hand, but resist and mordant stamping with pearwood blocks were also used.

As well as establishing an Art and Design School in Tehran Mirza Taq-i Khan revived the designers' award system for good Indian-styled work and brought in machinery to cut costs and speed up production. It was not enough: the stream of imports became a flood with cheap Manchester printed cotton designed specifically for the Iranian market. Polak noted in his book published in 1865 (Issawi 1971, p. 269):

> . . . manufacture is very laborious and costly, for the colors have to be printed separately, by hand, and then covered with resin to prevent them from mixing together. The most widely used calicoes in Persia are usually supplied by Manchester factories, where the goods are made to suit Persian taste and for sale in the Orient.

It was only a matter of time before the 284 textile-printing workshops of Isfahan closed, and with them over 7,000 craftspersons including dyers, washers, ironers and woodblock makers lost their jobs. Those in Yazd and Kashan were also in trouble, and eventually the related guilds, too, shut their doors.

Cotton-growers fared slightly better. The planting of South Sea cotton had been introduced and fostered by Taq-i Khan, and with the American Civil War interrupting New World supplies Europe eagerly took Iranian raw cotton, only to re-export it into the country as finished cloth. By the 1880s imports of cotton yarn and material accounted for 48 per cent of Iran's total import bill.

Resht work

While Benjamin enjoyed his *qalamkar* tent, royal tents were decorated with *resht* work. As Kirman was renowned for shawl manufacture, the town of Resht, south of the Caspian Sea, was famous in Qajar times for *gul-duzi-i resht* (flower embroidery of Resht) (Murdoch Smith in Wearden 1991b, p. 121):

> A peculiar kind of embroidery and patchwork. . . . It consists of a patch-work of minute pieces of broadcloth of different colours, the seams and some other portions of which are then covered with needlework also variously coloured, the whole forming a combination of geometric and floral ornamentation. The colours being of the brightest, the general effect is perhaps somewhat gaudy.

Similar work was done on a commercial scale in Karadagh, Isfahan and Shiraz, the work of the latter characterised by 'inlaid' shapes of velvet (Benjamin 1887). It was suitable for items such as saddle-cloths, or much larger pieces like floor coverings and tent panels, and thus the saddle- and tent-makers came under one guild.

The complexity and style of decoration are seen at their best on a royal tent dating from the second quarter of the nineteenth century, which when erected has a gable roof over a single chamber with an accompanying side wall. For such large-scale pieces the makers would have worked from full-size cartoons, drawing or pouncing the outlines on to the ground fabric. Pre-shaped pieces were placed on the field as appliqué, or more usually 'inlaid', in which case the exact image of the shape was removed from the ground fabric with a metal cutter. It then remained for the maker to sew the 'patch' to the field and decorate with chain-stitch.

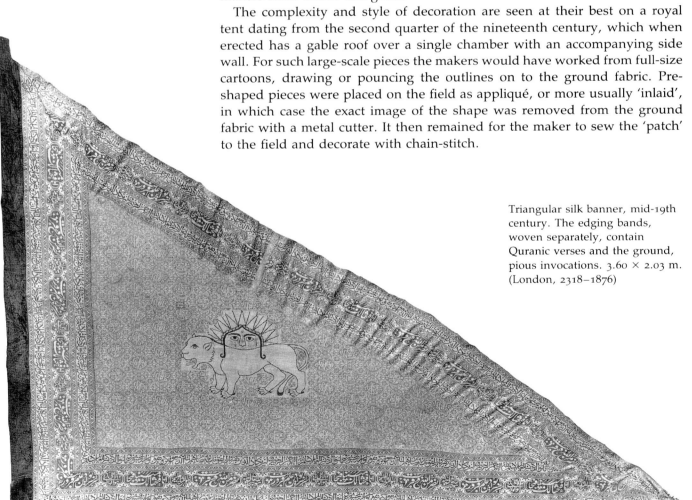

Triangular silk banner, mid-19th century. The edging bands, woven separately, contain Quranic verses and the ground, pious invocations. 3.60 × 2.03 m. (London, 2318–1876)

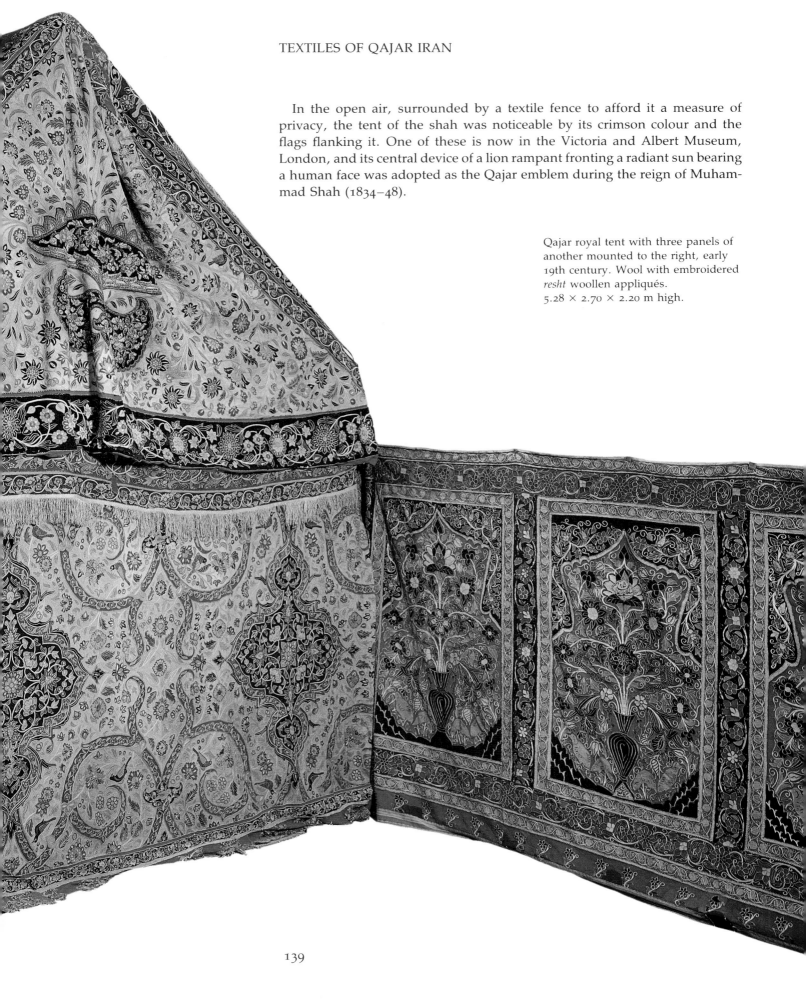

In the open air, surrounded by a textile fence to afford it a measure of privacy, the tent of the shah was noticeable by its crimson colour and the flags flanking it. One of these is now in the Victoria and Albert Museum, London, and its central device of a lion rampant fronting a radiant sun bearing a human face was adopted as the Qajar emblem during the reign of Muhammad Shah (1834–48).

Qajar royal tent with three panels of another mounted to the right, early 19th century. Wool with embroidered *resht* woollen appliqués.
5.28 × 2.70 × 2.20 m high.

Embroidery

Perhaps reflecting the difficulty in finding high-quality patterned fabrics at affordable prices, embroidery in nineteenth-century Iran was used extensively on a wide range of items, from saddle-cloths and furnishings for the home, including hangings, covers and cushions, to items of dress for men, women and children. As in Ottoman work, commercial and domestically produced work is indistinguishable. According to a 1877 history of Isfahan (Issawi 1971), embroidery purchased from the bazaar was priced according to the patterns, which were themselves designed and copied on to cloth in the bazaar. Colliver Rice (1923), writing after the First World War, describes taking fabric to the bazaar, where it was weighed to the nearest $^1/_6$ oz (5 g). The quality and colouring of embroidery thread were discussed and the pattern selected. Getting the designs transferred on to the fabric and buying the thread were the responsibility of the embroiderer. On completion the embroidery was reweighed in front of the customer and payment calculated on the difference. For the fine drawn-thread work which produced the open lattice (at eye-level) of the *ru-band* veil the weight difference was negligible, the silk embroidery barely registering over that lost by the removed threads.

In 'whitework', cream-white silk embroidery on similarly coloured cotton, the decorative effect was achieved by working the stitches, particularly satin-stitch, in different directions, so creating a quietly shimmering surface. However, to embellish the lower sections of women's trousers fifteen or so shades of silks were used. Tent-stitch worked in a series of diagonal stripes transformed a simple cotton backing to look like a miniature carpet '. . . in which the intricate medley of brilliant colors melt and harmonize, as the splendor of autumnal foliage loses itself in the quivering haze of an October sunset' (Benjamin 1887, p. 332). The pattern could take the form of flattened lozenges but more usually was composed of diagonal stripes, as may also be seen in Safavid album paintings, although such depictions of trouser fabrics may indicate printed cottons or patterned silks (also revived in Qajar times) rather than decorative stitching. By the late Qajar period this diagonal composition was also being employed in carpet designs and metalwork decoration.

Also reflected in carpet-weaving were the overall embroidery patterns of (Persian) Azerbaijan, north-west Caspian. On examples thought to date from the late seventeenth century onwards the composition is typically symmetrical, radiating from a central star or polygonal form. Cross-stitch, surface darning or more frequently surface darning on the diagonal is used in one of two palettes: the earlier pieces imitating Safavid patterns sport a dark field with strong colours for the details, whereas later examples have a golden-coloured ground and dusky pastel shades.

Some of the most intricate Qajar decorative stitching may be seen on women's garments associated with the Zoroastranian community. At first glance the *shalvar* and *qamis* in the Embroidery Guild, London, appear to be made of printed fabric, but close inspection reveals the small motifs are painstakingly embroidered. Hume Griffith (1909, p. 127) noted that young girls were taught as soon as they could hold a needle:

> These trousers are often made of very pretty pieces of embroidery joined
> together. As soon almost as a girl can sew she begins to embroider
> strips of brightly coloured materials in order to have them ready for her
> wedding trousseau.

Detail of Qajar *shalvar* (trousers), cotton cloth covered with tent-stitch in silks with slight z-twist and s-plied. Similar patterning is also found on certain dress-weight silks of the period. (London, 799–1876)

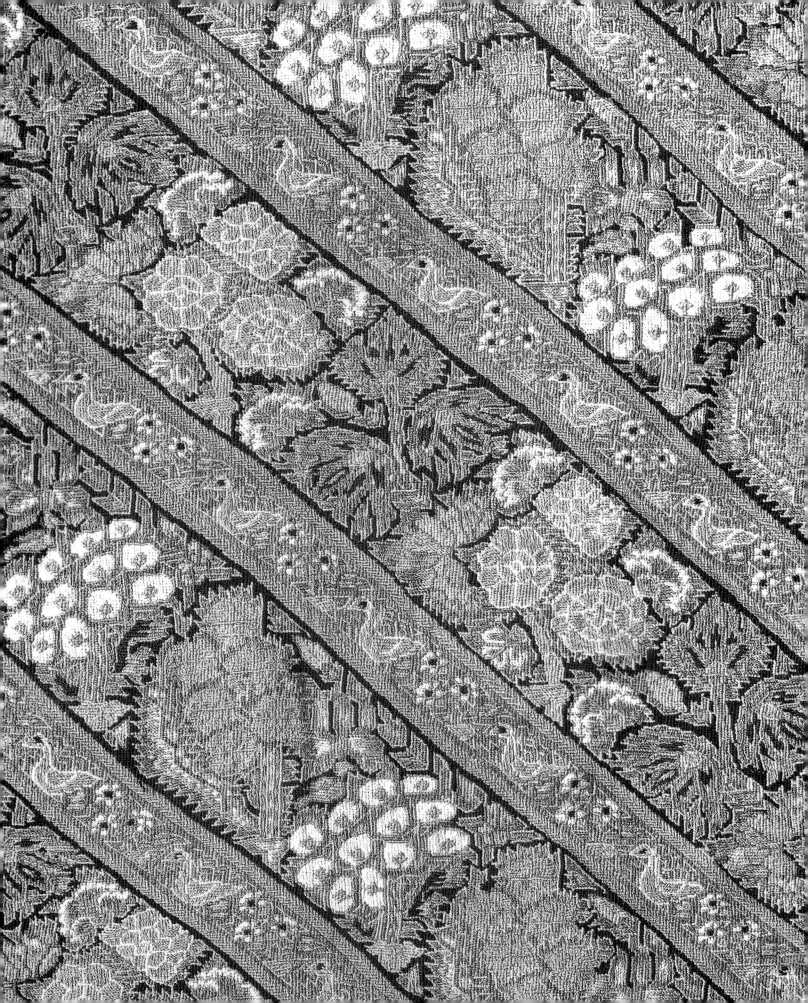

RIGHT Zoroastrian 'bridal' *shalvar* (trousers) and *qamis* (tunic) of silk with cotton facings and linings, with embroidered motifs, late 19th/early 20th century. (Hampton Court, EG 3454, 3459 and 3461)

ABOVE Cotton plain weave with silk embroidery 'whitework' in satin-stitch, late 19th/early 20th century. (Washington, DC, 3.2)

Tambour work (*qulab-duzi*: 'hook[ed-needle] stitching') was also produced in Iran at this time, but as this technique is associated with striking work produced in Ottoman Turkey it will be covered briefly in the next chapter.

The years of decline

The removal and assassination (January 1852) of Mirza Taq-i Khan set the seal on decline. Europe was interested only in Iran's raw materials and paying in manufactured goods; France eagerly purchased disease-free silkworm eggs

Cotton plain weave, with cross-stitch embroidery in two-plied
s-twisted silks, late 17th century, Azerbaijan. Such embroideries have
strong links with carpet design of the period and into the next century.
There was also conscious borrowing of certain design elements
and aspects of colouring in early 19th-century embroidery.
64 × 69 cm. (London, Circ. 535–1910)

until pebrine struck in Iran in 1864 but insisted on paying with French silk fabrics. As Iran lacks rich gold or silver deposits, this policy was an additional blow. Foreign importers benefited, too, from advantageous customs terms, while Iranian merchants paid at least 50 per cent extra, exclusive of provincial road tolls levied at each major city.

Home demand for the 'traditional' highly coloured and richly patterned silks and velvets steadily decreased every year, what with the great famine in 1869–72 and the regime's Europeanisation programme. In 1873 government officials were ordered to wear 'European' dress, styled like the Ottoman frock-coat in similar sombre colours, which naturally affected demand. Iranian commentators mourned: 'Whenever their [European] textile fabrics have had new designs and have appeared different to the eyes, the people of Iran have given up their body and soul and have pursued the color and scent of the others' (Mirza Husayn in Issawi 1971, p. 280). With increasing export sales of raw silk, cotton and wool, spinners and twisters lost their jobs along with the weavers, dyers and bleachers. Of the weavers who formed 10 per cent of the workforce in Isfahan only one in five remained in business by 1880; in Kashan, where a quarter of the citizens were involved in some aspect of silk manufacture, the situation was grave. Guilds closed as they lost members. Silk textiles which had formed 5 per cent of total exports in 1857 was a mere 0.5 per cent in 1889. Worse still were woollen textiles and cotton cloth export sales, declining from over 22 per cent to 1 per cent in 1889 (Foran 1989). As if that was not enough, a stiff tax levied in 1903 on dyes as well as white and grey cottons was 'a distinct blow to the already depressed printing and dyeing industries of Persia' (GB Parliamentary Accounts and Papers 1904, cd. 2146, p. 827). However, there was one bright spark in the otherwise unremitting gloom: Persian carpets which had not featured significantly in exports before the mid-nineteenth century formed 4 per cent of Iran's exports in the third quarter of the century and 12 per cent by 1912.

Carpets

During the 1850s carpet-making in Iran was in the doldrums. Admittedly there had been the occasional court commission for Kirman in the turbulent years of Nadir Shah's reign and the Qajar regime placed orders to furnish its palaces, but court patronage was a shadow of that in Safavid times. It was the showing of Persian carpets at the great international expositions in Europe and North America which changed matters. The massive surge in overseas demand resulted in the city of Tabriz alone seeing the value of its carpet exports more than double from £25,000 in 1873 to £65,000 six years later. European companies not only sent representatives over but quickly became involved directly in design development and workshop expansion. Ziegler of Manchester and Hotz of London were responsible for the increase in Sultanabad carpet looms, from about forty in 1874 to 1,200 in 1894, while a Russian venture in Tabriz gave employment to 1,500 workers. By the end of the century there were 30,000 looms in Isfahan alone with the Ziegler workshop there, known locally as The Fort, occupying almost 35,000 sq m.

Carpet-making remained essentially a cottage industry with the dealer supplying the weaver with the design, wool and a money advance, the balance paid on completion, although European companies increasingly opted to set up factory workshops employing men and boys. Such a system allowed greater quality supervision and yielded increased output, as weavers were removed from domestic disruptions. Details of the internal organisation of a Ziegler workshop were reported in British Parliamentary Papers, 1894 (Issawi 1971, p. 304):

> With quiet and order the various shades of wool are sorted out, weighed and given to the weaver, and at the same time a paper stating the amount of wool, the pattern of the carpet and its size; the same details are entered in a book, so that when he comes with the carpet his account is quickly made up. If he has made it true and well he gets a small reward, and if he has committed faults he is put under penalty.

Such supervision was designed to ensure that the weaver would not be tempted to substitute imported aniline-dyed yarn. The chemical dyes themselves had found a ready market in both the Ottoman world and Qajar Iran during the 1870s.

For designs the weavers relied at first on locally produced cartoons from the bazaar, but increasingly dealers and weavers reworked Safavid patterns and motifs, adjusting the size to suit European interiors and turning to art books for inspiration. Small pattern samplers (*vagira*s) containing the main border, guard-band and field motifs would be sent to importers for consider-

A wool 'Bijar' *vagira*, late 19th/early 20th century. This carpet sampler shows the main pattern elements and the colouring for some six types of border and two choices of field. Wool warp z-spun and two-plied in s-direction, wool weft and wool pile, symmetrical knot. 140 × 129 cm. (London, T.214–1989)

ation and the colouring adjusted according to requirements. Compositions of small repeat units, for instance, of the *buta* motif, are characteristic of early Qajar production and indeed may have been a feature of Zand production. A Qajar prince, one-time governor of Kirman (1891–4), was responsible for the vogue in court circles for pictorial carpets depicting episodes from the Persian classics (such as the *Shah-nama* and *Khamsa* of Nizami) and scenic views taken from European archaeological publications. One derived from Watteau's *Fête Vénitienne* was acquired by the Victoria and Albert Museum (Wilber 1979, Ittig 1985). Despite the general high technical quality, the passion for detail is not matched with a concern for the dynamics of the composition and the role of colour within it.

The late nineteenth-century client overseas was perhaps not overburdened with aesthetic considerations, but there was another problem. Increasingly complaints were voiced about the fugitive and garish nature of the imported aniline and chrome dyes employed extensively throughout Iran. European writers began to include advice to the reader on recognising vegetable-dyed yarn from chemically dyed stuff. Anxious to promote sales and reduce the import bill, the Qajar government acted. In 1882 importation of aniline dyes was prohibited, and three years later this ban was extended to yarns so dyed. However, supplies continued to be smuggled in from Germany via Baghdad in sugar sacks and via the Caucasus concealed in petroleum cans. In 1900 the edict was reissued but with little result; by 1913–14 exports of chemically dyed Persian carpets were over a third greater than those vegetable-dyed. This problem – and indeed the overall situation regarding home-manufactured textiles – was to exercise the Pahlavi regime during the two World Wars.

A wool Ziegler rug. The composition of the main field with palmettes, flower sprays and vase motifs is loosely derived from Safavid work, some two centuries earlier.
5.13 × 3.49 m. (London)

8

EIGHTEENTH-
AND NINETEENTH-
CENTURY
OTTOMAN FABRICS

An interior in the Yildiz palace, Istanbul, from a photographic album presented to Queen Victoria by Sultan Abdul Hamid II (1876–1909). The imperial factory at Hereke supplied many of the late Ottoman palaces and pavilions with furnishing silks and carpets to complement the 'European' interior decoration. (London, 7:25)

By the last quarter of the eighteenth century the Ottoman sultan had decided that modernisation on European lines was essential if the state was to withstand the interventionist and expansionist policies of the European powers and Russia. The first moves by Sultan Selim III (1789–1807) to retrain and re-equip the Janissary regiments only provoked his own downfall. Proceeding more cautiously, his successor Mahmud II (1808–39) inaugurated a programme of wide-ranging reforms from 1826. The New Order, as it was called, affected all aspects of court and government life and, following the accepted convention that dress proclaimed the wearer's political loyalty, it included dress laws which dramatically cut demand for 'traditional' fabrics. Taste in furnishing textiles also changed with the royal household leading the way, by transferring to new palaces constructed and increasingly furnished on European lines.

At the same time many of the established Ottoman manufacturing centres were lost as Russia advanced into eastern Europe and eastern Anatolia, France moved into Ottoman North Africa, and the independent Ottoman governor of Egypt, Muhammad ᶜAli (1805–49), controlled Egypt and much of Syria. By the terms of the Congress of Berlin (1878) the sultanate was forced to yield two-fifths of its territory (and one-fifth of its population), and with the consequent loss of tax revenue the Ottoman state tottered on the edge of bankruptcy. Ineffectual government under the constitution granted in 1876 only fuelled the frustration from the new intelligentsia, many of whom had been educated abroad.

'Frenkpesenk, Frenk beğendi'

During the eighteenth century the luxury weaves of the Ottoman 'classic age' were set aside. One underlying reason was the shortage of skilled workers in the industry, for throughout the century the Ottoman heartlands suffered recurring outbreaks of plague. Western Anatolia was one of the hardest-hit regions, with Bursa in 1778 losing a further one-thirteenth of its already

Pages from a stock-book, *c. 1790–1820*, containing in all some fifty silk fabric samples with occasional details about quantities written in Karamanladika (Ottoman Turkish written in Greek). (London, T.671–1919)

seriously depleted population (Panzac 1985, p. 60). Bursa did continue to produce some gold 'chekma' (? *çatma*) weaves and striped silk-cotton mixtures (Sestini 1785, White 1845, vol. 2), but overall, it seems, pattern weaving declined and increasingly decoration was added to the finished cloth by printing, needle-lace and embroidery. Perhaps it was the unavailability of high-quality woven gold and silver fabrics which lay behind the growing fashion for metal-thread embroidery.

It was also a matter of taste. In the first years of the eighteenth century the Ottoman Grand Vizier was already urging the Bursa manufacturers to season their work with a more European flavour in order to curtail imports (Issawi 1966). Increasingly the gentleman and lady of fashion were expressing their cultivated refinement by selecting European imports rather than domestic manufactures. In 1720–1 for the first time an Ottoman ambassador, Yirmi-sekiz Çelebi Mehmed Efendi, was sent to France, and his subsequent travel account greatly influenced court taste into the next century. New garden landscaping and palace construction work were carried out on French lines, while at a slower pace the palace interiors, too, underwent modification under the eye of Flachat of Lyons, the Bezirǧan Başa (Chief Purchaser) at court. By

Silk damask *çarşaf* with brocaded detail of crescent and star motif, last quarter of 19th century, Sivas (eastern Turkey). Similar fabrics have been classified as Elaziğ and Harput manufacture. In this period the crescent-star motif was strongly associated with the Ottoman court, appearing on royal jewellery and medals, palace chandeliers, etc. (Istanbul, 9722)

the mid-nineteenth century European furniture was being imported, and with it urban domestic habits (for example, eating and sleeping arrangements) altered radically.

By the 1750s Lyonnais textile manufacturers were deliberately designing for the Ottoman market (Evans 1988), and while sultans like Selim III considered using domestic fabrics for palace furnishings, there was no active policy to promote home manufacture (Issawi 1966). Ottoman weavers tried to adapt, but the silks and silk-cotton fabrics of the major Istanbul workshops were then dismissed as 'none remarkable for taste or originality of designs' (White 1845, vol. 2, p. 264). Evidence of contemporary taste may be found in a stock-book of *c.* 1790–1820, now in the Victoria and Albert Museum's textile collection, containing some fifty silk fabric samples with a few details in Karamanladika (Ottoman Turkish written in Greek). Most are patterned in the French style with small, repeated floral sprays held in broad stripes or squares. Perhaps it was the appearance of European ladies on the streets of Istanbul that spread the fashion for such silks and Indian chintzes, for by 1800 it was customary for such ladies to accompany their menfolk abroad. Acutely aware of the changing climate, shopkeepers proudly displayed textiles with the slogan *Frenkpesenk, Frenk beğendi* ('As favoured by Europeans', Küçükerman 1987) in order to motivate sales.

With the patterns came the colouring. Although banned by Selim III (1789–1807), pastel colours as favoured in Europe were preferred for outer cloaks worn by ladies of high rank; stronger, brighter colours were deemed more suitable for their servants; while less wealthy women of Istanbul wore darker tones. Plaids and tartans were fashionable in the following decades, but pastel shades were still in demand as Sultan Abdul-Aziz (1861–76) attempted to curtail use, arguing that the excessive cost of these dyestuffs was harming the national economy. Yet according to one commentator he was to blame (Dodd 1904, p. 389):

> Fashion is the greatest of all subverters. Since Adbul Aziz brought from France French notions about women's dress, and introduced to the women of his harem the intricacies and refinements of Parisian costumes, the tastes and desires of Turkish women, quite insensibly, have begun, in their turn, their retroactive influence upon Turkish life and finance.

However, the real instigator of change had been Mahmud II (1808–39) with his Dress Reform Laws.

Dress reform and consequences

The Dress Reform programme (Baker 1986) began quietly in 1826 with Mahmud II establishing a regiment kitted and trained on 'European' lines. The Janissaries rioted, ignoring his call to rally to the Prophet's flag (displayed for the first time for fifty years) and paid the price. Their disbandment on 17 June 1826 opened the way for full-scale military dress reform. The distinctive Janissary felt headgear with its long back 'sleeve', the colourful calf-length coat and the ceremonial dress were set aside, as was the flamboyant clothing of most other Ottoman military units. In their place 'modern' uniforms which in fact owed little to European military styling were supplied along with fezzes. This form of headgear became standard issue for all government and military officials. Within a century it was to become 'the emblem of Ottoman and Islamic traditionalism and orthodoxy' (Lewis 1966, p. 100).

A page illustrating four of the uniforms which replaced the traditional Ottoman military dress, as recorded by Brindesi, *c.* 1830. Although the stylings seem far removed from contemporary European army uniforms, they aroused much hostility in certain Ottoman circles.

At first fezzes, 50,000 of them, were imported from Tunis, but in 1832 manufacture was set up in the Eyub district of Istanbul. There 500 women outworkers knitted the woollen shapes which then were processed, dyed, boiled and blocked. Julia Pardoe's detailed account (1837) of the mid-1830s makes no mention of any workshop mechanisation used in the production of 15,000 fezzes each month, but photographs taken about sixty years later show work-benches with primitive machinery.

In 1829 the clothing decree was extended to include all men save the *ulema*; former sumptuary legislation relating to race and creed was abolished. Everyday wear for men was now a frock-coat or *setre* in plain dark cloth, a shirt with collar, cape, fez and European-style shoes. The demand for broadcloth soared, and as Ottoman production was insufficient Mahmud II attempted to control prices by restricting retail profits to 3 per cent (Reed 1951, p. 335). Spinning mills and weaving workshops were set up in the western Ottoman provinces, with machinery and staff imported to such an extent that one foreign employee commented (Macfarlane 1850, vol. 2, p. 453):

> It would be very odd . . . if we could not turn out a piece of finest cloth occasionally, seeing that we have the best machinery of England and France, that the finest wools for the purpose are imported . . . and that we, Frenchmen and Belgians, work it. You could not call it Turkish cloth – it was only cloth made in Turkey by European machinery, out of European material, and by good European hands.

The impact on turban-makers, tailors and silk-weavers was immediate. The market for patterned silks and fine cottons was suddenly halved (White 1845, vol. 2). The Üsküdar silk factory set up by Selim III (d. 1807) with over 1,000 looms and 1,500 hands reduced its looms to 250 in 1843, and production was limited to plain silks. Prices for such items as 'Kashmir' shawls were slashed: '. . . superb shawls at the price of $300, which five years ago would have readily sold for $800 or $1000 . . . of so fine a texture as to pass through the compass of a finger-ring' (De Kay 1833, p. 212).

The Dress Reform Laws did not cover female attire, but as noted above there was already a great demand for European floral, striped and chequered silks and printed cottons, and with these a desire for French styling in dress. With ladies' high fashion so influenced by the West, new workshops producing cotton stockings were established. Demand for European lace to decorate gowns rose steadily, and during the second half of the century some 7,600 new jobs were created in lace-making. The yarn (approximately 80,000 kg per annum) had to be imported, but much of the work was then exported back to Europe (Quataert 1986).

Decline of the Ottoman textile industry

The Ottoman textile workshops could offer little resistance to cheap mass-produced textiles flooding in from Europe and India. The guild pricing system, geared to protect the indigenous workforce, worked against price cutting among domestic manufacturers. As it was, opportunities for reducing production costs while maintaining technical quality were limited, unlike Europe where textile manufacturers were reaping the benefits of late eighteenth-century inventions. Domestic producers were further penalised by the 1838 Anglo-Turkish Commercial Convention terms whereby Turkish exports carried 12 per cent tax against a 5 per cent *ad valorem* duty on British imports; foreign merchants were also exempted from an 8 per cent internal transportation levy. Inevitably such favourable terms resulted in a massive influx of European manufactured goods into the Ottoman Empire, while cotton and silk were increasingly exported in the raw state, especially after the silkworm disease pebrine broke out in France around 1853.

Disease-free eggs, cocoons and filament were exported from Bursa to replace stock. French silk-workers came out to work in Bursa, and Italian steam-powered silk-reeling machinery and engineers were brought in, the mills alone providing employment for 5,000 workers (Macfarlane 1850, vol. 1). However, the boom years of the 1850s proved to be shortlived. Pebrine struck Ottoman sericulture, and tax revenue from this sector halved; Bursa production fell to 400,000 piastres in 1855 from 4 million piastres' worth around 1815 (Ubicini repr. 1973). Furnishing velvets were still woven in Bursa. Üsküdar (Istanbul) and Diyarbakir, but production had fallen, and while the cotton weft was now mechanically regular in thickness the dye was poor quality (Wearden 1986).

By the time a disease-free stock had been re-established and the economy was beginning to benefit from amendments to the 1838 Convention terms (1861–2), the newly opened Suez Canal (1869) was speeding shipments of cheap Japanese and Chinese silk through to the European markets. However, the Ottoman government's action in setting up a scientific station and training institute in Bursa, offering prizes, tax exemptions and encouraging a mulberry-planting programme did save the industry. The French consul in Bursa pushed for a joint industrial venture, arguing such an employment scheme would promote French (Catholic) interests and counteract British and American political influence and Protestant evangelicanism (Dutemple 1883). Output virtually tripled from the late 1880s to the 1900s, with France taking almost 80 per cent of total production of raw silk – but not of woven cloth. Silk-weaving so declined that by the 1900s only 2 to 7 per cent of Ottoman-produced silk filaments were being woven in Anatolia.

Hereke production

In 1843 a small mill to manufacture cotton and silk gauze was set up by the Ottoman Defence Minister, Riza Paşa, at Hereke outside Istanbul. When the sultan saw the establishment, the minister expeditiously handed it over. It was enlarged in 1850 and 100 Austrian Jacquard 'looms' installed, with the chief manager brought from Vienna along with other materials and designs, and the chief engineer a M. Rivière from Lyons, France. All the production was earmarked for the Imperial palaces and geared to contemporary taste (Macfarlane 1850, vol. 2, p. 467):

> The designs of some of the pieces we saw were very pretty and tasteful, but they had all been imported. They had now [1850], however, three designers, one . . . Italian, and the two others German; and we saw two or three Armenian boys copying ornaments and fancy drawings under their tuition.

Lack of planning and a poor training programme plagued production so that only a tenth of the looms were operational (Macfarlane 1850). However, at the 1851 Great Exhibition, London, some of the Hereke silks were shown and at the 1855 Exposition in Paris alongside Izmir cloth and military uniforms were fezzes from the Imperial factory at Eyub and printed cottons from Zey-

Cushion velvet in green and red pile on a yellow satin ground, late 19th century. Formerly known as 'Scutari' work (from the Üsküdar workshops, on the Asian side of the Bosphorus), these covers show reinterpretations of early 18th-century Ottoman 'medallion' patterns. 130 × 58.5 cm. (London, 630–1890)

ABOVE Silk dress fabrics purchased in Salonika, Ottoman Thrace, in the late 19th century. (Jerusalem, 956.81; 776–7.81; 646.84; 171.79; 172.79A; 992.85; 1040.85; 987.85)

RIGHT Hereke silk, compound weave, second half of 19th century. The strong colouring and the three-dimensional naturalistic representation of the floral sprays owe much to French and British fabrics of the 1850s. (Istanbul, Hereke 13/37)

OPPOSITE Household bedding fabrics, linens and silks, 19th century. (Jerusalem, 1051.85; 1053.85; 1058.85; 87.88; 814.82)

tinburu near today's Istanbul airport, Hereke velvets, damasks (or Damascus-styled silks), satins, taffetas, gauzes and ribbons. In 1857 it was decided to discontinue attempts to weave velvets with floral decoration in gold thread, as the quality had been sub-standard, and to begin production of a voided silk and cotton velvet with the approval of the Grand Vizier (Öz 1951, vol. 2,). Undated designs from Hereke (Küçükerman 1987) display French influence with a number of patterns derived from 'bizarre' silks of the early eighteenth century (Slomann 1953).

Much of the factory was destroyed by fire in 1878, and although it reopened some four years later the textile industry remained in the doldrums. Ten years earlier an Ottoman document recorded only twelve looms producing patterned and furnishing silks operating in Istanbul and Üsküdar where in the 1830s there had been 410 (Issawi 1966). These were probably not Jacquard 'looms', for outside the royal workshop their introduction was very late; Bilecik's cushion, furnishing and dress velvets were still being woven on ordinary drawlooms in 1883 (Öz 1951, vol. 2). By 1891 the Hereke factory had switched to carpet production (see p. 161).

Embroidery

If European visitors were dismissive of the domestic textiles, they were enthusiastic about the embroidered items available for purchase. Many more references to embroidery occur in nineteenth-century travel literature than before, and while this reflects the wider interests of the authors, which now included female writers permitted in the harem quarters in private and royal households, it also suggests that decorative stitching was acknowledged as a respectable or even preferred substitute to patterned woven fabrics.

While continuing to use the established repertoire of stitches, late eighteenth-century Ottoman embroiderers adopted, probably from the Far East or India, the time-saving tambour technique, using the special needle, shaped like a crochet hook. They were turning away from the 'classic' Ottoman embroidery patterns: the open placement of full flower heads and tight buds carried on thin stems or framed by broad leaves on a generous ground was increasingly replaced by a crowded profusion of overblown blossoms, rendered in a painterly manner as viewed from above, in two-thirds profile. Architectural and landscape motifs, isolated or repeated to form a narrative, were increasingly employed, perhaps mirroring the court's fascination for small landscape murals in the European mode. As if to emphasise such painterly associations many shades of silks are employed in the finest examples, carefully selected to enhance the chiaroscuro effect, with the tambour stitching creating an even textural quality. However, much work was still produced with stitches based on double-darning and double-running combinations.

As the official reform programme got underway, the influence of European pattern design grew more emphatic. Printed cottons were embellished with gold-thread embroidery to resemble French brocade silks. Motifs of knotted ribbons and bows with floral bouquets in late rococo style were greatly in vogue. On dress silks these are scattered across the surface, with elements repeated as delicate trimmings in needle-lace (White 1845, vol. 3, p. 186). This *iğne oya* work could be incredibly fine, as may be seen in minute orange blossoms, pansies and morning glories decorating a little seal-purse presented to Queen Victoria in 1845 by the Ottoman ambassador. However, for European clients the commercial embroidery workshops along the Bosphorus and the Marmara were careful to give their work an 'ethnic' quality with calligraphic legends 'with wreaths and palms of flowers, in coloured silks intermixed with gold, and ornamented at the ends with various devices in gold or silver, such as the Sultan's cipher, mosques, mashallahs, crescents and stars' (White 1845, vol. 2, pp. 102–3). Commercial work could be signed, as was the embroidery of the Hassan Ağa family displayed at the 1851 Great Exhibition, London: a piece now in the Victoria and Albert Museum, London, was sewn by the daughter.

In upper circles embroidered furnishings were found in every room. Bedding kept in cupboards during the daytime consisted of:

> mattresses . . . covered with a sheet of silk gauze, or striped muslin . . .
> – half a dozen pillows . . . all in richly embroidered muslin cases,
> through which the satin containing the down is distinctly seen – and a
> couple of wadded coverlets . . . carefully folded: no second sheet is
> considered necessary, as the coverlets are lined with fine white muslin
> (Pardoe 1838, vol. 1, p. 32).

At mealtimes servants spread embroidered cloths under the low tables to catch crumbs, then carried trays of china and glassware, food and drink, each covered with embroidered fabrics, handing individual napkins and towels similarly embellished to the company. Both guests and members of the household sat or reclined on divans covered in 'costly materials, such as silk or velvet, embroidered with gold or silver . . . At the back and extremities are thick cushions of the same materials . . .' (White 1845, vol. 3, pp. 170–1).

By the last decades of the century these covers and drapes were typically monochrome velvet of a deep, rich colour, worked in *dival*-stitch (the frequently used term *bindalli*, 'a thousand leaves', refers to the pattern), a derivation of the traditional *zerduz*-stitch, embellished with sequins and spangles. The metal thread is laid back and forth over padded shapes, caught around the edges with silk or linen thread which may criss-cross along the back of the fabric. The gold, silver-gilt or silver thread, wire and strips were increasingly

Detail of cotton kerchief, printed and embroidered with gold thread and pink and blue silk, 19th century. The embroidered decoration is clearly inspired by French silk brocade work, *c.* 1800. (Boston, 15.488)

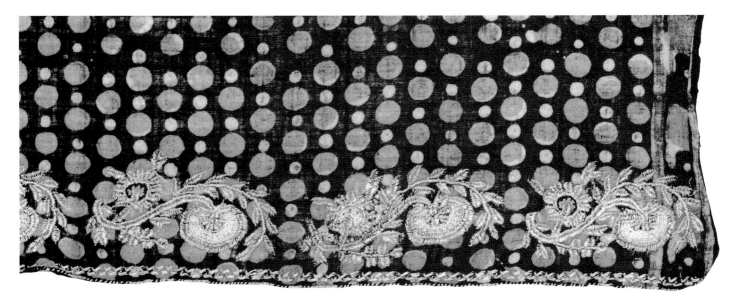

ABOVE Detail of *dival* embroidery on
a velvet cradle-hammock, lined with
leather, late 19th/early 20th century.

TOP Samples of needle-lace work,
arranged in roundels, from the
mid-19th century. Such intricate trims
decorated the front edges and cuffs of
Ottoman ladies' gowns of the period.
(Istanbul)

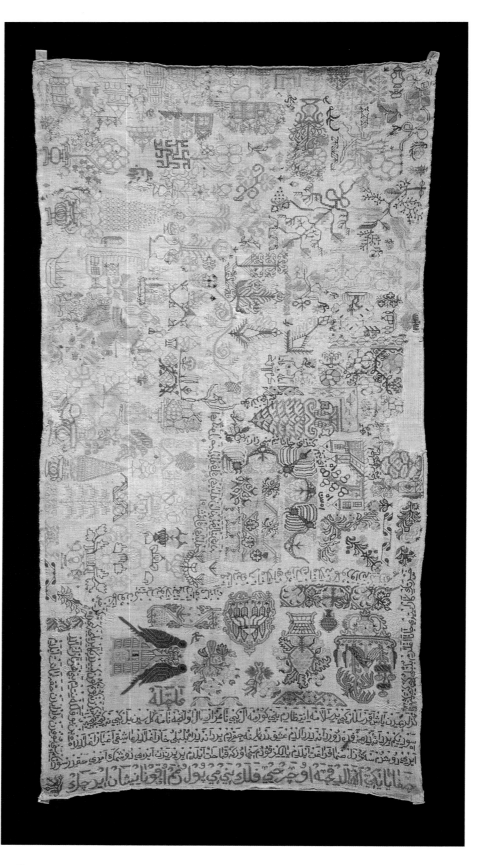

RIGHT Linen sampler, late 18th/early
19th century, with combinations of
double running-stitch and eyelet stitch
in floss silk. (Cambridge, T.1–1956)

Red silk with tambour work
in coloured silk and metal thread,
early 18th century.
Such flower heads are a feature of
18th-century work. 116 × 112 cm.
(London, Circ. 744–1912)

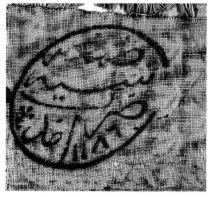

Samples (TOP) of Ottoman resist-printed cotton found among Marseilles custom archives of the late 18th century. The (?excise) stamp on the reverse of the leaf-spray print (ABOVE) reads 'stamped 1186 [1772–3] Amid [Diyarbakir]'. (Marseilles, C3374)

replaced by copper and nickel by the end of the century, no doubt reflecting growing monetary crisis in the Ottoman state. Such decorated velvets became the formal dress for Ottoman court ladies and recognised bridalwear.

By the close of the century German and American sewing-machines were being imported in large numbers, but Ottoman entrepreneurs showed no inclination to organise home manufacture. To one writer (Fesch 1907) this disinterest was symptomatic of the Empire's sorry decline. Machine chain-stitching provided a cheap substitute for tambour work: in both the earlier careful shading vanished as increasingly chemically dyed (and machine-twisted) silks were employed.

Printed cottons

The mid-seventeenth-century Turkish traveller Evliya Çelebi recorded twenty-seven printing workshops in Istanbul, employing some 200 workers producing fine handkerchiefs and dress fabrics (Mantran 1962); by 1725 there were 192 establishments of which thirty-three were in Muslim ownership, the rest Armenian. Traditionally these were sited on the banks of the Bosphorus and Dardanelles waterways. Cottons were manufactured in Ottoman Anatolia, the Levant and Cyprus and exported in vast quantities to Europe, especially France; and certain regions like Bursa, Tokat and Amasya were famous for their dyed and printed lengths. Aynteb (modern Gaziantep) supplied indigo-blue cottons, and Diyarbakir was another important centre selling the French its 'chafarcanis' (?şafakgun: 'twilight-coloured, red') cottons. Fukasawa's detailed research (1987) allows us to identify securely Diyarbakir work as resist cottons with red or violet fields dotted with simple floral motifs. The similarity to contemporary Indian prints was probably deliberate, as silver bullion had been flowing out of the Ottoman Empire from the second half of the seventeenth century to pay for such Indian printed cottons.

But without mechanisation Ottoman manufacturers could not match the low prices of Indian imports and the rapid reduction in English yarn prices which dropped sevenfold between 1792 and 1813. During 1823–43 there was a sixfold increase in British cloth exports to the Ottoman Empire, and Europe was determined it should stay that way: Ottoman government plans to establish a 4,000–5,000-loom workshop were forestalled by the British quickly and deliberately flooding the market with printed fabric (Inalcik 1987). Gradually mechanised looms replaced the traditional handlooms, but it still made financial sense to export raw cotton from the Ottoman Balkan provinces and reimport it from northern and central Europe in the form of yarn or cloth. In the 1820s the Ottoman Empire could have met home demand for cotton cloth, but by the early 1870s 80 per cent was imported.

The Istanbul printers struggled to compete, switching to French pattern-blocks as early as 1813, using flour paste to burnish the fabric (Hobhouse 1813). But by the 1840s Hamlin (1877, p. 59) sadly noted:

five thousand weavers in Scutari [?Istanbul or Albania] were without employ, and reduced to the most deplorable beggary. The fast colors and firm material of Di[y]arbekr disappeared . . . and Bursa towels [printed cottons] came from Lyons and Manchester . . . Thus all industries of Turkey have perished.

It was a similar story throughout the Empire: the textile printers of Baghdad, Aleppo and Cyprus were all suffering. Factory managers, especially of the

Imperial printed cotton factories at Bakirköy (Macrikoy) and Yesilköy (San Stefano), near to Zeytinburu, were not adverse to passing off high-quality imported fabrics as their own production to the court. However, by the last decade of the century imports slowed and by using women outworkers in Izmir, Trabzon (Trebizond), Tokat and Kayseri the Ottoman merchants of printed cottons witnessed a great increase in sales, with western Anatolia alone earning 15 million German marks by exporting vast quantities to Iran.

Carpet production

The one section of the Ottoman textile industry to flourish throughout the nineteenth century was carpet manufacture. A surge of demand from Europe and North America resulted from displays at the various international expositions. Prices for Uşak carpets increased by at least 50 per cent between 1846 and 1873, and the value of carpet exports virtually doubled from the late 1870s to the mid-1890s, as did the number of looms: by 1914 some 60,000 workers were employed in this sector. Most carpets went to Britain, with half that volume to France, and the United States taking a third.

Apart from late nineteenth-century attempts to mechanise spinning in particular, production remained essentially based in the home, working to the order of the commissioning merchant who sometimes even provided the loom. The men generally washed and bleached the wool, which was then spun by the women. In Uşak men dyed the yarn; in Kula it was women's work. Weaving was done by both sexes in Gördes and Kula, but by women only in Uşak. As demand threatened to outstrip supply, Greek and Armenian women were introduced to carpet-weaving in other areas (Quataert 1990). Unlike Muslim women they had no difficulty in adapting to male-supervised workshop environments.

As in Iran these workshops were set up by European agents to speed up production: it was estimated that a home worker averaged 5,000–6,000 knots a day, but once freed from domestic interruptions the weaver could increase that rate to 14,000 working on simple vertical two-beam looms. In Uşak the French Antoine Giraud workshop, set up around 1860, produced six types priced by the square metre, according to quality. Such establishments allowed the agents strict control of pattern and colour: from the 1850s the use of aniline dyes spread quickly throughout the textile industry.

It is not clear when the Imperial Hereke silk factory started producing carpets; Beattie (1981) suggests production was underway around 1890 or 1891 with weavers brought in from Anatolia. Then, as now, cotton was generally used for the warp, and both symmetrical and asymmetrical knots have been found as the pile. A knot count around 1,650 to the square inch is usual, though much finer work survives. As with Hereke silks the most important customer was the royal household, in order to furnish the numerous summer palaces being built on the shores of the Bosphorus. In keeping with the furniture and décor the colours, compositions and designs reflect contemporary French taste, although the pattern elements derive from both the Ottoman and Persian Safavid decorative repertoires.

9

THE CONTEMPORARY WORLD

Cotton *suzani* cloth with silk embroidery, late 19th century, Central Asia. Often the *suzani* is formed from a series of panels and worked before or after being sewn together. This example is embroidered in couching stitch including 'Bukhara' couching, chain and double chain.
2.49 × 1.95 m. (Glasgow, 30/4)

After the First World War the political map of the Islamic Middle East was redrawn, with the established ruling houses barely clinging on to the tattered remains of their authority. The European powers and Russia carved up the region into zones of political and economic interest, setting up regimes within new territorial boundaries, which generally paid scant regard to the ethnic groupings of the indigenous population. The Bolshevik revolution formally brought to an end the Central Asian khanates and reinforced control in and around the Black Sea area. Iran, for so many years a pawn in the great game between Britain and Russia, now attracted the attention of the United States of America, while Britain had extended its protectorate over Egypt and established mandates in former Ottoman Palestine, Transjordan and Iraq, as France did with Syria and Lebanon. North Africa and the Balkans, too, passed out of Ottoman control. It was the breakup of the old order, and commentators, though perhaps critical of the reorganisation programmes of Mustafa Kemal (Atatürk) and Riza Shah Pahlavi of Iran, have recognised that these two men saved their countries from complete absorption, as in all aspects – militarily, politically, economically and culturally – the domination of the Western and the Soviet blocs was apparent. What had been a challenge in the nineteenth century now seriously threatened the continued existence of the Islamic world.

Our knowledge of early twentieth-century non-industrial textiles of the Middle East is largely confined to work classed as 'tribal' and 'ethnic', especially that associated with nomadic groups. Yet just as foreign interest in the bedouin and nomad in the Middle East (seen to personify the noble savage concept) was stimulated by the writings of T. E. Lawrence and others, this tiny section (some 5 per cent) of the population was increasingly giving up the migratory lifestyle in the face of water shortages, official measures regarding state security, and implementation of taxation, land allocation, education and health programmes.

Ethnic differences were deliberately played down by national leaders, such

163

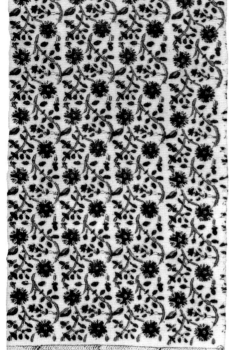

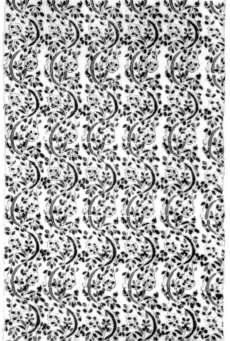

as Riza Shah of Iran (d. 1941), in the belief that this would promote a new sense of nationhood. Few were so determined as Stalin who ordered mass movements of peoples throughout the Soviet Union. Other resettlement programmes within national borders have taken place, perhaps occasioned by earthquakes, hydroelectric projects or internal security. Important demographic movements also occurred between the Wars and after 1948, when a number of Middle Eastern countries declared independence. International agreements, such as between Greece and Republican Turkey in the 1920s, resulted directly or indirectly in the transfer of peoples from one province or even country to another. And the establishment of the Jewish state of Israel in 1948 led to about 750,000 Arabs leaving their homes and then further disruption after the 1967 war. The impact on regional textile manufacture in terms of labour force and customers can be imagined.

Improvements in transport and advances in mass-communication also have been bringing about changes. Rural and village families now do not hesitate to search for better-paid work and improved lifestyle in cities. Formal educational and training programmes, organised by the authorities or development agencies, with training manuals and pattern-books, have also served to diffuse and disseminate regional decorative repertoires and techniques. Industrialisation of textile manufacture has also had repercussions on home demand and supply, but even with Turkey's active manufacturing programme only some 24 per cent of its domestically produced cloth was factory made between the Wars.

Yet with the attention of scholars and collectors firmly fixed on 'tribal' work little of village and town production has been recorded, except in the field of carpets. What information has been gathered is generally disparate and diverse. Fascinating glimpses may be caught: Iranian patterned sacking used to wrap carpet exports, later to be developed as a British textile design (G. P. and J. Baker archive collection, inv. no. z-004); a cotton length printed in a 1920s Hama workshop with blocks then available; a study on Syrian ikat-workers; another on felt manufacture. What follows is a short survey, region by region, highlighting certain common features.

Central Asia

Under Communist control the region supplied cotton for the whole of the Soviet Union, much as North Africa had been the granary for the Roman Empire. The damaging consequences of Kremlin economic and agricultural policies on the region fall outside the scope of this study, but it should be noted that shortages of industrial goods were nothing compared with the difficulty faced by individuals wishing to purchase basic equipment and materials for knitting, embroidery and tailoring, even in the perestroika period. Furthermore, personal exportation/importation of certain textile goods among other items was forbidden between the various republics.

Some handwork continued with official support such as the gold-embroidery workshops of Bukhara, Uzbekistan. For over a century ceremonial court robes in the region had been heavily embellished with metallic-thread embroidery, traditionally the work of male embroiderers (p. 32). After the Bolshevik overthrow of the provincial khanates and their courts, a small number of workers' co-operatives, increasingly employing women, were set up in Bukhara, the production going for export or official distribution. While design elements and compositions were based on the established decorative repertoire, the Cyrillic alphabet was now used for all calligraphic inscriptions as a matter of government policy alongside the symbols and devices of the Soviet Union. There has been no marked change in technique of couching metallic thread over padded card shapes, as in Ottoman *dival* embroidery; templates are occasionally on sale in the main Bukhara bazaar.

Aside from the difficulty (and thus expense) of obtaining materials and equipment, women were officially expected to work outside the home, so both opportunity and time for domestic craftwork were restricted. Thus the finest examples of embroidered covers and spreads date from the turn of the century. Most renowned are the lively, gaily coloured floral *suzanis* (hangings, covers, linings) with embroidery in floss (or, later, industrial twist) silk on a cream or white cotton ground. Soviet textile historians identify certain designs to particular regions, such as Samarkand, Shahr-i Sabz, Nurata and Bukhara, although there is little documentary evidence. Typically the central area of the *suzani*, edged with a series of narrow and wide borders, is filled with a strong axial and diagonal composition of stylised flowers, shown as full blooms on foliated scrolls or as isolated plant forms. It has been suggested that these are represented for their talismanic and medicinal qualities: the iris for its diuretic properties, the capsicum used against cholera, the willow (aspirin), and a form of garden rue (congestion relief and an aphrodisiac). Huge circular poppy-heads decorate another kind of *suzani* which features a form of couching known as 'Bukharan', in which the small stitches holding down the laid thread are arranged in diagonal lines; the palette is restricted to two or three sombre reds, a dull purple and black. Such artificial dyes first appear in Central Asia in the late 1870s.

This 'poppy' design also features on certain Central Asian ikat velvets, silks and silk mixtures, woven at the turn of the century and often lined with Russian roller-printed cotton. According to local tradition, the name *abrant* (Uzbek: 'cloudy') for these textiles came from a weaver seeing a reflection of the sky in water. The warp is tie-dyed, often white, yellow, rose-red and blue, with the weft rose-red. The dramatic patterning was exploited by Leon Bakst in his costumes for Diaghilev's Ballets Russes productions. In recent years the wearing of similar, more vivid, ikat satins has increasingly become a symbol of national, political and cultural identity; women of the Russian and German communities in Central Asia rarely wear such fabrics, and the men do not sport the black cotton cap with white-embroidered motifs of hot chillies, said by locals to represent the wearer has a sound mind.

Wishing to escape the Sovietisation of Central Asia in the late 1920s, many Turkoman families migrated and settled in Afghanistan, but carpet design in the region continues to be based on the Turkoman polygonal motif, the *gul* (literally, 'flower' or 'rose'), arranged in an axial grid on a red field. At the turn of the century a fugitive red dye was employed, but such 'Golden Bukharas', as these Tekke pieces were later labelled, proved suitable particularly for American interior design schemes. The origin of the motif and the provenancing of the many variations have exercised a number of critics. Some suggest that as occurred elsewhere the design originated in court work, as seen in fifteenth-century painting, to pass into 'provincial' carpet production; while others, pointing to its wide geographical distribution across Asia, argue

ABOVE Detail of 'Tree of Life' *kilim* woven, in 1958, by Fayek Nicolas (1931–58) at the Harraniya workshop, near Cairo.

LEFT Silk and cotton, warp ikat, 1992, Central Asia. In the early 1980s it was unusual to see young Uzbek women wearing ikat, but within a decade the fashion had spread across the generations. Comparatively expensive, the narrow-width fabric is purchased by the metre and privately made up in the latest fashions for everyday wear.

for a common and ageless tribal tradition. More recently parallels with seventh- and eighth-century Chinese and Sasanian 'pearl-roundel' silks and, perhaps more controversially, with the cloud-collar of Chinese Imperial robes have been drawn. Whatever the case, as has been noted elsewhere (Baker, 1993), the great volume and variety of production of carpets, storage bags, animal-trappings, door hangings and so on raise the question whether all pieces should be regarded as solely the work of nomadic tribal groups in the region, as is generally assumed.

Egypt

Interest in contemporary Egyptian textiles has centred on the Harraniya project outside Cairo, set up in 1952 by Ramses Wissa Wassef to encourage the creative talents of *fellahin* (peasant) children 'untouched by the age of technology', while providing basic schooling in *kilim*-weaving. The idea of a vocational training was nothing new in Egypt. Technical schools had been established in the nineteenth century and further supported by the government between the two World Wars, while import restrictions in force during the Nasser years encouraged many Egyptian carpet dealers to organise their own workshops. Wassef's ideas of utilising vegetable dyes, randomly selecting the children to be trained, and having them work straight on to the loom without cartoons has appealed to many who empathise with the craft philosophy of William Morris and others. Some have found the children's naïve imagery a refreshing alternative to the established decorative repertoire of Egyptian pile carpets. Favourable coverage in Western media and craft circles has resulted in the mushrooming of other workshops, producing related work but rarely underpinned by the Wassef philosophy.

Flat-woven rugs are also produced in various urban centres and by bedouin families in the Western and Eastern Deserts and the Sinai. However, the bedouin communities are famous for their embroidery, as are the oases families. Worked in cross- and running-stitch, or machine stitching, stylised motifs decorate women's dress on the shoulders, yoke and in the case of Dakhla oasis women the side and back panels of the black robes. Such garments are rarely seen in urban areas, where since 1967 Islamic fundamentalist dress is increasingly worn. The latter originated in the Egyptian context, it is said, after the demoralising 1967 defeat by Israel and became increasingly popular among students following the Egyptian military successes of 1973, when it seemed as if the return to high moral standards, signified by the adoption of such dress, far removed from current Western styling, was reaping its own rewards (Rugh 1986).

For centuries the shops of the Cairene tent-makers and appliqué-workers have been situated in the Bab al-Zuwayla area. The patchwork prepared for tourists is generally small in size with the decoration often based on Pharaonic motifs, whereas items made for the home market can range from cushion covers and small wall panels to large-scale work for public display, such as religious banners, tomb covers, tent hangings, backdrops and curtain fences used for large gatherings, in which case the patterns are calligraphic and geometric. Layers of various coloured fabrics (generally cotton) are placed on to the ground cloth, then cut as required, folded back and stitched so revealing the colour of the layer underneath. Conversely, as often seen on 'tourist' work, precut and folded shapes are applied on to the field and stitched into place. There is little textural contrast, since usually only monochrome cottons with some linen are used, but the juxtaposition of strong colours creates a visual tension.

A recent case-study of a Cairene village (Lynch and Fahmy 1984) reveals some of the problems faced by those producing such appliqué work and other textile activities. The merchant continually presses for lower prices, even at the cost of lower quality. Competition is stiff, and with design skills in short supply a large capital outlay is required to stock-pile new ranges in order to maximise profits before new work is imitated by others. Such competition is found at all levels, including within the family: relatives work separately rather than combining operations even for the production of *varsalia*, a heavy fabric used for suitcase and bag linings. There is a marked division of labour with little if any formal training, with equipment (such as looms and sewing-machines) and materials often supplied by the dealer or the head of the household.

Syria and Palestine

From medieval times the major cities of this region, such as Damascus, Aleppo and Hama, were not only important textile trading centres but also famous for their weaving. In the twentieth century small looms could be found in most villages, producing simple cloth to meet private and local demand. In Palestine before the Second World War the town of Majal, some thirty kilometres from Gaza, boasted 500 looms and this was not unique. Since then, of course, imported low-priced, mass-produced fabrics from Europe and Asia have swamped the bazaars, but local non-industrial manufacture, including the processes of spinning, reeling, dyeing (but with artificial dyes) and weaving, still continues. In Damascus, for instance, luxury brocaded silk incorporating gold thread is produced, some especially designed for Christian ecclesiastical vestments as considered for Westminster Abbey. An expanding tourist market has revived interest in the 'traditional' striped silk and cotton mixtures.

However, for many families it has proved difficult to interest young people in learning the techniques: they consider the financial return for such time-consuming and physically exhausting work is too low, and other occupations carry greater social kudos. In the late 1970s the last two ikat-dyers in Aleppo regretted that when they retired no one else in the area would be able to produce their distinctive hammam wraps in rayon. They had already virtually halted production of their silk ikats because of pricing constraints.

For the casual observer it might seem that the bedouin families are the sole guardians of indigenous textile tradition. In fact, much of the decorative work about the tent may be produced in the towns and not in the encampment. Even the goat-hair cloth used for the tent itself is often purchased ready-made, as are the reed screens interlaced with various coloured wools. And as items are often handed on from one camp to another, determining the origins of specific pieces is not easy (Weir 1976). Most are plain weave and warp-faced, with bands of warp-faced or weft-faced geometric patterning in red wool and white cotton, in sharp contrast to the dark blue or brown ground.

It is, however, still possible at times to distinguish regional differences in Palestinian embroidery, although the distribution of pattern-books and manuals of various missionary and development training centres has resulted in a wider diffusion of motifs, compositions and techniques. As Weir (1989) points out, although many observers view 'traditional' Middle Eastern society as static, a local community is constantly reacting and adjusting to the changing circumstances, and in turn this is mirrored in dress and ornament. On one level the presence of European troops in the mandate period occasioned a radical change in the tailoring of women's garments, while on another level national aspirations are given voice by the wearing of certain items of dress. Pattern motifs are 'traditional' (that is, established favourites), but brides in particular endeavour to have their wedding robes different from each other's in the selection and placing of embroidered patterning. Quality is measured in the fineness of the stitching and the number of repeated motifs within a certain grouping.

Iran

At his coronation in 1926 Riza Shah controlled a number of provinces rather than a nation. In a country three times the size of France what few roads existed were unsafe for travellers. Many village homes had private looms for producing coarse cotton plaids, used for women's *chador*s (full-length wraps),

LEFT Section of appliqué hangings for public assemblies, mid-1980s, Cairo.

RIGHT *Thawb al-Na'ani* Palestinian dress with couching stitch on the sleeves, yoke and side seams and cross-stitch motifs elsewhere, early 1930s, Bait Dajan, Gaza. Wedding robes of a decade earlier featured a deep front slit from the hem upwards, but post-war realisation of the sexual connotation resulted in such tailored detail being dropped. (London, Eth. 1969.AS.8-19)

BELOW Section of a Syrian reed screen with woven pattern in wool, 1970s. Such screens are made in the towns for use by the bedouins in their tents as space dividers or draught excluders. 7 × 1.65 m. (London, Eth. 1975.AS.7–1)

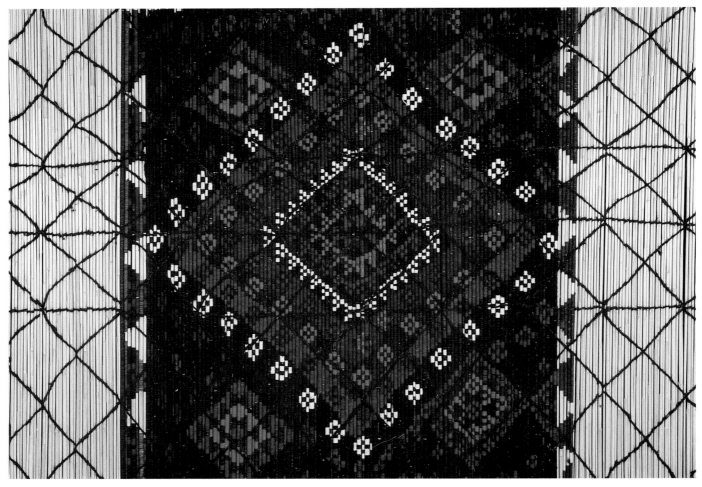

the choice of whichever two colours depending on village convention, but there was still great demand for colourful, floral Manchester cotton prints. In an effort to revitalise domestic textile manufacture and to cut imports Riza Shah had factories established across the provinces for cotton, wool and silk manufacture, and insisted army and government orders were placed with them; however, as late as 1977 about 70 per cent of all industrial workers were in workshops employing fewer than ten staff. The import of foreign silk fabrics was banned, but this only resulted in an active black market.

The Uniform Dress Reform Laws beginning in 1928 (Baker forthcoming), which stipulated European-style clothing for men and later women, put a grave strain on suppliers and retailers alike, let alone the lower-income groups. In a drive to weld the people together into a new nation Riza Shah forbade the use of ethnic languages other than Farsi in education and public speaking and tried to ban dress associated with those groupings. Indeed, the distinctive felt cap worn by men of the Qashqai tribe is a comparatively recent innovation, dating from the late 1940s, although many assume it is traditional (Whitworth Art Gallery 1976). The nomads purchased the caps and often the heavy shepherd mantles from village or town sources but produced flat felts themselves for personal use in the camps. Today it seems all felt manufacture is now based in towns and villages using elemental machinery.

While Iranian fabrics have largely failed to attract foreign custom, carpet exports rose steadily, except during the Great Depression which resulted in severe unemployment especially in Kirman and in the 1980s to date as the Islamic Republic of Iran has faced certain trade embargoes. By 1914 over half the total labour force was employed in carpet-making (Foran 1993, p. 127), generally working to commission with the agent taking between 5 and 20 per cent of the purchase price and providing the dyed yarn and a cash advance. The weaver either bought or rented the design for the making period at a price again calculated on the final purchase price, some 15 to 20 per cent.

To improve yarn quality, knotting and safeguard designs by copyrighting them Riza Shah established the Iran Carpet Company in 1935 to handle exports. Increasingly the work was geared to Western room sizes and trends in interior design, as noted by Edwards (1953): thus in the 1960s and 70s carpets for the vast US market were produced in unconventional pastel shades, with minimum dye variation in the pile and simplified compositions very different from those woven earlier in the century. Government support over the past decades has resulted in Persian carpet sales as of 1991 totalling 43 per cent of exports, excluding oil and petroleum-related products. Scarcely surprising, then, that we find the guilds associated with carpet-weaving (for example, dyers, cleaners, repairers, pattern-makers) very influential in politics, although less concerned with the protection of the craft and workers.

The post-war US Aid programme in Iran included support of certain crafts, and in the mid-1960s the Pahlavi regime established the Iranian Handicrafts Centre (later Organisation) to promote craftwork; to preserve the established crafts and develop new ones; to assist in the marketing and 'adjust the handicrafts to the current requirements and tastes of buyers' (Gluck 1977, p. 26); and thus generate more income for the craftworkers and so contain rural drift into cities. The work was sold in IHO shops in the capital and provincial towns, but was also available in the bazaars. Some ranges were clearly designed for metropolitan and foreign tastes, but other items had local or

Woodblock printer at work, 1993, Isfahan, Iran. A few doors away a wood-worker was fashioning and carving the blocks to order.

widespread appeal, such as the resist-printed silk or rayon squares worn by Qashqai women, Kirmani embroidery on red woollen cloth, the printed calicoes of Isfahan, Kashan and Yazd, and the needleworked cotton *givah* slippers with soles often made from vehicle tyres instead of leather.

Today the government of the Islamic Republic of Iran views the crafts in a similar light: jobs, extra income and possible export sales (after the 1990 repeal of a 1978 ban), yet requiring minimal financial investment in tooling and training. But official circles also argue that the crafts with their deep roots in tradition assist in fighting the cultural imperialism of the West (*Hands and Creativity*, vol. 1, p. 3). Resist- and block-printing still continue, but the once-famous cotton *zilus* (Wulff 1966) woven with a double warp of two different colours on drawlooms are difficult to find.

Turkey

From the outset Mustafa Kemal (Atatürk) was determined to strengthen the manufacturing base of the new Turkish republic, established in 1923. The Industrial Promotion Law of 1927 aimed at drastically reducing the crippling dependence on imported textiles and yarn. Widespread planting of long-staple cotton was instituted, and printing workshops (re)established. Costs were kept down by the extensive use of cheap pit-looms, while the govern-

Detail of cotton ikat wrap, known as *peştemal*, worn over the head and shoulders by Turkish women, young and old alike, in the Trabzon region, especially around the tea-growing area of Rize, eastern Turkey.

ment through the industrial and mining development bank Sümerbank began a programme of textile mill and factory construction (Linke 1938, p. 302) and carpet-weaving through the Sümerhali branch. During the Second World War the government organised training courses to popularise private weaving, distributing simple treadle looms and spinning-wheels, and offering financial incentives to weavers, dyers and workers' co-operatives.

After the War the emphasis returned to industrial production, but today certain textiles remain firmly associated with specific regions in Anatolia. In the area of Trabzon and Rize in the eastern corner of the Black Sea the local cherry red, black and white ikat *peştemals* (wraps), made from industrial cotton yarn, are often seen over the heads of young and old women alike, while Erzurum women are increasingly wearing the full-length woven wrap of fine fawn wool, sometimes dotted with small blue motifs, despite the expense.

Occasionally the fashion is shortlived, as with needle-lace *oya* which became very popular for printed *yazma* scarf trimmings among urban women in the 1980s; now it is rare to see this work being produced and openly on sale. Town brides no longer choose the deep rich colours and gold-embroidered motifs of the satin marriage-bed quilts and cushions, made in specialist workshops in the bazaar. Instead, pale pastel tones with deep rouching and machine-stitched floral decoration in like colouring are preferred. Likewise the custom of embellishing the circumcision-bed with embroidered quilts and curtains, as recorded between the Wars, has largely disappeared in the urban context, though the young Turkish boy still dresses up for the pre-circumcision visits accompanied by his proud parents. It is noticeable that following new stringent traffic laws boys pass over models of police uniforms for their circumcision outfits, deciding on versions of tuxedos worn by TV entertainers or, reflecting current enterprise culture, business suits complete with Filofax.

Public recognition of non-industrial textiles has dimmed over the last decade, although certain Turkish fashion designers find inspiration in the fabrics and designs. A leading bank, Akbank, has organised over twenty handicrafts competitions: in the 1980 one the *dival*-embroidery work of Maraş was promoted. In addition the Ministry of Tourism and Culture features craft textiles in its sales outlets, but for active support one must turn to carpet production and in particular the DOBAG scheme.

DOBAG (Turkish abbreviation: National Dye Research and Development Project) was formally set up in 1985 at the instigation of Dr Harald Böhmer in conjunction with Marmara University, Istanbul. For over half a century Turkish carpet production had been dominated by dealers: by the First World War one European company controlled up to 75 per cent of total output in Anatolia, using its own spun and dyed yarn. Böhmer was concerned that empirical knowledge of vegetable dyeing processes and 'traditional' designs would soon be lost, and he felt strongly that the makers should be adequately rewarded for their work.

The first carpet-weaving co-operative employing vegetable dyes was established in 1981 at Ayvacik in the Çannakale region and a second followed at Yuntdağ, near Manisa. At least 1,500 jobs have been created in this area of Anatolia. Weavers are paid by the number of knots (an inducement to produce finer knotting), and the work is for export only, all profits going to the members of the co-operative, except a small percentage assigned to Marmara

University. The project has won much acclaim at home and abroad, and the impact on the Turkish carpet world is apparent if only from the new emphasis placed on vegetable dyes in dealers' sales talk. However, the design problem remains: how to build 'on the existing pool of designs in their present form without altering them, fossilising them or trying to turn the clock back . . . [and] resisting the temptation to "improve" the designs in the light of a sophisticated knowledge of old carpets' (Thompson 1986, p. 19).

Aside DOBAG production the variety of carpet and *kilim* patterns woven today is immense, and as most work is destined for export sizes, colourings and compositions are usually adapted to satisfy the relevant markets: thus rugs loosely based on earlier 'Caucasian' designs in which blue, green and red dominated can now be found in pastel shades, further lightened by artificial means. However, weaving for private or local distribution may be found all over Anatolia, and Landreau's 1970s' fieldwork with the Yörük, south-east Anatolia, is but one of many post-war studies (1983). The researchers note that in a mere decade (1971-82) the number of Yörük nomadic families had

ABOVE Weaver working in the DOBAG project, Turkey.

A circumcision bed, 1920s–30s, Turkey, with gold- and silver-embroidered coverlet. Relatives pinned talismans and other auspicious objects, needlework lace and embroidered sashes on to the bed curtains. (Istanbul)

dropped by over 40 per cent, and that with various resettlements 'traditional' pattern compositions and motifs were no longer exclusive to any one region. While the women weavers often gave names to certain design elements, these could vary even within the same village, and certainly no symbolic interpretation (excluding prayer-rug design) was offered by the weaver. Goat-hair and wool were spun in the community but largely dyed elsewhere by professional dyers, with the weaver ambivalent towards vivid artificial dye colours and man-made yarns.

Felt-making is also widespread across Anatolia, from the deep brown inlaid floor-coverings of eastern Turkey to the creamy-white shepherd mantles and rugs of the western provinces. Although Burkett (1979) saw little evidence of the making and use of felt in the late 1970s, compared with some fifteen years earlier, today in Afyon alone there are some ten or so workshops situated in one minor road, all producing felt on the premises with a small steam room for fulling and smoothing and elemental machinery for compression. The items are for local sale and geared specifically to that market.

Conclusion

Throughout the Middle East governments and development agencies have recognised in the post-war period the value of local small-range production units, while acknowledging that the needs of today's society totally outstrip the capacity of such units. There is always the hope that the work itself will engender keen customer demand at home and abroad, thereby reducing dependency on imported products and expanding the export market, but in the mean time such workshops provide much needed employment and income into the regions while requiring only low-level capital investment.

Wishing to encourage textile crafts, governments and official agencies have sought advice and guidance from consultants often far removed geographically, socially and economically from the working community concerned. As wider markets are sought for the products, this 'trawling' has certain advantages, provided the consultants are aware of prevailing technical, social and cultural constraints faced by the maker in the locale. Training schemes and projects organised at regional level operate under these disciplines, but formal art education in the Middle East is still largely based on nineteenth-century European models. Students gain little direct experience with either material or process; design work is purely a paper exercise. To enhance the social status of the craftsperson sometimes a system of national awards has been introduced, although the usefulness of such schemes has been questioned. Rarely do these titles earn international recognition, as the concept and evaluation of craft differ throughout the world.

To some the nomadic society is the guardian of tradition. For over 100 years the world of the nomad, the bedouin, has provided those living elsewhere, perhaps in a densely populated and polluted environment, a glimpse of sublime spiritual as well as territorial freedom. The myth of the medieval craftsman, so lovingly fashioned by William Morris reacting to the late nineteenth-century industrial world, has become inextricably bound up with the romance of the nomadic tribesman. Influential artists and critics in the West marvelled at the unity and consistency of pattern styles, which they considered were products of non-urban societies (Owen Jones 1854, p. 16):

It is far different with ourselves. We have no principles, no unity . . .

each craftsman runs each his independent course; each struggles fruitlessly, – each produces in art novelty without beauty, or beauty without intelligence.

As the lifestyle of the nomadic pasturalist seemed increasingly threatened, so the wish has grown to identify and authenticate the textiles and other material goods of this grouping as if to guarantee their continued existence, if only on record. However, if we are concerned with the ethnic origins of a particular pattern weave or embroidery, it is clear that the maker and the local community are not. Observers may read symbolic interpretations into the work, but as the makers themselves rarely offer such meanings and often within the same community give different names to the same motif, the idea that the makers 'live' the symbols and pattern in their work is highly controversial. As Spooner writes (1986, p. 230) concerning Turkoman carpets:

> . . . they worked with designs embodying symbols that were for them extensions of their own social identity. They did not understand these symbols [n]or need to know their origins. Now these symbols have become the property of others. To repossess them they must now find out from others what they mean. They are concerned only with how they will look to others . . . They market their ethnicity, their culture, as a commodity. Our search for authenticity in their carpets will not help them find it again. It is part of the cause of the problem.

Perhaps one can overlook social diversity (tribal, peasant, merchant, land-owner) within a given ethnic group which necessarily affects the interpretation and manipulation of symbols (the concept of space to a nomad and to a town-dweller will obviously differ); but the impact of political and social changes in the twentieth century cannot be ignored.

For centuries in order to maximise sales the Islamic textile worker (as elsewhere) has adjusted output to satisfy the preferences of the urban clientele, home and abroad, as well as those of the local customer. So, as is apparent in recent times, new colours, colour harmonies and sometimes motifs have been introduced into the established local repertoire. Sizes, shapes and styles are adapted: dimensions of most carpets and rugs are now linked to European room sizes rather than domestic measurements. Palestinian embroiderers work square cushion covers, rather than the traditional rectangular shape (Weir 1989), while garments incorporate elements of European styling. To those keen to ensure the survival of indigenous craft manufacture and design such adaptation interferes with and endangers the local tradition and 'natural' evolution of pattern and technique. In certain quarters (usually foreign) the appearance of helicopter and gun motifs on Iranian and, more recently, Afghan carpets was a matter for censure, as such imagery was not part of the established decorative repertoire. The prevailing political reality in which the makers were then living and working was not to influence their 'tradition' and so confuse the quest for 'authenticity'.

At the same time the danger of fossilising both the craft and patterns is being recognised to a degree. The most fervent craft *aficionado* finds it difficult to argue for the retention and use of equipment and materials now proven hazardous to the worker's health. Likewise it is clear that while endless repetition of a pattern may demonstrate its survival such work can quickly become stereotyped and lifeless as proportions, contours, colours and positioning within the composition lose clarity and nuance. Needless to say, lifeless designs are not improved, let alone transformed just by the use of vegetable-dyed yarn instead of synthetic colours. Conversely, while the technical ability of the craftsperson may be indisputable, the finished work is frequently diminished by the use of low-quality, cheap processed yarns, as today governments see that most high-quality grades of home-produced wool, cotton and silk go for export.

Many casual observers may see traditional Middle Eastern society as unchanging, but Weir's study on Palestinian costume (1989) has traced how one local community's sensitivities have been reflected in subtle changes in dress over the decades. It is ironic, therefore, that while scholars and collectors have documented and acquired the weaving, the embroideries, the felts and the costumes associated with nomadic groups (a tiny fraction of the total population), the home-produced textiles of the contemporary village, town and city have gone largely unrecorded. And while we know something of regional textile manufacture in earlier centuries, these were rarely described and even less frequently preserved, unlike the costly luxurious fabrics designated for courtly use and export.

At the turn of the century the life of the urban woman of the Middle East revolved around the home; she rarely left its confines, often occupying herself with textile work in some form. Now it is usual for her to work outside and contribute to the family budget, leaving little time for such interests. Knowledge and information about the world outside the local community have dramatically increased with the rise in literacy and advances in telecommunications, which in turn have influenced aspirations and expectations. Centuries ago the luxury textiles of medieval Egypt and Syria, of the Ottoman world and of Safavid Iran were recognised as superior to many fabrics originating in Europe and elsewhere. Today home-produced textiles are generally associated with bad quality in design and manufacture, whereas European fabrics represent status and wealth, taste and education. The label of foreign manufacture is flaunted in public and in private, whether it is on jeans worn in Cairo, on Givenchy outfits in Riyadh homes, or on selvages of Sudanese *thawb* (dress) lengths. In the past European textile terminology was enriched by Arabic, Persian and Turkish words; now the traffic is reversed with, for instance, *blusa* and *mini* appearing in Arabic, *ceket* and *maksi* in Turkish, and *mantu* and *kravat* in Persian. Yet while foreign-made fabrics dominate the market, some textiles have become a recognised statement of identity.

Throughout Islamic history it has been accepted convention that one's clothing proclaimed the wearer's allegiances, profession and social rank. In the twentieth century it could be said that clothing had become an explicit expression of nationhood. To be denied such clothing is akin to losing group identity: thus before opening peace negotiations with Riza Shah both the Qashqai and Kurdish tribal representatives demanded exemption from the dress laws and the right to wear their characteristic clothing. More recently the Palestinian checked *kaffiya*s and embroidered robes are an 'increasingly self-conscious statement of . . . Palestinian identity and national aspirations' (Weir 1989, p. 273), just as ikat satin, frequently styled in the latest fashion, has become for Uzbek women of all ages since the late 1980s and the dying years of the Soviet Union.

Slight differences in, say, folding the head-covering or in the tailoring of men and women's clothing often reveal regional identity, so the wearer makes

Wool wrap, 1994, Erzurum, eastern Turkey. These fine woollen plain-weave wraps, sometimes decorated with small blue motifs, are reportedly made locally. Despite their price, over a week's wages, they are donned for everyday wear among certain middle-aged and older women in the region.

a conscious decision whether to appear conspicuous or anonymous in a given locale. Thus a Qashqai woman of the 1970s resplendent in her colourful tabard, resist-printed silk turban scarf and multiple lurex petticoats was anonymous in the encampment; in the bazaars of Shiraz she was identifiable but commonplace, though shockingly conspicuous on Tehran streets.

Often the fabric itself has not been produced in the region nor even within the national borders, being industrially manufactured abroad. It is the patterning and reworking that give it that special identity. This is also found in Islamic fundamentalist dress in the Middle East. The source of the fabric is immaterial, but the garment's styling and distinct monochrome colouring identify the wearer as rejecting contemporary Western fashions and thus implicitly its social values. It may be argued that the dress is 'traditional', which implies a timeless, unchanging quality, but since the 1970s several styles have come and gone. Presently the cut of Islamic clothing is generally based on urban costume, as worn at the turn of the century.

In Egypt the Muslim authorities have not defined what exactly constitutes Islamic dress, but in the first year of the Islamic Republic of Iran Ayatollah Khomeini announced that it was 'the personal duty' for Iranian women to wear the full-length black *chador*, adding that it was 'to be honoured as the black flag of revolution' (see p. 50). As in some Muslim Pakistani circles, ties (and collars) are not now generally worn by Iranian men. *Kravati* was a derogatory term for intellectuals and sophisticates in the last days of Pahlavi rule, but today the absence of a tie is associated with fundamentalist dress with some Muslims believing the tie is a Christian symbol of the crucified Jesus.

Nevertheless, while the origin of the dress fabric may be currently immaterial, there are indications that crafts in general are becoming linked with national identity. Mahatma Gandhi in his campaign for Indian independence had stressed the importance of indigenous textile production, and recently the Iran Handicrafts Organisation has drawn attention to the deep cultural roots of crafts, pointing out that they could be instrumental in combating 'the deceiving allures of foreign cultures' (*Hands and Creativity*, vol. 1 (spring), 1992, p. 3) or, as the late Ayatollah Khomeini called it, Westoxication (*gharbzadgi*).

Ribbon-tying at the Hacibektaş shrine complex, 1993, central Turkey. Haci Bektaş, 13th-century founder of the Bektaşi dervishes, was said to have inspired the distinctive felt head-dress of the Ottoman Janissaries.

Despite the changing world a number of textile traditions remain. Most are associated with established ritual, orthodox and otherwise. While there is no specific religious requirement for a prayer-rug in the performance of *salat*, the gift of a beautiful prayer-rug is generally appreciated by a Muslim. Similarly, it is the custom that a cloth, today often green with embroidered or machine-stitched Quranic verses, will cover the coffin on its journey from the home to the cemetery. The age-old tradition of tying prayer-ribbons on the grilles protecting a shrine or on 'wishing-trees' is an echo of shamanist rites and is not confined to the Middle East, as the 1970s American popular song 'Tie a Yellow Ribbon' reminds us.

In rural areas and villages bridal dress is in accord with local convention, although the urban bride will choose to wear a white gown based on Western modes. The matrimonial bed with its decorative quilted counterpane, cushions and pillows still features in many homes, although modern taste has influenced the colouring and decoration of the bridal bed set. In 'traditional' households the woman is often careful to conceal her transparent nightwear and embroidered sheets from visiting friends and relatives, should her husband be travelling away from home, displaying instead plain bedlinen and nightdress; to do otherwise might provoke gossip. While the gaily decorated circumcision bed may have disappeared in Turkish urban society, young boys still proudly dress up in special outfits for their pre-circumcision visiting.

As the governments of the Islamic Middle East react to the new world economic order largely controlled by multinational corporations, to many visiting the region it might seem as if the domination of the West is virtually complete. The old mercantile peasant economy with royal monopolies ordering the major (textile) production sectors is history. But there is a new interest among young and old alike in the 'national heritage' of the country and region. It is noticeable that this often manifests itself through a deliberate and conscious selection of textiles and dress. While the Islamic Middle East may never regain its formidable hold on textile manufacture and trading of medieval and post-medieval times, designers and artists throughout the world will continue to be inspired and influenced by this work, just as Bellini, William Morris, Bakst, Matisse and others were in the past.

BIBLIOGRAPHY

This listing, compiled to be of use to both general and specialist readers, includes references to recent research, often in article format, and also to works with useful bibliographies or illustrations. The most accessible translation of Arabic, Turkish or Persian source material has been noted, where applicable, for the general reader; the specialist reader will be aware of the merits and demerits of varius editions. It should be noted that dates given for Ph.D. theses refer to university submission and examination, rather than microfilm publication.

ABBREVIATIONS

AO Ars Orientalis
BCIETA Bulletin de Liaison, Centre internationale de l'Etude des Tissus anciens, Lyon
EI¹, EI² Encyclopaedia of Islam, 1st edn, Brill, Luzac, Leiden, London, 1913 on; 2nd edn, Brill, Luzac, Leiden, London, 1960 on
E. Iran. Encyclopaedia Iranica, Routledge, Kegan and Paul, London, 1985 on
IJMES International Journal of Middle East Studies
IS Iranian Studies
JESHO Journal of the Economic and Social History of the Orient
JRAS Journal of the Royal Asiatic Society of Great Britain and Northern Ireland
OCTS Oriental Carpet and Textile Studies, Hali, London
TMJ Textile Museum Journal
WSSH Woven from the Soul, Spun from the Heart, ed. C. Bier, Textile Museum, Washington, DC, 1987
ZDMG Zeitschrift der Deutschen Morgenlandischen Gesellschaft

General

ARTS COUNCIL OF GREAT BRITAIN 1976. *Arts of Islam,* exh. cat, Hayward Gallery, London
BOSWORTH, C.E., 1980. *The Islamic Dynasties,* Edinburgh University Press
FOLSACH, KJELD VON, and BERNSTED, A.-M. KEBLOW, 1993. *Woven Treasures – Textiles from the World of Islam,* David Collection, Copenhagen

Introduction and Chapter 1

ASHTOR, ELIYAHU, 1983. *Levant Trade in the Late Middle Ages,* Princeton University Press
BAER, G., 1970. 'Monopolies and restrictive practices of Turkish Guilds', *JESHO,* 13, pp. 145–65
BAER, G., 1977. 'The Organisation of Labour', *Wirtschaftsgeschichte des Vorderen Orients in Islamischer Zeit,* Brill, Leiden, pp. 31–52
BALDRY, JOHN, 1982. *Textiles in the Yemen . . . ,* British Museum Occasional Papers, no. 27, London
BALFOUR-PAUL, JENNY, 1987. 'Indigo – an Arab curiosity and its Omani variations',

Omani Economic, Social and Strategic Development, ed. B.R. Pridham, Croom Helm, London, pp. 79–93
BIER, C. MANSON, 1978. 'Textiles', *The Royal Hunter: art of the Sasanian Empire,* ed. P. Oliver Harper, Asia House, New York, pp. 119–40
BOSWORTH, C.E. (ed.), 1968. *The Lata'if al-Ma'arif of al-Tha'alibi,* Edinburgh University Press
BRUNELLO, FRANCO, 1973. *The Art of Dyeing in the History of Mankind,* Vicenza
BUCKLEY, R.P., 1992. 'The Muhtasib', *Arabica,* 39, pp. 59–117
CARROLL, DIANE LEE, 1988. *Looms and textiles of the Copts . . . ,* Memoirs of the California Academy of Sciences, no. 11, San Francisco
ÇIZAKÇA, M., 1980. 'A short history of the Bursa Silk Industry (1500–1900)', *JESHO,* 23, pp. 142–52
CLINTON, JEROME W., 1972. *The Divan of Manchihri Damghani . . .* Bibliotheca Islamica, Minneapolis
COOPER, R.S., 1973. *Ibn Mammati's rules for the Ministries . . . ,* Ph.D. thesis, Ann Arbor, Michigan State University
CRAFTS COUNCIL, 1988. *Ikats – woven silks from Central Asia: the Rau collection,* Blackwell, London
DAY, FLORENCE, 1954. 'The Inscription of the Boston "Baghdad" silk', *AO,* 1, pp. 191–4
DOZY, R.P.A., 1845. *Dictionnaire detaillé des noms des vêtements chez les arabes,* Amsterdam
EASTWOOD, GILLIAN M. VOGELSANG-, 1990. *Resist Dyed textiles from Quseir al-Qadim, Egypt,* A.E.D.T.A., Paris; preface by Krishna Riboud; to be read in conjunction with review by J. Herald, *Hali,* 67 (Feb./Mar. 1993), pp. 105, 107
EI², 'Harir', 'Kutn', 'Lawn', 'Mahmal'
E. Iran, 'Abrisam', 'Colour', 'Cotton'
FLOOR, WILLIAM M., 1975. 'The Guilds in Iran . . .', *ZDMG,* 125, pp. 99–116
FLOOR, WILLIAM M., 1985. 'The office of Muhtasib in Iran', *IS,* 8(i), pp. 53–74
FRENCH, D., 1972. 'A sixteenth century English Merchant in Ankara?', *Anatolian Studies,* 22, pp. 241–7
GAUDEFROY-DEMOMBYNES, 1918. 'Notes sur la Mekke et Médine', *Revue de l'histoire des religions,* 77, pp. 316–44
GEIJER, A., 1963. 'A Silk from Antinoe and the Sasanian Textile Art', *Orientalia Suecana,* 12, pp. 3–36
GITTINGER, MATTIEBELLE, 1982. *Master Dyers to the World . . .* Textile Museum, Washington, DC
GOITEIN, S.D., 1978. *The Mediterranean Society,* vol. 3, University of California Press, Berkeley
HAKLUYT, RICHARD, 1903. *The Principal Navigations, Voyages . . . ,* vol. 3, Hakluyt extra series, Glasgow
HALD, MARGRETHE, 1980. *Ancient Danish*

Textiles from Bogs and Burials, Publications of the National Museum Archaeological-Historical series 21, Copenhagen
HOOPER, D., and FIELD, H., 1937. *Useful Plants and Drugs of Iran and Iraq,* Field Museum of Natural History, Chicago
IBN AL-UKHUWWA, ed. and trans. Reuben Levy, 1938. *The Ma'alim al-Qurba fi ahkam al-hisba . . . ibn al-Ukhuwwa,* E.J.W. Gibb Memorial series, Cambridge University Press, London
IBN KHALDUN, ed. and trans. F. Rosenthal, 1967. *The Muqaddimah: an Introduction to History,* Princeton University Press, vol. 2
JAYAKAR, A.S.G. (ed.), 1908. *Hayat al-Hayawan of al-Damiri,* Luzac, London, Bombay, vol. 1
KUHN, DIETER, 1981. 'Silk Technology in the Sung Period (969–1278)', *Toung Pao,* 67 pp. 48–90
KUHN, DIETER, 1988. *Science and Civilisation in China,* ed. J. Needham, vol. 5(ix), Textile Technology: Spinning and Reeling, Cambridge University Press
LAMM, CARL JOHAN, 1937. *Cotton in Medieval Textiles of the Near East,* Paul Geuthner, Paris
LANE, EDWARD WILSON, 1874. *An Arabic-English Lexicon,* vol. 1(v), Williams and Norgate, London, Edinburgh, 1863–93
LAPIDUS, I.M., 1967. *Muslim Cities in the later Middle Ages,* Harvard University Press, Cambridge, Mass.
LEWIS, BERNARD, 1974. *Islam from the Prophet Muhammad to the Capture of Constantinople,* vol. 2, Harper and Row, New York
LOMBARD, MAURICE, 1978. *Etudes d'économie médiévale: Les Textiles dans le Monde Musulman du VIIe au XIIe siècle,* Mouton, Paris
LOPEZ, R.S., and RAYMOND, I.W., 1955. *Medieval Trade in the Mediterranean World,* Oxford University Press, London
MINORSKY, VLADIMIR F., 1943. *Tadhkirat al-Muluk: a manual of Safavid administration,* E.J.W. Gibb Memorial series, N.S. 16, Luzac, London
MUKMINOVA, R.G., 1992. 'Craftsmen and Guild Life in Samarqand', *Timurid Art and Culture . . . ,* ed. L. Golombek and M. Subtelny, Brill, London, pp. 29–35
MUNRO, JOHN H., 1983. 'The medieval Scarlet and the Economics of Sartorial Splendour', *Cloth and Clothing in Medieval Europe . . . in memory of Prof. Carius Wilson,* ed. N.B. Harte and K.G. Ponting, Pasold Studies in Textile History 2, London, pp. 13–70
MUSLIM 1973. *Salih Muslim,* trans. Abdul Hamid Siddiqi, Muhammad Ashraf, Lahore
NICHOLSON, R.A., 1906. 'A Historical enquiry concerning the origin and development of Sufism', *JRAS,* pp. 303–48
PARET, RUDI, 1968. 'Das Islamische Bilderverbot und die Schia', *Festschrift*

Werner Caskel, ed. Erwin Graf, Brill, Leiden, pp. 224–32

PFISTER, R., 1938. *Les Toiles imprimées de Fostat et l'Hindoustan*, Editions d'Art et d'Histoire, Paris

QASTALLANI, SHAHIB AL-DIN, 1323/1905. *Irshad al-Sari fi sharh al-Bukhari*, Bulaq

RABI(E), H., 1972. *The Financial System of Egypt, AH 564–741/AD 1169–1341*, Oxford University Press, London

REENEN, DAAN VAN, 1990. 'The Bildverbot: a new survey', *Der Islam*, 67, pp. 27–77

RICHARDS, D.S. (ed.), 1970. *Islam and the Trade of Asia*, Bruno Cassirer, Oxford

SEYF, A., 1983. 'Silk Production and Trade in Iran in the 19th century', *IS*, 16, pp. 51–71

SERJEANT, R.B., 1972. *Islamic Textiles . . .*, Librairie du Liban, Beirut

TSIEN, TSUEN-HSUIN, 1985. *Science and Civilisation in China*, ed. J. Needham, vol. 5(i), Paper and Printing, Cambridge University Press

WARNER, A.G. and E. (trans.), 1912. *Shahname (Firdawsi)*, vol. 6, sect. 11, Trübner, London

WATSON, A.M., 1977. 'The Rise and Spread of Old World Cotton', *Studies in Textile History*, ed. V. Gervers, Royal Ontario Museum, Toronto, pp. 355–68

WEIR, S., 1970. *Spinning and Weaving in Palestine*, British Museum Publications, London

WHITFIELD, RODERICK, 1985. *The Art of Central Asia: the Stein Collection in the British Museum*, vol. 3, British Museum, Kodansha, Tokyo

WHITFIELD, RODERICK, and FARRER, ANNE, 1990. *Caves of the Thousand Buddhas: Chinese art from the Silk Route*, British Museum Publications, London

WILSON, SAMUEL G., 1896. *Persian Life and Customs . . .*, Oliphant, Anderson and Ferrier, Edinburgh

WULFF, HANS E., 1966. *The Traditional Crafts in Persia*, The M.I.T. Press, Cambridge, Mass.

Chapter 2

ACKERMANN, PHYLLIS, 1964 repr. 'Textiles through the Sasanian period', *A Survey of Persian Art*, ed. A.U. Pope, vol. 2, Oxford University Press

BAKER, PATRICIA L., 1991. 'An Abbasid Silk Fragment', *Hali*, 59 (Oct.), p. 100

BAMBERG, 1987. *Textile Grabfunde aus der Sepulchur des Bamberger Domkapitels*, Bayerisches Landesamt für Denkmalpflege, Arbeitsheft, 33, Munich

BERNUS, M., MARCHAL, H., and VIAL, G., 1971. 'Le suaire de St Josse', *BCIETA*, pp. 22–57

BIER, C. MANSON, 1978. 'Textiles', *The Royal Hunter: art of the Sasanian Empire*, ed. P. Oliver Harper, Asia House, New York, pp. 119–40

BLAIR, SHEILA S., BLOOM, JONATHAN M., and WARDWELL, ANNE E., 1993. 'Re-evaluating the Date of the "Buyid" Silks', *AO*, 22, pp. 1–42

BOSWORTH, C.E. (ed.), 1968. *The Lata'if al-Ma'arif of al-Tha'alibi*, Edinburgh University Press

CARROLL, DIANE LEE, 1988. *Looms and Textiles*

of the Copts . . . Memoirs of the California Academy of Sciences, no. 11, San Francisco

CHIRVANI, A.S. MELIKIAN, 1991. '*Parand* and *Parniyan* identified . . .', *Bulletin of the Asia Institute*, 5, pp. 175–9

COOPER, R.S., 1973. *Ibn Mammati's rules for the Ministries . . .*, Ph.D. thesis, Ann Arbor, Michigan State University

CROWFOOT, ELISABETH, forthcoming. *The Cathedral Burials and their Textiles* (Qasr Ibrim excavations), Egypt Exploration Society

DAY, FLORENCE, 1954. 'The Inscription of the Boston "Baghdad" Silk', *AO*, 1, pp. 191–4

DE MOOR, A. (ed.), 1993. *Koptisch Textiel/ Coptic Textiles . . .*, Provinciaal Archeologisch Museum van Zuid-Oost-Vlaaderen, Zottegem

DODDS, JERRILYNN (ed.), 1992. *Al-Andalus: the Art of Islamic Spain*, Metropolitan Museum of Art, New York

EI[1], 'Dibadj'; *EI*[2], 'Harir', 'Mandil'

E. Iran., 'Abrisam'

GENEVA, 1994. Musée d'art et d'histoire, *Tissus d'Egypte: témoins du monde arabe VIIIe-XVe siècles*, exh. cat.

GOITEIN, S.D., 1967. *The Mediterranean Society*, vol. 1, University of California Press, Berkeley

GOLOMBEK, L., and GERVERS, V., 1977. 'Tiraz fabrics in the Royal Ontario Museum', *Studies in Textile History*, ed. V. Gervers, Royal Ontario Museum, Toronto, pp. 82–126

HEYD, WILHELM VON, 1923. *Histoire du commerce du Levant au moyen age*, vol. 2, Harrossowitz, Leipzig

HOFFENK-DE GRAAFF, J.H., 1973a. 'Dye-stuffs Analysis of the Buyid Silk fabrics . . .', *BCIETA*, 37, pp. 120–33

HOFFENK-DE GRAAFF, J.H., 1973b. 'About Dyestuff Analysis of the Buyid Silks', *BCIETA*, 38, pp. 39–40

HOFFENK-DE GRAAFF, J.H., 1976. 'Comments on comments', *BCIETA*, 43–4, pp. 101–23

IEROUSSALIMSKAJA, A.A., 1966. 'Trois soieries byzantines anciennes', *BCIETA*, 24, pp. 11–39

INDICTOR, NORMAN, n.d. 'Carbon-14 Dates for "Buyid" Silks by Accelerator Mass Spectrometry' (unpub.), Brooklyn, New York

KAWAMI, TRUDY, 1991. 'Ancient Textiles from Shahr-i Qumis', *Hali*, 59 (Oct.), pp. 95–9

KING, DONALD, 1987. 'The Textiles found near Rayy about 1925', *BCIETA*, 65, pp. 34–59

KÜHNEL, ERNST, 1957. 'Abbasid Silks of the Ninth century', *AO*, 2, pp. 367–71

KÜHNEL, ERNST, and BELLINGER, LOUISE, 1952. *Catalogue of Dated Tiraz Fabrics: Umayyad, Abbasid, Fatimid*, Textile Museum, Washington, DC

LAMM, CARL JOHAN, 1937. *Cotton in Medieval Textiles of the Near East*, Paul Geuthner, Paris

LAMM, CARL JOHAN, 1941. *Oriental Glass . . .*, Wahlström and Widstrand, Stockholm

LANE, EDWARD WILSON, 1874. *An Arabic-English Lexicon*, vol. 1(v), Williams and Norgate, London, Edinburgh

LEMBERG, M., 1973a. 'Les soieries bouyides . . .', *BCIETA*, 37, pp. 11–54

LEMBERG, M., 1973b. 'Opening of the discussion about the Buyid silks', *BCIETA*, 38, pp. 17–19

LEMBERG, M., 1976. 'More about the Persian silks in the Abegg-Stiftung', *BCIETA*, 43–4, pp. 7–26

LOMBARD, MAURICE, 1978. *Etudes d'économie mediévale: Les Textiles dans le Monde Musulman du VIIe au XIIe siècle*, Mouton, Paris

MARTINIANI-REBER, M., 1986. *Soieries sassanides, coptes et byzantines V-XIe siècles*, Musée historique des tissus, Lyon, Paris

MAS'UDI, 1984. *The Meadows of Gold: The Abbasids*, ed. and trans. Paul Lunde and Caroline Stone, Kegan Paul International, London

MEISTER, MICHAEL W., 1970. 'The Pearl Roundel in Chinese Textile Design', *AO*, 8, pp. 255–67

MUTHESIUS, ANNA, 1984. 'A practical approach to the History of Byzantine silk weaving', *Jahrbuch der Oesterreichischen Byzantinistik*, 34, pp. 235–54

PICARD-SCHMITTER, M.-TH., 1973. 'The condemnation of 31 silks in the Abegg collection . . .', *BCIETA*, 38, pp. 87–111

REENEN, DAAN VAN, 1990. 'The Bilderverbot: a new survey', *Der Islam*, 67, pp. 27–77

RIBOUD, KRISHNA, 1977. 'Some Remarks on the Face Covers (Fu-Mien) discovered in the Tombs of Astana', *Oriental Art* (winter), pp. 438–54

ROSENTHAL, F., 1971. 'A Note on the Mandil', *Four Essays on Art and Literature in Islam*, Brill, Leiden, pp. 63–99

SERJEANT, R.B., 1972. *Islamic Textiles . . .*, Librairie du Liban, Beirut

SHEPHERD, D., 1957. 'A dated Hispano-Islamic silk', *AO*, 2, pp. 373–82

SHEPHERD, D., 1973. 'In defense of the Persian silks', *BCIETA*, 37, pp. 138–42

SHEPHERD, D., 1974. 'Medieval Persian Silks in Fact and Fancy', *BCIETA*, 39–40, pp. 1–239

SHEPHERD, D., 1975. 'The archaeology of the Buyid textiles', *Archaeological Textiles*, Irene Emery Roundtable 1974 Proceedings, ed. Patricia L. Fiske, Textile Museum, Washington, DC, pp. 175–90

SHEPHERD, D., 1981. 'Zandiniji Revisited', *Documenta Textilia Festschrift für Sigrid Muller-Christensen*, ed. M. Flury-Lemberg and M. Stollers, Munich, pp. 105–22

SHEPHERD, D., and HENNING, W.B., 1959. 'Zandaniji identified?', *Aus der Welt der Islamischen Kunst: Festschrift für Ernst Kühnel*, ed. R. Ettinghausen, Verlag Gebr. Mann, Berlin, pp. 15–40

SHEPHERD, D., and VIAL, G., 1965. 'La chasuble de St Sernin', *BCIETA*, 21, pp. 19–31

STILLMAN, YEDIDA, 1972. *Female Attire of Medieval Egypt . . .*, Ph.D. thesis, University of Pennsylvania

STILLMAN, YEDIDA, 1979. 'New Data on Islamic Textiles . . .', *Textile History*, 10, pp. 184–95

STORM-RICE, D., 1959. 'Thomas à Becket Cope', *Illustrated London News* (3 October), pp. 356–8

TRILLING, J. 1982. *Roman Heritage Textiles from*

Egypt and the Eastern Mediterranean, 300–600 AD, Textile Museum, Washington, DC

TRITTON, A.S., 1930. *The Caliphs and their non-Muslim Subjects*, Oxford University Press, London

VIAL, G., 1961. 'Le tissu aux elephants . . .', *BCIETA*, 14, pp. 29–34

VIAL, G., 1967. 'Un lampas bouyide . . .', *BCIETA*, 25, pp. 55–68

VIAL, G., 1973. 'Etude technique des soieries bouyides . . .', *BCIETA*, 37, pp. 70–102

VIAL, G., 1976. 'Etudes techniques', *BCIETA*, 43–4, pp. 41–100

WARDWELL, A., 1983. 'A Fifteenth-century Silk Curtain from Muslim Spain', *Bulletin of Cleveland Museum of Art* (Feb.), pp. 58–72

WHITFIELD, RODERICK, 1985. *The Art of Central Asia: the Stein Collection in the British Museum*, vol. 3, British Museum, Kodansha, Tokyo

WHITFIELD, RODERICK, and FARRER, ANNE, 1990. *Caves of the Thousand Buddhas: Chinese art from the Silk Route*, British Museum Publications, London

Chapter 3

BIERMAN, IRENE A., 1980. *Art and Politics: the Impact of Fatimid Uses of Tiraz Fabrics*, Ph.D. thesis, Chicago University

BRITTON, NANCY, 1938. *A Study of Some Early Islamic Textiles . . .*, Museum of Fine Art, Boston

COOPER, R.S., 1973. *Ibn Mammati's Rules to the Ministries . . .*, Ph.D. thesis, Ann Arbor, Michigan State University

DAY, FLORENCE, 1952. 'The Tiraz Silk of Marwan', *Archaeologica orientalis in memoriam Ernst Herzfeld*, ed. G.C. Miles, J.J. Augustin, New York, pp. 39–61

DODDS, JERRILYNN (ed.), 1992. *Al-Andalus: the Art of Islamic Spain*, Metropolitan Museum of Art, New York

EI[1], 'Tiraz' and also supplement

GLIDDEN, HAROLD W., and THOMPSON, DEBORAH, 1988. 'Tiraz Fabrics in the Byzantine collection, Dumbarton Oaks: part One', *Bulletin of the Asia Institute*, 2, pp. 119–39

GLIDDEN, HAROLD, W., and THOMPSON, DEBORAH, 1989. 'Tiraz Fabrics in the Byzantine collection, Dumbarton Oaks: parts Two and Three', *Bulletin of the Asia Institute*, 3, pp. 89–105

GOLOMBEK, LISA, 1988. 'The Draped Universe of Islam', *Content and Context of Visual Arts in the Islamic World*, ed. Priscilla Soucek, Pennsylvania University Press, pp. 25–38

GOLOMBEK, LISA, and GERVERS, VERONIKA, 1977. 'Tiraz fabrics in the Royal Ontario Museum', *Studies in Textile History*, ed. V. Gervers, Royal Ontario Museum, Toronto, pp. 82–126

HAMBLIN, WILLIAM J., 1985. *The Fatimid Army during the early Crusades*, Ph.D. thesis, Ann Arbor, Michigan State University

HINDS, MARTIN, 1971. 'The Banners and Battle Cries of the Arabs at Siffin (657 AD)', *Al-Abhath*, Beirut, 24, pp. 3–42

IBN KHALDUN, ed. and trans. F. Rosenthal, 1967. *The Muqaddimah: an Introduction to History*, Princeton University Press, vol. 2

KÜHNEL, ERNST, and BELLINGER, LOUISE, 1952. *Catalogue of Dated Tiraz Fabrics: Umayyad, Abbasid, Fatimid*, Textile Museum, Washington, DC

LANE, EDWARD WILSON, 1874. *An Arabic-English Lexicon*, vol. 1(v), Williams and Norgate, London, Edinburgh, 1863–93

LE STRANGE, GUY, 1897. 'A Greek Embassy to Baghdad in 917 AD', *JRAS*, pp. 35–45

MAYER, LEO A., 1952. *Mamluk Costume: a survey*, Albert Kundig, Geneva

MARZOUK, M.A.A., 1954. 'The Turban of Samuel b. Musa', *Bulletin of the Faculty of Arts, Cairo*, 16(ii), pp. 143–51

QUATREMÈRE, ETIENNE M. (ed.), 1838. *Mesalek alabsar fi memalek alamsar . . . al-'Umari*, Académie des Inscriptions et Belles Lettres, Notices et Extraits, Paris, vol. 13(i), pp. 151–384

SADAN, J., 1976. *Le Mobilier au Proche Orient médiéval*, Brill, Leiden

SALEM, ELIE A., 1977. *Hilal ibn al-Muhassin al-Sabi 'Rustum dar al-Khilafah'*, American University of Beirut

SANDERS, PAULA, 1984. *The Court Ceremonial of the Fatimid Caliphate in Egypt*, Ph.D. thesis, Princeton University

SERJEANT, R.B., 1972. *Islamic Textiles . . .*, Librairie du Liban, Beirut

SHEPHERD, DOROTHY, 1957. 'A dated Hispano-Islamic Silk,' *AO*, 2, pp. 373–82

STILLMAN, YEDIDA, 1972. *Female Attire of Medieval Egypt . . .*, Ph.D. thesis, University of Pennsylvania

STORM-RICE, D., 1959. 'Thomas à Becket Cope', *Illustrated London News* (3 Oct.), pp. 356–8

WARDELL, ANNE, 1983. 'A Fifteenth-century Silk Curtain from Muslim Spain', *Bulletin of Cleveland Museum of Art* (Feb.), pp. 58–72

Chapter 4

ABD AR-RAZIQ, A., 1973. *La femme au temps des mamlouks en Egypte*, Institut Français d'Archéologie Orientale du Caire, Cairo

ATIL, E., 1981. *Renaissance of Islam: Art of the Mamluks*, Smithsonian Institution, Washington, DC

AYALON, DAVID, 1957. 'The System of Payment in Mamluk Military Society', *JESHO*, 1, pp. 37–65

AYALON, DAVID, 1958. 'The System of Payment in Mamluk Military Society – Concluded', *JESHO*, 1, pp. 257–96

BARNES, RUTH, 1990. 'Indian Trade Cloth in Egypt: the Newberry collection', *Textiles in Trade: Proceedings of the Textile Society of America Biennial Symposium*, Washington, DC, pp. 178–91

BARNES, RUTH, 1993. *Indian Block Printed Cotton Fragments in the Kelsey Museum, the University of Michigan*, Ann Arbor, Mich.

BELLINGER, LOUISA, 1954. 'Patterned Stockings: Possibly Indian, found in Egypt', Workshop Notes Paper no. 10, Textile Museum, Washington, DC (Dec.)

CROWFOOT, ELISABETH, 1977. 'The Clothing of a Fourteenth century Nubian Bishop', *Studies in Textile History*, ed. V. Gervers, Royal Ontario Museum, Toronto, pp. 43–51

DARRAG, A., 1961. *L'Egypte sous le règne de*

Barsbay . . ., Institut Français de Damas, Damascus

DOLS, MICHAEL W., 1977. *The Black Death in the Middle East*, Princeton University Press

EASTWOOD, GILLIAN, 1983. 'A medieval Face-veil from Egypt', *Costume*, 17, pp. 33–8

EASTWOOD, GILLIAN M. VOGELSAND-, 1990. *Resist Dyed Textiles from Quseir al-Qadim, Egypt*, A.E.D.T.A., Paris; to be read in conjunction with review by J. Herald, *Hali* 67 (Feb./Mar. 1993), pp. 105, 107

ETTINGHAUSEN, RICHARD, 1959. 'An early Ottoman Textile', *First International Conference on Turkish Art*, Türk Tarih Kurumu, Ankara, pp. 134–40

ETTINGHAUSEN, RICHARD, 1977. 'Originality and conformity in Islamic Art', *Individuality and Conformity in Classical Islam*, 5th Giorgio Levi Della Vida Biennial Conference, ed. A. Banani and S. Vryonis, Wiesbaden, pp. 83–114

GENEVA, 1994. Musée d'art et d'histoire, *Tissus d'Egypte: témoins du monde arabe VIIIe–XVe siècles*, exh. cat.

GERVERS, VERONIKA, 1978–9. 'Rags to riches: medieval Islamic textiles', *Rotunda*, Royal Ontario Museum, vol. 11(iv), pp. 22–31

GITTINGER, MATTIBELLE, 1982. *Master Dyers to the World . . .*, Textile Museum, Washington, DC

HALDANE, DUNCAN, 1978. *Mamluk Painting*, Aris and Phillips, Warminster

IBN KHALDUN, ed. and trans. F. Rosenthal, 1967. *The Muqaddimah: an Introduction to History*, Princeton University Press, vol. 2

IBN SASRA, trans. William Brinner, 1963. *A Chronicle of Damascus 1389–97*, vol. 1, University of California Press, Berkeley

INDICTOR, NORMAN, n.d. 'Carbon-14 Dates for "Buyid" Silks by Accelerator Mass Spectrometry' (unpub.), Brooklyn, New York

'IZZI, WAFIYYA, 1974. 'Objects bearing the name of An-Nasir Muhammad and his Successors', *Colloque internationale sur l'Histoire du Caire 1969*, Ministry of Culture, General Egyptian Book Organisation, Cairo, pp. 235–41

KING, DONALD, and SYLVESTER, DAVID, 1983. *The Eastern Carpet in the Western World . . .*, Hayward Gallery, Arts Council, London

KLESSE, BRIGITTE, 1967. *Seidenstoffe in den Italienischen Malerei des 14 Jahrhunderts*, Stampfli, Bern

LABIB, SUBHI, 1970. 'Egyptian Commercial Policy in the Middle Ages', *Studies in the Economic History of the Middle East from the Rise of Islam to the Present Day*, ed. M.A. Cook, Oxford University Press, London, pp. 63–77

LAMM, CARL JOHAN, 1937. *Cotton in Medieval Textiles of the Near East*, Paul Geuthner, Paris

LAMM, CARL JOHAN, 1937. 'Some Mamluk Embroideries', *Ars Islamica*, 4, pp. 65–76

LAPIDUS, I.M., 1967. *Muslim Cities in the Later Middle Ages*, Harvard University Press, Cambridge, Mass.

LOWRY, G., and LENTZ, T. (eds), 1989. *Timur and the Princely Vision . . .*, exh. cat., County Museum of Art, Los Angeles

MACKIE, LOUISE, 1984. 'Toward an Understanding of Mamluk Silks: National and International Considerations', *Muqarnas*, 2, pp. 127–46

MACKIE, LOUISE, 1989. 'Textiles' in W. Kubiak and G.T. Scanlon (eds), *Fustat Expedition Final Report vol. 2 Fustat-C*, American Research Center in Egypt, Eisenbrauns, Winona Lake, Minn., pp. 81–97

MARZOUK, M.A., 1955. *History of the Textile Industry in Alexandria . . .*, Alexandria University Press

MARZOUK, M.A., 1965. 'Tiraz institutions in Medieval Egypt', *Studies in Islamic Art and Architecture in honour of Prof. K.A.C. Creswell*, ed. C.L. Geddes, American University in Cairo Press, London, pp. 157–62

MAYER, LEO, A., 1933. *Saracenic Heraldry: a survey*, Clarendon Press, Oxford

MAYER, LEO, A., 1952. *Mamluk Costume: a survey*, Albert Kundig, Geneva

NEWBURY, ESSIE, 1940. 'Embroideries from Egypt', *Embroidery*, 8(i), pp. 11–18

PFISTER, R., 1936. 'Tissus imprimées de l'Inde mediévale', *Revue des Arts Asiatiques*, 10, pp. 161–4

PFISTER, R., 1938. *Les Toiles imprimées de Fostat et l'Hindoustan*, Editions d'Art et d'Histoire, Paris

RABI(E), H., 1972. *The Financial System of Egypt, AH 564–741/AD 1169–1341*, Oxford University Press, London

SCHMIDT, H., 1934. 'Damaste der Mamlukenzeit', *Ars Islamica*, 1, pp. 99–109

STILLMAN, YEDIDA, 1972. *Female Attire of Medieval Egypt . . .*, Ph.D. thesis, University of Pennsylvania

STOWASSER, K., 1984. 'Manners & Customs at the Mamluk Court', *Muqarnas*, 2, pp. 13–20

WARDWELL, ANNE, 1987. 'Flight of the Phoenix: crosscurrents in late Thirteenth to Fourteenth century Silk Patterns and Motifs', *Bulletin of Cleveland Museum of Art*, 74(i) (Jan.), pp. 1–35

WARDWELL, ANNE, 1989a. 'Panni Tartarici: Eastern Islamic Silks woven with Gold and Silver (13th and 14th centuries)', *Islamic Art*, 3, pp. 95–173

WARDWELL, ANNE, 1989b. 'Recently Discovered Textiles Woven in the Western Part of Central Asia before A.D. 1220', *Ancient and medieval textiles: Studies in Honour of Donald King*, ed. L. Monnas and H. Granger-Taylor, Pasold, Leeds, pp. 175–84

Chapter 5

ANDERSON, SONIA, 1989. *An English Consul in Turkey: Paul Rycaut at Smyrna, 1667–78*, Clarendon Press, Oxford

ATIL, E. (ed.), 1987. *The Age of Sultan Suleyman the Magnificent*, exh. cat., National Gallery of Art, Washington, DC

BAKER, PATRICIA, WEARDEN, JENNIFER, and FRENCH, ANN, 1990. 'Memento Mori: Ottoman Children's Kaftans in the Victoria and Albert Museum', *Hali*, 51 (June), pp. 130–40, 151–2

BAUDIER, MICHEL, 1652. *Histoire générale du Serrail . . .*, La Rivière, Lyon

BELDICEANU, NICOARA, 1960. *Les actes des premiers sultans conservées dans les manuscrits turcs de la Bibliothèque Nationale à Paris*, vol. 1, Mouton, Paris

BUSBE(C)Q[UIUS], OGIER GHISELIN DE, 1694. *The Four epistles of . . .*, London

CAMMANN, SCHUYLER, 1977. 'Ming Mandarin Squares', 4(iv), pp. 5–14

CELAL, MELEK, 1939. *Turk Islemeleri*, Istanbul

ÇIZAKÇA, M., 1980. 'A short history of the Bursa Silk Industry (1500–1900)', *JESHO*, 23, pp. 142–52

COOK, M.A. (ed.), 1976. *A History of the Ottoman Empire to 1730*, Cambridge University Press

COVEL, JOHN, 1893. 'Extracts from the Diaries of . . .', *Early Voyages and Travels in the Levant*, Hakluyt series I, no. 87, London

DENNY, WALTER, 1971. Review of publications by Öz and Geijer, *TMJ* 3(ii), pp. 38–42

DENNY, WALTER, 1972. 'Ottoman Turkish Textiles . . .', *TMJ* 3(iii), pp. 55–66

DENNY, WALTER, 1974. 'A Group of Silk Islamic Banners', *TMJ* 4(i), pp. 67–81

DENNY, WALTER, 1982. 'Textiles', *Tulips, Arabesques and Turbans: decorative arts from the Ottoman Empire*, ed. Y. Petsopoulos, Alexandria Press, London, pp. 121–44

EBIED, R.Y., and YOUNG, M.J.L., 1980. 'An 18th century Ottoman Commercial Phrase Book', *Oriental Studies presented to B.S. Isserlin*, ed. Ebied and Young, Brill, Leiden, pp. 139, 143

ERBER, CHRISTIAN (ed.), 1993. *A Wealth of Silk and Velvet*, Edition Temmen, Bremen

ETTINGHAUSEN, RICHARD, 1959. 'An early Ottoman Textile', *First International Conference on Turkish Art*, Türk Tarih Kurumu, Ankara, pp. 134–40

FAROQHI, SURAIYA, 1984. *Towns and Townsmen of Ottoman Anatolia*, Cambridge University Press

FORSTER, EDWARD S., 1968. *The Turkish Letters of Ogier Ghiselin de Busbecq*, Oxford University Press

FRENCH, D., 1972. 'A Sixteenth Century English Merchant in Ankara?', *Anatolian Studies*, 22, pp. 241–7

GALANTÉ, ABRAHAM, 1931. *Documents officiels turcs concernant les juifs de Turquie*, Haim, Rozio, Istanbul

GERBER, HAIM, 1988. *Economy and Society in an Ottoman City, Bursa 1600–1700*, Hebrew University, Jerusalem

GERVERS, VERONIKA, 1982. *The Influence of Ottoman Turkish Textiles and Costume in Eastern Europe . . .*, Royal Ontario Museum, Toronto

GOFFMAN, DANIEL, 1990. *Izmir and the Levantine world 1550–1650*, University of Washington Press, Seattle

GOODWIN, GODFREY, 1971. *A History of Ottoman Architecture*, Thames and Hudson, London

HILL, AARON, 1710. *A Full and Just Account of the Present State of the Ottoman Empire . . .*, London

MACKIE, LOUISE, 1980. 'Rugs and Textiles', *Turkish Art*, ed. Esin Atil, Washington, DC, pp. 299–374

MANSEL, PHILIP, 1988. 'Travelling Palaces', *Hali*, 37, pp. 30–5

MANTRAN, ROBERT, 1962. *Istanbul dans le second moitié du XVII siècle . . .*, Maisonneuve, Paris

MANTRAN, ROBERT, 1965. *La Vie quotidienne à Constantinople . . . XVIe et XVII siècles*, Hachette, Monaco

MENINSKI, FRANCISCUS À MESGNIEN, 1680–7. *Thesaurus Linguarum Orientalium Turcicae, Arabicae, Persicae . . .*, Vienna

NOUR, RIZA, 1933. 'L'histoire du Croisant', *Revue de Turcologie*, iii, pp. 233–410

ÖZ, TAHSIN, 1950. *Turkish Textiles and Velvets*, Turkish Press, Broadcasting and Tourist Department, Ankara

PANZAC, DANIEL, 1985. *La Peste dans l'Empire Ottoman*, Editions Peeters, Louvain

PFISTER, R., 1938. *Les Toiles imprimées de Fostat et l'Hindoustan*, Editions d'Art et d'Histoire, Paris

RABY, JULIAN, 1986. 'Court and Export: part I, Market demands in Ottoman Carpets 1450–1550', *OCTS*, 2, pp. 29–38

REATH, ANDREWS NANCY, 1927. 'Velvets of the Renaissance from Europe and Asia Minor', *Burlington Magazine*, 50, pp. 298–304

ROGERS, J.M., 1986a. 'Carpets in the Mediterranean Countries, 1450–1550', *OCTS*, 2, pp. 13–28

ROGERS, J.M., 1986b. 'Ottoman Luxury Trades and Their Regulation', *Osmanistische Studien . . . in memoriam Vanco Boskov*, ed. H.G. Majer, Otto Harrassowitz, Wiesbaden, pp. 135–55

ROGERS, J.M., and WARD, R.M., 1988. *Süleyman the Magnificent*, British Museum Publications, London

SANDERSON, JOHN, ed. William Foster, 1931. *The travels of . . . 1584–1602*, Hakluyt second series, no. 67, London

SERJEANT, R.J., 1972. *Islamic textiles . . .*, Librairie du Liban, Beirut

SCHIMMEL, ANNE-MARIE, 1976. 'The Celestial Garden in Islam', *The Islamic Garden*, ed. R. Ettinghausen, Dumbarton Oaks, Washington, DC

TEZCAN, HÜLYE, and DELIBAŞ, S., 1986. *Topkapi: Costume, embroideries and other textiles*, ed. J.M. Rogers, Thames and Hudson, London

THOMPSON, CHARLES, 1744. *The Travels of . . .*, J. Newbery, Reading

TIETZE, ANDREAS, 1982. 'Mustafa ᶜAli on Luxury and the Status Symbols of Ottoman Gentlemen', *Studia Turcologica memoriae Alexii Bombasi dicati*, eds. A. Gallotta and U. Marazzi, Instituto Orientale di Napoli, Naples, pp. 577–91

WEARDEN, J., 1986. 'Saz', *Hali*, 30 (Apr.–June), pp. 22–9

WEARDEN, J., n.d. [1986]. *Turkish Velvet Cushion Covers*, Victoria and Albert Museum, London

WHITE, CHARLES, 1845. *Three Years in Constantinople: or the Domestic manners of the Turks in 1844*, vols 1–3, Colburn, London

WITTEK, PAUL, 1936. 'Deux chapitres de l'histoire des turcs de Roum – part II', *Byzantion*, 11, pp. 285–319

Chapter 6

ANON. [H. Chick], 1939. *A Chronicle of the Carmelites in Persia*, vol. 1, Eyre and Spottiswoode, London

ACKERMAN, PHYLLIS, 1964 repr. 'The Textile Arts', *A Survey of Persian Art*, ed. A.U. Pope, vol. 5, Oxford University Press

AGA-OGLU, MEHMET, 1941. *Safawid Rugs and Textiles*, Columbia University Press, New York

ANDERSON, SONIA, 1989. *An English Consul in Turkey: Paul Rycaut at Smyrna, 1667–78*, Clarendon Press, Oxford

BEATTIE, MAY, 1976. *Carpets of Central Persia*, World of Islam Festival Trust, Westerham

CHARDIN, JOHN, 1711. *Voyages de M. John Chardin en Perse*, vols 1–3, De Lorme, Amsterdam

DELLA VALLE, PIETRO, 1663. *Les Fameux Voyages de . . .*, vols 1–4, Clovzier, Paris

DIBA, LAYLA S., 1987. 'Visual and Written Sources: dating eighteenth-century silks', *WSSH*, pp. 84–96

DU MANS, PÈRE RAPHAEL, 1890. *Estat de la Perse en 1660*, ed. C. Schefer, Ernest Leroux, Paris

E. Iran., 'Abrisam', 'ʿAbdullah', 'Carpets'

FERRIER, R.W., 1976. 'An English view of Persian Trade in 1618 . . .', *JESHO*, 19, pp. 182–214

FERRIER, R.W., 1986. 'Trade from the mid-14th century to the end of the Safavid period', *Cambridge History of Iran*, ed. P. Jackson and L. Lockhart, vol. 6, Cambridge University Press, pp. 412–90

FORAN, JOHN, 1993. *Fragile Resistance: Social Transformation in Iran from 1500 to the Revolution*, Westview Press, Boulder, Colorado

FLOOR, WILLEM, 1987. 'Economy and Society: Fibers, Fabrics, Factories', *WSSH*, pp. 20–32

FOSTER, WILLIAM, 1901. *Letters received by the East India Company . . .*, vol. 5, Sampson and Low, London

GEIJER, AGNES, 1951. *Oriental Textiles in Sweden*, Rosenkilde and Bagger, Copenhagen

HAKLUYT, RICHARD, 1903. *The Principal Navigations, Voyages of . . .*, vol. 3, Hakluyt extra series, Glasgow

HERBERT, THOMAS, ed. William Foster, 1928. *Travels in Persia 1627–9*, George Routledge, London

INALCIK, HALIL, 1973. *The Ottoman Empire, the Classical Age 1300–1600*, trans. N. Itzkowitz and C. Imber, Weidenfeld and Nicolson, London

KAEMPFER, ENGELBERT, 1977. *Am Hofe des persischen Grosskönigs 1684–85*, Horst Erdmann, Tübingen

KEYVANI, MEHDI, 1982. *Artisans and Guild Life in the later Safavid period . . .*, Klaus Schwarz, Berlin

KIANI, M.Y. (ed.), 1981. *(Discoveries from) Robat-e Sharaf*, National Organisation for the Preservation of Iranian Monuments, Tehran

KING, DONALD, and SYLVESTER, DAVID, 1983. *The Eastern Carpet in the Western World . . .* Hayward Gallery, Arts Council, London

KRUSINSKI, JUDAS THADDEUS, 1728. *The History of the Revolution of Persia . . .*, vol. 1, London

MINORSKY, VLADMIR, 1943. *Tadhkirat al-Mulk: a manual of Safavid administration*, E.J.W. Gibb Memorial, N.S. 16, Luzac, London

MORTON, A.H., 1993. *Mission to the Lord Sophy of Persia (1539–42): Michèle Membre*, School of Oriental and African Studies, London

OLEARIUS, ADAM, 1669. *The Voyages and travells of the Ambassadors sent by Frederick Duke of Holstein*, London

REATH, N., and SACHS, E.B., 1937. *Persian Textiles and their Techniques*, Philadelphia Museum of Art

ROSS, E. DENISON, 1933. *Sir Anthony Sherley and his Persian Adventure*, George Routledge, London

SAVORY, ROGER, 1980. *Iran under the Safavids*, Cambridge University Press

SONDAY, MILTON, 1987. 'Pattern and Weaves: Safavid Lampas and Velvets', *WSSH*, pp. 57–83

STEENSGAARD, N., 1975. *The Asian Trade Revolution of the Seventeenth century*, University of Chicago

STEINGASS, F., 1892. *A comprehensive Persian-English Dictionary*, W.H. Allen, London

TASZYCKA, MARIA, 1990. *Pasy Wschodnie*, 1 (with English trans.), Museum Naradowe, Krakow

VAN VLOTEN, M.G., 1892. 'Les drapeaux en usage à la fête de Huçein à Teheran', *Internationales Archiv für Ethnographie*, 5, pp. 105–11, plus illus

WILLS, CHARLES J., 1883. *In the Land of the Lion and Sun*, Macmillan and Co., London

WOODS, JOHN E., 1976. *The Aq Quyunlu Clan Confederation Empire*, Bibliotheca Islamica, Minneapolis

Chapter 7

AMANAT, ABBAS (ed.), 1983. *Cities and Trade: Consul Abbott . . . Iran 1847–66*, Ithaca Press, London

BENJAMIN, S.G.W., 1887. *Persia and the Persians*, John Murray, London

BRYDGES, H.J., 1834. *An Account of the . . . Mission, . . . 1807–11*, vol. 1, James Bohn, London

COLLIVER RICE, C., 1923. *Persian Women and their Ways*, Seeley, London

CURZON, G.N., 1892. *Persia and the Persian Question*, vol. 2, Longman, London

DELLA VALLE, PIETRO, 1663. *Les Fameux Voyages de . . .*, vols 1–4, Clovzier, Paris

DIBA, LAYLA S., 1987. 'Visual and Written Sources: dating eighteenth-century silks', *WSSH*, pp. 84–96

DU MANS, PÈRE RAPHAEL, 1890. *Estat de la Perse en 1660*, ed. C. Schefer, Ernest Leroux, Paris

EDWARDS, A.C., 1953. *The Persian Carpet*, Duckworth, London

FALK, S.J. 1972. *Qajar Paintings: Persian Oil Painting of the 18th and 19th centuries*, Faber and Faber, London

FORAN, JOHN, 1989. 'The Concept of Dependent Development . . . Qajar Iran (1800–1925)', *IS*, 22(ii–iii), pp. 5–56

FLINN, LEONARD, 1987. 'Ziegler's Man', *Hali*, 36, pp. 18–21

FLOOR, W.M., 1975. 'The Guilds in Iran', *ZDMG*, 125, pp. 99–116

FRASER, J.B., 1826. *Travels and Adventures in the Persian provinces . . .*, Longman, London

GILBAR, G., 1978. 'Persian agriculture in the late Qajar Period . . .', *Asian and African Studies*, 12(iii), pp. 312–65

GOLDSMID, F.J., 1876. *Eastern Persia, an Account of the Journeys 1870, 1871 and 1872*, vol. 1, Macmillan, London

GRIFFITH, M. HUME, 1909. *Behind the Veil in Persia and Turkish Arabia*, Seeley, London

IRWIN, JOHN, 1973. *The Kashmir Shawl*, HMSO, London

ISSAWI, C. (ed.), 1971. *The Economic History of Iran, 1800–1914*, University of Chicago Press

ITTIG, ANNETTE, 1985. 'The Kirman Boom – A study in Carpet Entrepreneurship', *OCTS*, 1, pp. 111–23

ITTIG, ANNETTE, 1992. 'The Carpets and Textiles of Iran . . .', *IS*, 25 (i–ii), special issue

KEYVANI, MEHDI, 1982. *Artisans and Guild Life in the late Safavid Period . . .*, Klaus Schwarz, Berlin

OTTER, JEAN, 1748. *Voyage en Turquie et en Perse*, vol. 1, Paris

PARLIAMENTARY ACCOUNTS AND PAPERS, GB 1904, Cd. 2146 McLean

PHILIPP, T., 1984. 'Isfahan 1881–1891: a close up view of Guilds and Protection', *IS*, 17, pp. 391–411

PIEMONTESE, ANGELO M., 1972. 'The photographic album of the Italian diplomatic mission to Persia (Summer 1862)', *East and West*, 22, pp. 249–311

SARRAF, MORTEZA, and CORBIN, HENRY, 1973. *Traites des Compagnons-Chevaliers: Rasa'il-e Javanmardan*, Paris

SCARCE, JENNIFER, 1988/9. 'The Persian Shawl Industry', *TMJ*, 27/28, pp. 23–39

SEYF, A., 1983. 'Silk Production and Trade in Iran in the 19th century', *IS*, 16, pp. 51–71

SEYF, A., 1992. 'The Carpet Trade and the Economy of Iran, 1870–1906', *Iran*, 30, pp. 99–106

TAVERNIER, JEAN BAPTISTE, 1682. *Les Six Voyages de . . .*, vol. 1, Paris

WARING, EDWARD SCOTT, 1804. *A Tour to Sheeraz . . .*, Bombay

WEARDEN, JENNIFER, 1991a. 'A Synthesis of Contrasts' (Azerbaijan embroideries), *Hali*, 59 (Oct.), pp. 102–11

WEARDEN, JENNIFER, 1991b. 'Rasht Textiles', *Hali*, 59 (Oct.), pp. 121–2

WILBER, DONALD, 1979. 'The Triumph of Bad Taste: Persian Pictorial Rugs', *Hali*, 2, pp. 192–7

Chapter 8

BAER, GABRIEL, 1970. 'Monopolies and Restrictive Practices of Turkish Guilds', *JESHO*, 13, pp. 145–65

BAKER, PATRICIA L., 1986. 'The Fez in Turkey: a symbol of modernization?', *Costume*, 20, pp. 72–86

BEATTIE, M., 1981. 'Hereke', *Hali*, 4(ii), pp. 128–34

CLARK, E.C., 1974. 'The Ottoman Industrial Revolution', *IJMES*, 5, pp. 65–76

DE KAY, J.E., 1833. *Sketches of Turkey in 1831 and 1832*, New York

DODD, ANNA B., 1904. *In the Palace of the Sultans*, Heinemann, London

DUTEMPLE, EDMOND, 1883. *En Turquie d'Asie*, Tours, Paris

EVANS, GUY, 1988. 'From West to East', *Hali*, 38, pp. 28–31

FESCH, PAUL, 1907. *Constantinople aux derniers jours d'Abdul Hamid*, Rivière, Paris

FUKASAWA, KATSUMI, 1987. *Toilerie et Commerce du Levant: d'Alep à Marseilles*, Editions du Centre National de la Recherche Scientifique, Paris

GÖCEK, FATMA M., 1990. 'Encountering the West: French embassy of Yirmisekiz Çelebi Mehmet Efendi', *III Congress on the Social and Economic History of Turkey* (Princeton), ed. H. Lowry and R. Hattox, Isis Press, Istanbul, pp. 79–84

HAMLIN, CYRUS, 1877. *Among the Turks*, Carter and Bros, New York

HOBHOUSE, J.C., 1813. *A Journey through Albania . . . 1809 and 1810*, Cawthorn, London

INALCIK, HALIL, 1987. 'When and how British cotton goods invaded the Levant markets', *The Ottoman Empire and the World Economy*, ed. H. Islamoğlu-Inan, Cambridge University Press, pp. 374–83

ISSAWI, C., 1966. *The Economic History of the Middle East, 1800–1914*, University of Chicago Press, Chicago and London

ISSAWI, C., 1980. *The Economic History of Turkey, 1800–1914*, University of Chicago Press, Chicago and London

JOHNSTONE, PAULINE, 1985. *Turkish Embroidery*, Victoria and Albert Museum, London

JUHASZ, ESTHER (ed.), 1989–90. *Sephardi Jews in the Ottoman Empire: Aspects and Material Culture*, exh. cat., Israel Museum, Jerusalem

KÜÇÜKERMAN, ONDER, 1987. *Hereke Fabrikasi*, Sümerbank, Ankara

LEWIS, BERNARD, 1966. *The Emergence of Modern Turkey*, Oxford University Press, London

MACFARLANE, C., 1850. *Turkey and its Destiny . . .*, vol. 2, London

MANTRAN, ROBERT, 1962. *Istanbul dans le second moitié du XVII siècle . . .*, Maisonneuve, Paris

ONUK, TACISER, n.d. [post 1977]. *Needleworks; Iğne Oyalari*, Turkiye Iş Bankasi, Istanbul

ÖZ, TAHSIN, 1951. *Türk Kumas ve Kadifeleri*, vol. 2, Istanbul

PAMUK, S., 1987. *The Ottoman Empire and European Capitalism, 1820–1913 . . .*, Cambridge University Press

PANZAC, DANIEL, 1985. *La Peste dans l'Empire Ottoman, 1700–1850*, Editions Peeters, Leuven

PARDOE, JULIA S.H., 1837. *The city of the Sultan and domestic manners of the Turks in 1836*, vols 1 and 2, London

QUATAERT, DONALD, 1983. 'The Silk Industry of Bursa 1880–1914', *Contributions à l'Histoire économique et sociale de l'Epoque Ottoman*, Collection Turcica, III, ed. J.L. Bacque-Grammont and Paul Dumont, Editions Peeters, Leuven, pp. 481–503

QUATAERT, DONALD, 1986. 'Ottoman Handicrafts and Industry 1800–1914: a reappraisal', *Osmanistische Studien . . . in memoriam Vanco Boskov*, ed. H.G. Majer, Otto Harrassowitz, Wiesbaden, pp. 128–34

QUATAERT, DONALD, 1990. 'The Carpet makers of Uşak, Anatolia (1860–1914)', *Congress on the Social and Economic History of Turkey* (Princeton), ed. H. Lowry and R. Hattox, Isis Press, Istanbul, pp. 85–91

REED, HOWARD A., 1951. *The Destruction of the Janissaries . . .*, Ph.D. thesis, Princeton University

SESTINI (Abbé), DOMINIQUE, 1789. *Voyage dans la Grèce asiatique*, Pingeron, London

SLOMANN, VILHELM, 1953. *Bizarre Designs in Silks*, Munksgaard, Copenhagen

T.C. KÜLTÜR BAKANLIĞI ANITLAR VE MÜZELER GENEL MÜDÜRLÜĞÜ, 1993. *Çağlarboyu Anadolu'da Kadin: Anadolu Kadininin 9000 Yili*, exh. cat., Istanbul

TEZCAN, HÜLYE, 1993. *Atlaslar Atlasi: Pamuklu, Yün ve Ipek Kumaş Koleksiyonu* (with English text), Yapi Kredi Collections–3, Istanbul

UBICINI, M.A., 1973 repr. *Letters on Turkey*, vol. 1, Arno Press, New York

WEARDEN, JENNIFER, n.d. [1986]. *Turkish Velvet Cushion Covers*, Victoria and Albert Museum, London

WHITE, CHARLES, 1845. *Three Years in Constantinople*, vols 1–3, Colburn, London

Chapter 9

BAKER, PATRICIA L., 1993. 'Carpets of the Middle and Far East', *5000 Years of Textiles*, ed. Jennifer Harris, British Museum Press, London, pp. 118–32

BAKER, PATRICIA, forthcoming. 'Iranian Dress Reform Laws in the 1920s and 1930s', *The Language of Dress in the Middle East*, ed. B. Ingham

BOROUJERDI, MEHRZAD, 1992. 'Gharbzadgi: the dominant intellectual discourse of Pre- and Post-Revolutionary Iran', *Iran: Political culture in the Islamic Republic*, ed. S. Farsoun and M. Mashayekhi, Routledge, London, pp. 30–56

BROWN, LUANNE, and RACHID, SIDNA, 1985. *Egyptian Carpets*, American University in Cairo Press

BURKETT, M.E., 1979. *The Art of the Felt Maker*, Abbot Hall Art Gallery, Kendal, Cumbria

CADOUX, ALDYTH M., 1990. 'The Burrell Collection – Asian Domestic Embroideries', *Arts of Asia* (May–June), pp. 138–45

COSTELLO, V.F., 1979 repr. *Kashan: a city and region of Iran*, Centre for Middle Eastern and Islamic Studies Press, University of Durham

CRAFTS COUNCIL, 1988. *Ikats – woven silk from Central Asia: the Rau collection*, Blackwell, London

EDWARDS, A.C., 1953. *The Persian Carpet*, Duckworth, London

E. Iran., 'Asnaf', 'Carpets', 'Cotton', 'Crafts'

ENGLISH, P.W., 1966. *City and Village in Iran . . .*, University of Wisconsin Press, Madison

FORAN, JOHN, 1993. *Fragile Resistance: Social Transformation in Iran from 1500 to the Revolution*, Westview Press, Boulder, Colorado

FORMAN, W. and B., and WASSEF, RAMSES WISSA, 1968 repr. *Tapestries from Egypt woven by the children of Harrania*, Paul Hamlyn, London

GERVERS, MICHAEL and VERONIKA, 1974. 'Felt-making Craftsmen of the Anatolian and Iranian Plateaux', *TMJ*, 4(i), pp. 14–29

GLUCK, J. and S.H., 1977. *A Survey of Persian Handicraft . . .*, Bank Melli, Tehran

IRAN HANDICRAFTS ORGANISATION, 1992. *Hands and Creativity*, vol. 1 (spring)

JONES, OWEN, 1854. *The Alhambra Court in the Crystal Palace*, London

KAÇITÇI, MEHMED ALI, 1978. *Yazma*, Grafik Sanatlar Matbaacilik, Istanbul

KALTER, JOHANNES, 1992. *The Arts and Crafts of Syria*, Thames and Hudson, London

LANDREAU, ANTHONY N., and YOHE, RALPH S., et al., 1983. *Flowers of the Yahla: Yörük Weaving of the Toros Mountains*, Textile Museum, Washington, DC

LINKE, L., 1938. *Allah dethroned*, Constable, London

LYNCH, PATRICIA D., and FAHMY, HODA, 1984. *Craftswomen in Kerdassa, Egypt*, International Labour Office, Geneva

MOSER, R.J., 1974. *Die Ikattechnik in Aleppo*, Pharos Verlag, Basel

ONUK, TACISER, 1981. *Needleworks: Iğne Oyalari*, Turkiye Iş Bankasi, Istanbul

PETERSON, JANE, 1991. 'A Passion for Color' (DOBAG project), *Aramco World* (May–June), pp. 2–9

RUGH, ANDREA B., 1986. *Reveal and Conceal: Dress in Contemporary Egypt*, American University in Cairo Press, Syracuse/Cairo

SIDORENKO, A.I., ARTYKOV, A.R., and RADJABOV, R.R., 1981. *Gold Embroidery of Bukhara*, Tashkent

SPOONER, BRIAN, 1986. 'Weavers and Dealers: the authenticity of an oriental carpet', *The Social Life of Things . . .*, ed. Arjun Appadurai, Cambridge University Press, pp. 195–235

STILLMAN, YEDIDA KALFON, 1979. *Palestinian Costume and Jewellery*, University of New Mexico Press, Albuquerque

TEKELI, I., and ILKIN, S., 1988. 'War economy of a non-belligerent country – Cotton textiles', *Turcica*, 20, pp. 113–57

THOMPSON, JON, 1986. 'A Return to Tradition' (DOBAG project), *Hali*, 30 (Apr.–June), pp. 14–21

WASS, BETTY, 1982. 'The Tent-makers of Cairo', *Islamic Art from the Michigan Collections*, ed. C.G. and A.W. Fisher, Michigan State University, pp. 17–26, items 18a–i

WEIR, SHELAGH, 1976. *The Bedouin: Aspects of Material Culture of the Bedouin of Jordan*, World of Islam Festival Trust, London

WEIR, SHELAGH, 1989. *Palestinian Costume*, British Museum Publications, London

WHITWORTH ART GALLERY, 1976. *The Qashqa'i of Iran*, World of Islam Festival Trust, Manchester

WULFF, HANS E., 1966. *The Traditional Crafts of Persia*, The M.I.T. Press, Cambridge, Mass.

ILLUSTRATION ACKNOWLEDGEMENTS

Illustrations are reproduced on the page numbers listed by courtesy and with permission of the following institutions and individuals.

ABBREVIATIONS: BM (Trustees of the British Museum); BL (Trustees of the British Library Board); CMA (Cleveland Museum of Art); TKS (Topkapi Sarayi Müzesi, Istanbul); TM (Textile Museum, Washington, DC); V&A (Board of Trustees of the Victoria and Albert Museum, London)

1   Photo Sotheby's, London

2–3   Metropolitan Museum of Art, New York (52.20.22), purchase Joseph Pulitzer Bequest, 1952, © 1986/95 by the Metropolitan Museum of Art

6   © CMA, 1995 (82.16), Leonard C. Hanna Jr Fund

Introduction

10   Museum of Fine Arts, Boston (33.371), Ellen Page Hall Fund

12   The John Work Garrett Library, Johns Hopkins University, Baltimore

Chapter 1

15   After Dr Saleh Soubhy, *Le pèlerinage à la Mecque et à Medine*, 1895, facing p. 28, photo University of London

18–19   Photo © TRIP, Epsom

19   Photo © TRIP, Epsom

20   Photo Christie's, London

21   Photo author

22   © Photo Bibliothèque Nationale de France, Paris (MS 13030 suppl. persan 775, f. 152v)

23   TKS (MS H. 1344, f. 330b–331a), photo author

24–5   Photo author

27   V&A (D. 1656–1904)

30   Photo Dr Jenny Balfour-Paul

31   BM (OA MAS 876)

Chapter 2

34   © CMA, 1995 (50.526), John L. Severance Fund

35   TM (73.213), acquired by George Hewitt Myers, 1935

36   After Diane Lee Carroll, *Looms and Textiles of the Copts*, memoir no. 11, p. 40, © 1988 California Academy of Sciences

37   Whitworth Art Gallery, University of Manchester (T. 8358)

38 *top*   BM (EA T. 29)

38 *bottom*   © CMA, 1995 (51.91) gift of the Textile Arts Club

39 *top*   V&A (1314–1888 and T.13–1960), photo Daniel McGrath

39 *bottom*   BM (OA MAS 862a and b)

41   V&A (8230–1863)

42   V&A (8579–1863)

43 *left*   BM (OA MAS 858)

43 *right*   Musée National du Moyen Age, Thermes de Cluny, Paris (CL 12869), © photo RMN

45   © CMA, 1995 (39.506), purchase from the J. H. Wade Fund

46–7   Musée National du Louvre, Paris (AO 7502), © photo RMN

Chapter 3

48   © Photo Bibliothèque Nationale de France, Paris (MS arabe 5847, f. 19r)

51   © Photo Bibliothèque Nationale de France, Paris (MS arabe 5847, f. 58v)

54   Museo de Telas Medievales, Monasterio de Santa Maria la Real, Burgos, photo supplied and authorised by the Patrimonio Nacional, Madrid

55   © CMA, 1995 (59.48), purchase from the J. H. Wade Fund

56   BM (EA 1990.1–27.4410)

57 *top*   Church of St Anne, Apt, Vaucluse, photo Archives Photographiques, Paris, © DACS 1995

57 *bottom*   After G. Marçais and G. Wiet, 'Le ''Voile de Sainte Anne'' d'Apt', *Monuments et mémoires de la fondation Eugène Piot*, Academie des Inscriptions et Belles Lettres, vol. 34, 1934, pp. 179–94, fig. 9

58   BM (OA 1901.3–14.52)

59   Royal Ontario Museum, Toronto (970.364.2B)

61   Fermo Cathedral, photo © David Storm-Rice, courtesy Museum for Islamic Art, L. A. Mayer Memorial, Jerusalem

62   Real Academia de la Historia, Madrid (292)

63   Musée des Tissus, Banque d'Images Textiles, Lyons (29686)

Chapter 4

64–5   V&A (1269–1864)

66   Museum of Islamic Art, Cairo (3899), photo Dr Bernard O'Kane

67   BM (EA 1990.1–27.439)

69   Bouvier Collection (I 68), photo © Musée d'Art et d'Histoire, Geneva

70   TM (73.693), acquired by George Hewitt Myers, 1953

71 *top*   © CMA, 1995 (83.121), purchase from the J. H. Wade Fund

71 *bottom*   © CMA, 1995 (19.28), Dudley P. Allen Fund

72   Ashmolean Museum, Oxford (1990.441), Newberry Textile Collection

73   © CMA, 1995 (83.120), purchase from the J. H. Wade Fund

74–5   Art Institute of Chicago (1983.746), Grace R. Smith Textile Endowment

75   Ashmolean Museum, Oxford (1984.479)

77   Bouvier Collection (M 117), photo Musée d'Art et d'Histoire, Geneva

78   Museum of Islamic Art, Cairo (23903), photo author

79   TM (R16.1.3), acquired by George Hewitt Myers, 1951

81   Erzbischöfliches Dom-und Diözesanmuseum, Vienna

82–3   Germanisches Nationalmuseum, Nurnberg (Gew 488)

Chapter 5

84–5   V&A (T.99–1923)

88 *top*   Deutsches Textilmuseum, Krefeld (00976/Ku 54)

88 *bottom*   TKS (13/6-2/3228), photo author

90   TKS (13/37), photo author

91   Musée des Tissus, Banque d'Images Textiles, Lyons (29420)

94 *left*   Państwowe Zbiory Sztuki na Wawelu, Krakow (3981)

94 *right*   TM (1.84), gift of Mrs Hoffman Philip

95   TKS (13/9)

96   TKS (13/866)

97   V&A (86–1878)

98–9   TKS (MS H.1609, ff. 68B–69A)

101   Ashmolean Museum, Oxford (1990.467), Newberry Textile Collection

102   TKS (13/1150)

103 *top*   TM (R34.18.4), acquired by George Hewitt Myers

103 *bottom*   Państwowe Zbiory Sztuki na Wawelu, Krakow, photo General Sikorski Museum, London

Chapter 6

106–7   Danske Kunstindustrimuseet, Copenhagen (B21/1931), photo © Ole Woldbye

109   After van Vloten, 'Les drapeaux en usage à la fête de Hucein à Teheran', *Internationales Archiv für Ethnologie*, Bd V, 1892, pl. X, photo University of London

111   Fitzwilliam Museum, Cambridge (T.48–1912)

112   TKS (MS H.762), photo author

113   TKS (13/2088), photo author

114 *left*   TM (3.103A), acquired by George Hewitt Myers, 1927

114 *right*   Petworth House, photo National Trust Photographic Library/Roy Fox

115   Musée des Tissus, Banque d'Images Textiles, Lyons (30157)

117   Danske Kunstindustrimuseet,

Copenhagen (D 1227), photo © Ole Woldbye

118 *top*   BM (OA 1985.5–4.1)

118 *bottom*   David Collection, Copenhagen (13/1991), photo © Ole Woldbye

119   Musée des Tissus, Banque d'Images Textiles, Lyons (27960)

120   V&A (313–1907)

122–3   Museo Poldi-Pezzoli, Milan (d.t.1/154)

Chapter 7

124–5   © CMA, 1995 (16.1483), gift of J. H. Wade

126   Photo Sotheby's, London

127   David Collection, Copenhagen (38/1992), photo © Ole Woldbye

128   V&A (T.333–1920)

129   © CMA, 1995 (15.660), gift of the John Huntington Art and Polytechnic Trust

130–1   Musée des Tissus, Banque d'Images Textiles, Lyons (24392/79)

131   V&A (287–1884), photo author

133   V&A (884–1887)

134   V&A (513–1874)

135   TM (1980.8.5), gift of Dr Isabel T. Kelly

137   V&A (2318–1876)

138–9   *Hali* 79, October 1991, p. 118, photo

Jeremy Richards/Sotheby's, London

141   V&A (799–1876)

142 *left*   TM (3.2), acquired by George Hewitt Myers, *c.* 1940

142 *right*   Embroiderers' Guild Collection, Hampton Court (EG 3454; 3459; 3461), gift of Lady Evelyn Sykes, photo Julia Hedgecoe

143   V&A (Circ. 535–1910)

145   V&A (T. 214–1989)

146   Photo Sotheby's, London

Chapter 8

148   BL, Oriental and India Office Collections (Abdul Hamid photo album 7, f. 25)

150   V&A (T. 671–1919)

151   Sadberk Hanim Müzesi, Istanbul

152   After Jean Brindesi, *Elbicei Antika*, 1830, photo University of London

153   V&A (630–1890)

154 *top*   Israel Museum, Jerusalem (956.81; 776–7.81; 646.84; 171.79; 172.79A; 992.85; 1040.85; 987.85)

154 *bottom*   TKS (Hereke 13/37)

155   Israel Museum, Jerusalem (1051.85; 1053.85; 1058.85; 87.88; 814.82)

157   Museum of Fine Arts, Boston (15.488), gift of Denman Waldo Ross

158 *top left*   Sadberk Hanim Müzesi, Istanbul

158 *bottom left*   Marianne Ellis

158 *right*   Fitzwilliam Museum, Cambridge (T.1–1956)

159   V&A (Circ. 744–1912)

160 *top*   Archives départementales des Bouches-du-Rhône, Marseilles (C3374, 28 and 29)

160 *bottom*   Archives départementales des Bouches-du-Rhône, Marseilles (C3374, 29v)

Chapter 9

162   Glasgow Museums: Burrell Collection (30/4)

164   Museum of Fine Arts, Boston (47.1029), gift of Mrs George Sarton

166   Photo author

167   Photo Werner Forman Archive, London/Ramses Wissa Wassef Art Centre, Cairo

170 *top*   Photo author

170 *bottom*   BM (Eth. 1975.AS.7–1)

171   BM (Eth. 1969.AS.8–19)

173   Photo author

174   Photo author

175 *left*   Photo © Gayle M. Garrett, Washington, DC, 1995

175 *right*   Sadberk Hanim Müzesi, Istanbul

179   Photo author

180   Photo author

INDEX

Page numbers in italic refer to illustrations

ᶜAbbas I 108–9, 117, 136
ᶜAbbasid(s) 36–8, 40, 44, 49–50, 53, 56, 60, 65–6, 68–9; court 44, 50, 52; dynastic colour *48*, 50, 60, 66; textiles 41, 52, 56, 60–1
ᶜAbd al-Malik 53
ᶜAbd al-Rahman III 61
Abdul Aziz 151
ᶜAbdullah 117
Abu Saᶜid 80, *81*
Afghan(istan) 36, 107–8, 113, 117, 165, 178
Africa 9, 16, 31; *see also* North Africa, Tunisia
Afshar 108, 117, 120, 125–6; dynastic dress 117, *120*; textiles 117, *120*
Afyon 21, *21*, 176
Ahmed III 86
ᶜAisha 17
ᶜalam 52–3, 109
Aleppo 70, 78, 160, 168–9; galls 28
Alexandria 29, 36, 68, 78
ᶜAli (caliph) 35, 49–50, 52, 59, 61, 68, 92
Almohad(s) 36, 52, *54*, 62, 72
Almoravid(s) 36, 62
alum 28–9, 31, 73; *see also* monopoly
Amasya 160
America(n) *see* North America
Anatolia(n) *see* Turkey, Ottoman
Andalusia(n) *see* Iberia
Ankara 21, 104
appliqué(s) 21, 69, *70*, *103*, 103–4, *113*, 128, 137, *138–9*, 168, *170*
Aq Qoyunlu 107–8
Arabia 14, 16, 20, 36, 41, 49, 65, 86, 179; imports 20; *see also* Mecca, Najran, Yemen
architecture(al) 69, 104, 150, 156, *159*; Gujerati 76
Ardabil 107, 112, 121; carpet *121*
Armenia(n) 38, 108–9, 111, 153, 160–1
al-Ashraf Shaᶜban 70
Asyut 71
Atatürk 163, *173*
al-ᶜAttabi 40
Austria(n) 131, 153
Aynteb 160
Ayyubid(s) 49, 65–6, 69–70; dynastic colour 66; textiles 71, *71*
Azerbaijan 108, 140, *143*

Baalbek 70, 78
Baghdad 14, 36, 38, 40–1, 44, 49, 61, 147, 160
Bahnasa 53, *55*
Bakst, Leon 165, 180
Balkan(s) 85, 100, 104, 149, 151, *154–5*, 160–1, 163–4
baraka 15–16; *see also* talisman
Barquq 68
Barsbay 66, 68
batik *see* print
Baybars I 65; Baybars II 68
Bayezid 87–8
bed(s) 33, 53, 100, 104; marriage- 33, 53, 174, 180;

-linen *155*, 157, 180; *see also* circumcision, furnishings
bedouin(s) *see* nomad
Bilecik 86, 156
Black Sea 85, 163, 174
blazon 69, *70–1*, 73, 80, *88*, 89; *see also* emblem, symbol(ism)
bleach(ers)/bleached 20, 28–9, 57, 78, 87, 144, 161, 176
block-printing *see* print
Britain/British 23–4, 125, 131, 144–5, 153, 157, 160, 163; exports 104, 131, 136, 152–3, 160, 172; imports 23–4, 104, 161
brocade(s) 93, 111, 126, *130*, 156, 169
Bukhara 40, 81, 164–5
burial/reliquary fabrics *see* shrouds
Bursa 25, 85–7, 89, 93, 97, 104, 109, 149–50, 153, 160
Buyid 36, 44, 60, 81; controversy 11, 44–5, *45–7*
byssus 41, *41*
Byzantine(s) 20, 24, 35–7, 50, 52–3, 85; ceremonial 35, 52; clergy 37; exports 20, 53; iconoclasm 37; textiles 24, 39–40, 45, 53; *see also* Istanbul

Cairo 11, 14, 29, 49, 53, 56, 59–61, 65–6, 68, 70, 76, 78, 80, 104, 167, *167–8*, *170*, 179
calligraphy 10, 19, 35, 40, 44–5, 52–3, 56–7, *58*, 59–60, 73, 76, 80–1, *81*, 92, 101, *102*, 113, 117, 136, *137*, 157, 168; Cyrillic 165; Kufic *20*, *39*, *43*, 44–5, *56*, 57, 59, 59–60, 62, 77; Maghribi 52; Naskhi 52, *54*, 60, 69; *thuluth* 62, 92, *94*
camel-hair 20–1, 131
carbon-14 dating 38, 45, *45*, 81
carpet(s) 7, 9, 13, 26, 38, *38*, 107, 120–1, 144–5, 161, 164–5, 167, 172, 174, 176–9; DOBAG 176, *176*; Mamluk 79, 79–80, 104; Ottoman 97, *103*, 104–5, 116, 121, *148*, 156, 158, 161; Qajar 126, 140, 144–5, *145–6*, 147; Safavid 110, 116–17, 120–1, *122–3*; *see also* kilim, knot, loom, prayer-rug
Caspian Sea 28, 108–9, 126, 137, 140
Caucasus 39, 65, 100, 108, 114, 125, 147, 176
Central Asia(n) 11, 13, 16–17, 24, 26, 32, 36, 39–40, 62, 65, 72, 80–1, 89, 109, 132, 163–5; exports 164; imports 164; textiles *12*, 31, 39, 40, 42–3, 62, 80–1, 87, 105, 129, 142, *162*, 164–5, *166*, 167; *see also* Buyid
ceramics 7, 11, 41, 53, 69, 88–9, 92, 100, 157
China/Chinese 20, 23–5, *25*, 28, 35, 39–40, 50, 70, 72, 105, 156; dress 57, 113, 167; exports 20, 72, 80–1, 153; textiles 27, 31, 32, 40, 66, 72, 80–1, 167; *see also* design
Chingiz (Genghis) Khan 80
chintz *see* cotton, India, print
Christian(s) 13, 17, 36–8, 44, 68, 85, 97, 108, 169; church 39; *see also* Byzantine, Coptic, *dhimmi*
circumcision 175, 180; -bed 33, 174, *175*, 180
collector(s) 11, 56, 89, 164, 178
colour(s) *passim*, especially: dynastic 15, 50, 87, 112; symbolism: black 17, *48*, 50, 60, 66, 112–13,

180; blue 68; green 17, 68, 92–3, 113, 180; red 17, 50, 66, 89, 92, 112, 139; turquoise 17; white 16–17, 50, 66, 68, 112; yellow 17, 37, 50, 66, 66, 68, 112; *see also* dye, mordant, sumptuary regulation
Constantinople *see* Istanbul
Copt(s)/ic 38; clergy 37–8, 67, 68; design 37, 57, 59; dress 36–8, 68; textiles 36–8, 68; *see also* dhimmi
Cordoba 44, 61
cotton *passim*, especially: 13, 15, 17, 20, 23–4, 37, 40, 57, 164–5, 168–9, 172–3; ᶜAbbasid 60; British 131, 169; cultivation 23–4, 70, 76, 101, 136, 173; dyeing 23, 31–2, 76, 174; exports 23, 136, 144, 153, 160; Fatimid 76–7, *77*; India 24, 32, 70, 76–8, 131, 136, 151, 160; Iranian 24, 109, 113, 126, 131, *135*, 135–7, 140, *142–3*, *173*; Mamluk 68, 70, 76–8, *77*; Ottoman 24, 100–1, 152–3, *157*, 160; Yemeni 35, 60–1, 76; *see also* print
court ceremonial 15, 49–50, 52, 68, *98–9*; dress *1*, 15, 26, 39, 50, 53–9, 66, 68, 88–9, 92–3, 97, *98–9*, *102*, 112, 112–13, *114*, 117, 120, 126, *126*, 128, 131–2, 144, 149–51, 160; furnishings 6, *12*, 15, 50, 56, 62, 80, 86, 104, 108–9, *138–9*, 147, *148*, 149–51, 153, *154*, 161, 178; painting/illumination 23, *71*, 79, 80–1, 88–9, 90, 100, 104–5, *112*, 113, 116–17, *117*, 126, *126*, 132, 140, 165; patronage 17, 24, 78, 92, 104, 108–10, 120–1, 131, 136, 144, 153, 172; workshop(s) 17, 29, 78, 86, 89, 97, 104, 108–10, 113, 120, 153, *154*, 156; *see also* flag, *khalat*, parasol, *tiraz*, individual dynasties
craft, concept of 167–9, *169*, 172–3, 176–8, 180; handicraft organisation 167, 168–9, 172–6, *179*, 180
Crusades/Crusaders 36, 49, 65, 70
customs, excise 24, 66, 70, 78, 86, 126, 144, 152–3; *see also* seals, tax

Damascus 13, 68, 70, 78, 156, 168–9
damask (weave) 13, *66*, 92, 97, 110–11, 113, 126, 156
Damietta 57, 59
design *passim*, especially: arabesque 88, 103, 117, *118*, 121, 126, 136; *buta* 128, *129*, 132, 147; cartoon 89, 104, 121, 137, 145, 168; cartouche 57, 59, 69, 73, 79, 80; Chinese/chinoiserie 57, 66, 72, 80, 88; *çintemani* 88, 88–9; Coptic 37, 57, 59; floral *2*, 38, 72, 88–9, *90–1*, 92, 101, 103–4, 111, *115*, 117, *119*, 126, 128, *130*, 136–7, *141*, 149, 156, *158–9*, 165; geometric 62, *63*, 70, 72, 72, 76, 88, 137, *143*, 168, *170*; human figures 37, 57, *61–2*, 62, 92, 106, 113–14, 116–17, *117–18*, *120*, 121, *123*, *130*, 147, *see also* Islamic law; lattice *2*, 68, 88, 92, 117, *124*, 126, 129, *130*; medallion 36, *71*, 73, 76, 80, 97, 101, 113, *123*, 153; Pharaonic 79, 80, 168; roundel 10, 39, 39–40, 44, 57, 61, 61, 167; stripes 36, 40, 62, 70–1, *71*, 80, 87, 111, 116, 126, 132, *133*, 140, *141*, 150–1, *150–1*, *155*, 169; zoomorphic 10, 38–9, 39–40, *43*, 44–5, *45–7*, 52,

design – *cont.*
59, 61–2, 70, 72–3, 76, 92, *106*, 116, 121, *123*; *see also* blazon, calligraphy, Europe, Sasanian
design education 136, 167, 169, 176–7
dhimmi(s) 17, 37, 50, 66, 68, 93, 105, 108, 152; *see also* Christian, Jew, Zoroastrian
diasper weave *10*, 44
Diocletian edict 24
Diyarbakir 153, *160, 160*
double/triple cloth 70, *71*, 110, 116–17, *118*, 173
dress *1*, 13, 15–17, 23, 25–6, 32, 36–8, 45, *48*, 50, *51*, 56–7, *57*, 71, 96, *98–9*, 109, 111, *112, 114*, 126, 140, 142, *151*, 151–2, 165, *166*, 168–9, *171*, 174–5, 178–9, *179*; fundamentalist 168, 179–80; Muslim 16–17, *18*, 93, 179–80; *see also* court, *dhimmi*, Europe, *khalat*, shawl, sumptuary regulation, terminology, *tiraz*, turban, veil
dye(s) *passim*, especially: 13, 20, 29, 31–2, 50, 70, 87, 113, 144, 151, 153, 167–8, 176, 178; 'artificial' 29, 145, 147, 160–1, 165, 169, 176, 178; fading 73, 77, 78, 87, *106*, 114; henna 13, 29, 31; indigo 29, *30*, 31, 73, 76, *106*; madder 29, 31, 76, *112*; *qirmiz* 13, 31; saffron 13, 31; tannic 45; *see also* alum, colour, *hisba*, ikat, mordant, price, print
dyer(s) 20, 23, 29, *30*, 109, 136, 144, 161, 164, 172, 174, 176; workshop(s) 29, 108, 110

earnings *see* salaries
East India Companies 25, 107–8, 110, 113, 116
Egypt(ian) 9, 16–17, 20, 23–4, 26, 28–9, 35–7, 44, 49, *55*, 57, 60–1, 65–80, *77*, 149, 163, *167*, 167–8, *170*, 179; exports 28, 86; imports 24, 167; textiles 27, 31–2, 36–9, 41, 44; *see also* Ayyubid, Cairo, Coptic, Fatimid, Mamluk
embargoes *see* trade
emblem(s) 15, 109, *137, 139*, 151; *see also* blazon, flag, parasol, *tiraz*
embroiderer(s) 19, 32–3, 109, 140, 156
embroidery 9, *15*, 25, 32–3, *35*, 36, 41, 53, *113*, 164–5, 168–9, 173, 177–8, 180; back-stitch 60, *69*; blanket- 60; chain- 60, 66, 137, *162*; couching 25, 57, 61, 62, 76, 100, 157, *162*, 165; cross- 140, *143*, 168, *171*; darning 75, 76, 84, 100, 140, 156; *dival* 157, *158*, 165, 175; drawn thread 140; Fatimid 60–1; herring-bone 76; *kum iğnesi 84*, 100; machine stitching 33, 160, 168, 174, 180; Mamluk 66, 68, 73, 75, 76; Ottoman *84*, 100, 103–4, 140, 150, 156–7, *158, 159*, 160, 168; Palestinian 169, *171*; Qajar 132, 137, 140, *141, 142*, 143; running-stitch 76, 156, *158*, 168; Safavid *113*, 113; satin- 140, *142*; split-stem 39, 57, 76; tambour- 142, 156, *159*, 160, 165; tent- 140, *141*; Umayyad 39; whitework 140, *142*; *zerduz* 100, 157; *see also* sampler
Erzurum 174, *179*
Ethiopia 23
etiquette 17, 41, 180
Europe(an/s) 14, 17, 23–5, 29, 70, 86, 93, 97, 107, 109–11, 113, 116, 126, 136, 142, 144–5, 149, 153, 156, 160–1, 163, 169, 176–9; design 121, 125–6, 147, 150–2, *151, 154*, 156, 172, 178–80; Europeanisation 125, 144, *148*, 149, *151*, 151–3, *154*, 168, 172–3, 178–80; exports 79, 104, 125, 137–8, 142, 151–2, 169, 179; imports 21, 23, 109, 136, 137, 142, 152; technology 25, 28, 78, 131, 152, 167
evil eye 17; *see also* magic
exhibition(s) 121, 144, 153, 157, 161

factory (production) 28, 131, 144, *148*, 152–3, *154*, 156, 160–1, 164, 172, 174; *see also* carpet, machinery
fake(s) *see* fraud, *hisba*
Fath ʿAli Shah 131, 136
Fatima 35, 49
Fatimid(s) 49–50, 56–7, 62, 68–9, 76, 103; ceremonial 50, 52, 56; cotton 76–7, *77*; dynastic colour 50; textiles 56–7, *56–9*, 59–60, 76; *see also* flag, parasol
felt(makers) 15, *21*, 21, 28, 38, 101, 103, 126, 151, 164, 172, 176, 178
flag(s) 6, 15, 35, *48*, 50–3, *54*, 59, 66, 69, 89, 92, 94, 109, 109, 113, *137*, 139, 168, 180; Prophet's flag 52, 151
fraud *10*, 11, 17, 20, 44–5, 86; *see also hisba*
France/French 23–4, 109, 112, 135, 149–50, 153, 161, 163, 169; exports 24, 142, 144, 151–3, 163; imports 23–4, 142, 153, 160–1; silks 144, 151, 156, *157*; style *150*, 150–1, 156, *157*, 160–1; *see also* Lyons
furnishings 13, 15–16, 21, 23, 32, 50, 52–3, *55*, 62, 86, 93, 97, *97*, 100, 104, 140, *148, 149*, 151, *153*, 153, 156–7, 165, 167–8, 174, 178, 180; *see also* bed, nomad, quilt
Fustat 76–7

Gandhi, Mahatma 180
garden 89, 117, 120, 150; *see also* Paradise
gauze 153, 156–7
Georgia(n) 100, 108–10
German(y) 131, 147, 153, 160, 165
Ghiyas *106*, 117
glass 41, 69–70, 72, 112, 157
goat-hair 15, 20–1, 104, 169, 176; exports 21, 104; *see also* mohair, shawl
Greece/Greek *see* Balkan
guild(s/men) 20, 23, 29, 70, 86–7, 89, 101, 108–10, 109, 135–7, 144, 152, 172
Gulf 14, 23, 108

Haci Bektaş 101, 103, *180*
hadith 16–17, 21, 50
Hajj 15, *15–16*, 17; *see also* dress (Muslim)
al-Hakim 59–60
Hama 78, *164*, 164, 168
Hapsburg 80, 97
Harraniya *167*, 167–8
Harun al-Rashid 36
Haydar 112
Hereke *148*, 153, *154*, 156, 161
hisba 17, 20, 29, 44; *muhtasib/muhtesib* 17, 20, 22, 86
Hisham 50, 53; Hisham II (Spain) 61
Hotz 144
Hungary 85, 100
Husayn 113; Husayn Quli Khan 132–4

Iberia 23–5, 31, 35–6, 44, 52, 76; textiles 6, *10*, 39, 44–5, *54*, 57, 61–2, *61–3*, 72, 80, 87, 89
Ifriqiya *see* Tunisia
ikat 20, 29, 31–2, *35*, 36, 60–1, 76, *114*, 129, 164–5, *166*, 169, 174, *174*, 179
il-Khanid(s) 20, 29, 80, *81*
image(s), lawfulness of *see* Islamic law
Imam(ate) 49, 59, *112*, 112
India(n) 28, 32, 66, 92, 107, 117, 132, 156, 180; cotton 24, 32, 76–7, *77*, 136, 160; exports 24, 29, 32, 70, 76–7, 125, 131, 136, 151–2, 160, 169;

imports 31; *see also* architecture, Mogul
Iran(ian) 9, 13–14, 23–4, 26, 28–9, 35–6, 38–41, 44, 80, 85–6, 89, 92–3, 107–47, 161, 163–4, 169–73, 179–80; carpets 161, 164; exports 20, 23, 28, 86, 92, 104, 109, 126, 132, 136, 142, 144, 147, 172–3; imports 131–2, 136–7, 147, 161, 172; textiles 25, 41, 76, 80–1, 86, 89, 107–47; *see also* Afshar, Islamic Republic, mythology, Pahlavi, Qajar, Safavid, Sasanian
Iraq 14, 24, 35–6, 38, 41, 65, 76, 85, 163
ironing 39, 117; ironers 136
Isfahan 107–10, 116, 120, 126, 131, 136–7, 140, 144, *173*, 173
Islam *passim*, especially: 15–17, 49–50, 65, 85, 89, 117, 126, 163; *see also* Paradise, Prophet Muhammad, Quran, Shiʿi, sunni
Islamic law 15–17, 20; on colour 16–17; on figural representation 16, 37, 62, 92, 116; Hanafi 16, 85, 92, 116; on pollution 20, 29–30, 32; on selling 17; on silk 16, 68; *see also dhimmi*, dress, *hisba*, Shiʿism, sumptuary regulation, sunni, *ʿulama*, workforce
Islamic Republic 172–3, 180
Ismaʿil 107–8, *112*, 112–13
Ismaʿili(ya) 49; *see also* Fatimid
Israel 107, 112–13, 164, 168; *see also* Jordan, Levant, Palestine, Syria
Istanbul 17, 21, 23, 37, 52, 85, 93, 104, 111, 131, *148*, 151–3, 156, 160, 176
Italy 15, 23, 25, 28, 76, 79–80, 92, 108, 110, 153; exports 79, 92, 153; imports 15, 23, 25; painting 73, 75, 76, *103*, 105, 180
Ithna ʿAshari 49, 107, 112, 116, 135
Izmir 28, 86, 89, 153, 161

Jabbal ʿAdda 71, *77, 78*
Jacquard device *see* loom
Janissary(ies) 85, 92, 94, 97, 101–3, 149, 151
Jews/Jewish/Judaism 13, 17, 31, 36, 68, 85, 97, 108, 112, 164; *see also dhimmi*
Jordan 163; *see also* Israel, Levant, Palestine, Syria

Kaʿba 15–16, *18–19*, 36, 66, 92, 105
Karamanladika *150*, 151
Kashan 108–10, 116, 120–1, 126, *130*, 131, 136, 144, 173; ceramics 11
Kashmir shawls 21, 126–8, 131–2, 135, 152
Khadija 20
khalat/hilat/khilʿa (honorific garments) 13, 15, 50, 53, 57, 57, 68, 93, 96, 97, 113, *114*, 132; *see also tiraz*
Khirbat al-Mafjar 38
Khomeini, Ayatollah 180
Khurasan 108, 110, 125
Khusrau (Shah) 38–9; Spring of 38; *see also* mythology
khutba 49, 52–3
kilim 26, 121, 167, 167–8, 176
Kirman 120, 135, 137, 144, 147, 172–3; *rang-i* 29; shawls 21, 126, 131–2, *133–4*, 135
kiswa 15–16, *18, 19*, 32, 36, 66, 92
Kitbugha 72
knitting 77, *77*, 152, 164
knot 38, 80, 121, 161, 172, 176; *see also* carpet, pile

lace 152; needle- 150, *155*, 156–7, *158*, 174
lampas (weave) *2*, 6, *10*, 44, 61–2, *63–4*, 73, *73–4*, 81, *81–3*, 90–1, 92–3, 94, *106*, 116–17, 119, 127, 129

Lawrence, T.E. 163
Lebanon 163; *see also* Levant
Levant 23, 26, 49, 56, 65, 160; *see also* Israel,
Jordan, Lebanon, Palestine, Syria
linen(s) 9, 13, 17, 20, 38, 41, 53, 56–7, 56–7, 59,
60–1, 62, 68, 70, 168; Coptic 36–8; cultivation
24; dyeing 31; imports 20, 24; Mamluk 68, 69,
72, 73, 75, 76–8; Ottoman 84, 100, 101–2, 155,
158
loom(s) 20, 26, 28, 32, 68, 70–1, 78, 86–7, 93, 109,
116, 131–2, 135, 152–3, 156, 160–1, 168–9;
backstrap 26; band 26; drawloom 27, 28, 32, 37,
70, 89, 156, 173; horizontal 26, 28; Jacquard
device 28, 153, 156; pit 28, 37, 173; tax on 20;
treadle 28, 31, 174; tubular 26; vertical 26, 37,
161, 176; warp-weighted 26, 37; *see also* Hereke
Luxor 37
Lyons 28, 45, 150–1, 153, 160

machinery 21, 25, 78, 131, 136, 152–3, 160, 172,
176; sewing machine 160, 168; *see also*
embroidery, factory
magic 15–16; -worm 24; *see also* baraka, evil eye,
talisman
Mahmud II 149, 151–2
Mamluk(s) 17, 32, 57, 65–80, 88, 103; blazon 69,
70–1, 73, 80; court dress 66, 68; textiles 65–80,
66–7, 70–5, 78–9, 87, 89, 104
al-Mamun 38
mandil see napkin
Manisa 20, 176
al-Mansur 50, 53
Marco Polo 108
market inspector *see* hisba, sumptuary regulations
Marwan 57; silk 39, 39–40, 57
Mashhad 126, 132, 135
Mazandaran 131; *see also* Caspian Sea
Mecca(n) 15–16, 18, 19, 32, 52, 66, 113
Mehmed II 85–6, 89, 92, 103
Mesopotamia *see* Iraq
metallic lustre 41
metal(lic) thread 10, 17, 19, 23, 24–6, 32–3, 34, 38,
41, 44, 50, 52–7, 54, 61–2, 61–2, 64, 66, 67, 70,
72, 81, 82–3, 87, 88, 90–1, 92–3, 95, 98–9, 100,
103–4, 109–111, 112, 113, 115, 116–17, 118, 121,
126, 150, 156–7, 157, 159, 160, 164–5, 169, 174,
175; quality 26, 113; supervision 26, 32, 56;
symbolism 50, 52
metalwork 7, 11, 39–41, 69–72, 81, 88, 100, 137,
140
military (textiles) 16–17, 52, 56, 66, 68, 92, 101,
103, 131, 137, 151, 151, 153, 172; *see also* flag,
tent
Mirza Taq-i Khan 131–2, 136, 142
Mogul 92, 107, 116–17, 128
mohair 13, 21, 104, 131; *see also* goat-hair
moiré 21, 40, 104, 110, 113
Mongol(ian) 25, 36, 57, 65–6, 70, 72–3
monopoly/ies 14, 24–5, 28–9, 86, 107–9, 136, 180
mordant(s) 13, 28–9, 31–2, 100, 136; *see also* alum,
print
Morris, William 121, 168, 177, 180
Mosul 13; muslin 9, 13, 157; *see also* cotton
Mu'awiya 35–6
Muhammad *see* Prophet Muhammad
Muhammad 'Ali 149; Muhammad Khudabanda
113; Muhammad Shah 139
al-Mu'izz 49, 60

mulberry leaves/tree(s) 25, 86, 153
Murad III 100, 104; Murad IV 93
al-Musta'li 57, 57
al-Mutawakkil 37, 40
al-Muti' 60
mythology: classical 37, 45; Arab and Iranian 24,
26–7, 89, 106, 116, 118, 147; mythical beast(s)
10, 42, 72

Nadir (Khan) Shah 108, 117, 120, 144
napkin 37, 41, 68–9, 70, 100, 157, 160
Nasrid(s) 6, 36, 52, 62, 63, 72, 80
natron 29
New Order 149, 151; *see also* Europe
Nile 38, 57, 65–6, 70
nomadic society 15, 26, 36, 87, 107, 109, 167–9,
172, 176–9; textiles 11, 121, 163–4, 167–9, 170–1,
172, 176–7; *see also* tents, Turkoman
non-Muslim(s) *see* dhimmi
North Africa 24, 35–6, 41, 49–50, 53, 62, 65, 68,
76, 89, 149, 163–4; *see also* Tunisia
North America 136, 144, 153, 160–1, 163, 165, 172

Osman 85
Ottoman(s) 7, 14, 16–17, 26, 28, 52, 65–6, 80,
85–105, 107–9, 113, 125, 144–63, 179; carpets 97,
104–5, 116, 121, 156, 158, 161; ceremonial 23,
86, 97, 98–9; court dress 16, 86–9, 93, 97, 98–9,
101–4, 149–51; embargoes 14–15, 86; textiles 2,
9, 26, 80, 84, 85–105, 88, 90–1, 94–6, 98–9,
101–3, 114, 116, 148, 149–61, 150–5, 157–60

Pahlavi 147, 163, 169–73
painting 1, 7, 22–3, 39, 48, 51, 53, 57, 70, 80–1, 88,
92, 98–9, 103, 105, 112, 113, 116–17, 126, 126,
140, 156, 165; on fabric 26, 41, 60–1, 101, 102,
124, 129; *see also* court
Palestine/ian 26, 29, 163, 168–9, 170–1, 178–9; *see
also* Israel, Jordan, Levant, Syria
Paradise 16–17, 52
parasol, royal 52, 56, 66
patronage 17, 24, 29, 78, 86, 93, 97, 108, 121, 144;
see also court, khalat, tiraz
pattern-book(s) 150, 151, 164, 169; *see also* court,
design
Persia(n) *see* Iran
pile 116, 121; loop 37–8; *see also* knot, velvet
pilgrim(age) *see* dress (Muslim), Hajj
plague 23, 66, 78, 86, 149
plain weave 31, 37, 40, 41, 45, 57, 59–60, 62, 71,
73, 101, 104, 110–11, 118, 128, 169; *see also*
al-'Attabi, kilim, taffeta, tapestry
poet(ry) 11, 41, 87, 89, 116, 132
Poland/ish 111, 121
Portugal/Portuguese 14, 66, 79, 109
potash wash 21; *see also* alum, natron
prayer 15; -mats/rugs 15, 92, 105, 109, 176, 180;
-ribbons 180, 180
prices 20, 29, 31–2, 40–1, 53, 56, 68, 78–9, 87,
92–3, 97, 103–4, 109–10, 131, 135–6, 140, 144,
152, 160–1, 168–9
print/printer(s) 9, 20, 29, 31, 31–2, 70, 72, 76–7,
78, 100–1, 101, 131, 135, 135–7, 140, 144, 150–3,
156, 157, 160, 160–1, 164, 165, 172–3, 173;
blocks 32, 76, 136, 160, 164, 173; *see also*
painting, stamp
Prophet Muhammad 15–17, 20–1, 35–6, 49–50,
59, 68, 89, 92

Prophet(s) (biblical, Quranic) 26, 49–50, 87, 92,
116, 118

Qait Bay 80
Qajar(s) 108, 117, 125–47; carpets 126, 140, 144–5,
145–6, 147; court dress 1, 126, 126, 128, 130,
131–2; textiles 109, 124, 125–47, 127–30, 133–5,
137–9, 141–3
qalamkar *see* cotton, print
Qalawun 17; house of 66, 69
Qansuh al-Ghawri 79
Qara Qoyunlu 107
Qasr Ibrim 38, 38, 56, 56, 66, 67, 68
Qazvin 107, 126
qizilbash 108, 112, 116; *see also* nomad
quality/quantity (control) 17, 27, 56, 86–7, 93, 97,
113, 156, 169, 179; *see also* guild, hisba,
monopoly
quilt cover/making 20, 33, 100, 155, 157, 174, 180;
see also bed
Qum 108, 126
Quran(ic) 15–16, 19, 52, 54, 92, 94, 101, 102, 105,
136, 137, 180
Qusayr 'Amra 39; al-Qadim 77

Ramadan 15, 50, 52, 97, 113
Rashidun caliph(ate) 35–6, 50, 92, 117
Red Sea 14, 66, 79
reed screen(s) 169, 170
Resht 126, 137, 138–9
Ribat-i Sharaf 112
Riza 'Abbasi 117, 117
Riza Paşa 153
Riza Shah Pahlavi 163–4, 169, 172, 179
Rize 174, 174
Russia(n) 14, 108, 111, 125, 131, 144, 149, 163–5

saddle-cloth(s) 21, 105, 109, 137, 140
Safavid(s) 7, 14, 45, 107–21, 125–6, 179; carpets
110, 116–17, 120–1, 122–3, 145; court 108–9,
112–13, 112–14, 115–17, 117, 120–1, 144; textiles
9, 45, 87, 92, 107–21, 111, 113–15, 117–20, 126,
128–9, 135, 140, 143, 144, 146, 161
St Thomas à Becket 61, 62
salaries/earnings 32, 41, 53, 56, 100, 109, 145, 176
Samarkand 68, 81, 103, 165
Samarra 39
sampler(s) 73, 75, 145, 145, 150, 158
San'a 36, 60
Sasanian(s) 24, 35–6, 39, 53; carpets 38, 58;
ceremonial 35, 50, 52; design(s) 35, 37–8, 38–9,
42–4, 57, 167; textiles 24, 40, 167
sash 57, 100, 111, 111, 132
satin (weave) 52, 68, 73, 86, 93, 97, 100, 108,
110–11, 113, 116, 126, 156–7, 165, 174, 179
Savah 108
seal(s) 20, 20, 86, 92; *see also* stamp
Selim I 97; Selim III 149, 151–2
Seljuk(s) 17, 36, 45, 50
al-Shafi' 56
Shafi' (Safavid) 117
shahada 15, 92, 94
Shahr-i Qumis 38; Shahr-i Sabz 165
Shari'a 15
shawl 57, 109, 126; *see also* Kashmir, Kirman
Shi'i, shi'ism 16–17, 35–6, 44, 49–50, 59, 107,
112–13, 116; *see also* 'Ali, 'Abbasid, Buyid,
Fatimid, Islamic Republic, Qajar, Safavid

Shiraz 137, 179

shroud(s), reliquary textiles *10*, 11, 40, 43, 44–5, *56*, 56, *67*, 68, *78*, 80, *81*, 92, *94*, 136, 168, 180; Shroud of St Josse 44, *46–7*, 60; *see also* colour (black, turquoise)

silk *passim*, especially: 13, 16, 20, 24–5, 28, *31*, 35, 38–41, *39*, *42–3*, 50, 53, 57, 80, 86–7; ʿAbbasid 34, 60; Afshar 117, *120*; Ayyubid *71*, 71; Buyid 44–7; Central Asian 40, *42–3*, 62, 80–1, *81–3*, 87, 165; cocoon 24, 86, 110, 153; exports 110, 142, 144, 153; Iberian 6, *10*, 43, *54*, 60–2, *61*, *63*; imports 20, 25, 87, 172; Mamluk 64, *66–7*, 66–79, *71*, *73–4*, *78*; mixture(s) 16, 40, 60, 82–3, 92, 104, 124, 131, 150–1, 156, 165, *166*, 169; monopoly 14–15, 86, 107–9; Ottoman *2*, 16, 25, 86–101, *90–1*, *94–5*, *97–9*, 104, 108–10, 126, *148*, 150–6, *150–1*, *154–5*, *159*; pebrine 25, 114, 153; Qajar *124*, 126, *127–30*, 131, *134*, *137–9*, 144; Safavid 86, 89, *106*, 107–21, *111*, *114–15*, *118–19*; Sasanian 24, *42*; sericulture 24–5, 86, 108, 126; Silk Road 13, *14*, 32, 38; silkworm 24–5, 86–7, 142; Timurid 80–1, *82–3*; *see also* carpet, embroidery, Islamic law, taffeta, velvet

silver (-gilt) *see* metallic threads

soap 21, 136

South-East Asia 9, 16, 31, 76, 109

Spain 23, 41, 44, 62; *see also* Iberia

spinner(s) 20, 24, 87, 131, 144, 161, 169, 174

stamp(ing) *20*, 26, 60, 62, 70–1, 76, 86, 101, *160*; *see also* customs, painting, seal

Sudan(ese) 23, 65, 86, 179

sufi(s) 21, 101, 107

Sulayman (caliph) 29

Suleyman (the Magnificent) 86

sumptuary regulations 17, 37, 57, 66, 68, 93, 112, 149, 151–2, 172, 179; *see also dhimmi, hisba*

sunna 16, 35; sunni(s) 14, 16–17, 21, 35–6, 49–50, 68, 85, 107–8, 116–17

symbol(ism) 21, 50, 52, 73, *88*, 88–9, 92, 94, 105, *112*, 112–13, 117, 120, *130*, 135, 151, 165, 168, 176–80; *see also* blazon, colour, design, flag

Syria(n) 9, 16, 23–4, 26, 28–9, 31, 35–9, 49, 65–6, 70, 72, 76, 78, 80, 85–6, 149, 163–4, *164*, 168–9, 179; *see also* Israel, Jordan, Levant, Palestine

Tabaristan 38, 53

Tabriz 80, 86, 100, 107–8, 120, 126, 144

taffeta 13, 40, 110–11, 113, 126, 136, 156

Tahmasp 107, 113, 120

tailor(s)/tailoring 20–1, 26, 87, 97, 109, 113, 152, 164, 169

talisman 101, *102*, 165; *see also* magic

tanners/ing 20, 28; tannic acid 28, 45

tapestry (weave) 28, 37, 39, 44, *55*, 57, *58*, 59–62, *62*, 67, 68, 70; *see also* kilim, loom

Tarim Basin 14, 24, 31, 32, 39, 40, *42–3*

tax(es) 20, 24–5, 38, 71, 78–9, 85–6, 109, 131, 144, 149, 152–3, 163; *see also* customs (excise)

Tehran 44, 125–6, 131, 136, 179

tents 12, 15, 21, 56, 76, 101, *103*, 103–4, 109, 136–7, *138–9*, 139, 168–9, *170*; *see also* military, nomad

terminology, loan words 13, 89, 92, 179–80; pattern- 40–1, 88–9, 132; textile-: *passim*, especially 31, 33, 40–1, 89, 92–3, 110

tie-dyeing *see* ikat

Timur Leng 12, 65, 81, 85, 89, 103, 107; textiles 12, 45, 80–1, *82–3*; Timurid(s) 25, 45, 78, 80–1, 121

tiraz 23, 33, 39, 49–50, *51*, 53–63, *55–9*, 68, 76, 80, *81*; official(s) 17, 56, 62; workshops 17, 53, 56, 59, 62, 68–9

Tokat 160–1

Trabzon 85, 161, *174*, 174

trade embargoes 14, 86, 101, 107–9, 147, 164, 172, *see also* monopoly; roads/routes 13–14, 32, 38, 66, 108–9, 126, 153, 169, 173

tribal society *see* nomad

tribute 14, 35–47, 38, 85

triple cloth *see* double cloth

trousseau (lists) 15, 53, 140, *142*, 142, 169, 174

Tunis 24, 41, 152; Tunisia 38, *49*, 57

turban (cloth) 36, *48*, 50, *51*, 57, 59, 68, 97, *98–9*, 100, *112*, 112–13, 152

Turkey 9, 16, 21, 24–6, 28, 31, 36, 39, 65, 85–105, 149–61, 164, 173–6, 180; carpets 174, *176*; exports 28, 101, 104, 152, 160–1, 176; imports 86, 150, 152–3, 160, 173, 178; *see also* Ottoman

Turkistan 39, 117

Turkoman 66, 107–8, 116, 121, 165, 177; *see also* nomad

twill (weave) 28, 38, *38–9*, 40, *42–3*, *46–7*, 60, 62, 68, 73, 81, *115*, 116–17, 132, *133*

twister(s)/twisting 23, 25, 87, 144

ʿUbaydallah 49

ʿulama/ulema 16–17, 21, 29, 41, 50, 53, 68, 93, 97, 105, 152, 179; *see also hadith*, Islamic law, Islamic Republic, Shiʿi, sunni

Umayyad(s) 35–6, 38–9, 49–50, 53, 57; ceremonial 50, 52; *tiraz* 39

Üsküdar 152–3, *153*, 156

Uzbek(istan) 39, 107, 164, *166*, 179

veil 66; of Hisham 44, 61, 62; of St Anne 57, *57*; *çarşaf* 151; *chador* 169, 172, 180; *see also* dress

velvet (weave) 7, 9, 37, 41, 126; Central Asian 165; Ottoman 16, 87–8, *88*, 92–3, 97, *97*, 116, *148*, 153, *153*, 156–7, 160; Qajar 126–7, 137, 144; Safavid 108, 110–11, 113, 116–17, *117*, 121

Vienna 86, 103, 153

Walid II 50

wax *see* print

weave/weaving *passim*, especially: 26, 36–7, 40, *42–3*, 57, 60–2, 65, 70, 73, 76, 81, 92, 104, 116, 121, 129, 150, 153, 161, 176; *see also* carpet, loom, terminology

weaver(s) 20, 23–4, 26, *27*, 32, 38, 87, 97, 104, 109, 117, 121, 132, 144, 150–1, 165, 174, 176

weight 20, 23, 25–6, 28–9, 32, 86, 100, 110, 131, 140

Wissa Wassef (school) *167*, 167–8

wool 15, 20–1, 28, 31, 36, 37, 38, 68, 78, 87, 103–5, 109, 152, 174, 176, 179; exports 21, 104, 144; sea- 41; symbolism 21; *see also* felt, Kashmir shawl, Kirman shawl, *sufi*

workforce, demography 14, 38, 70, 80, 85–7, 104, 109, 126, 132, 144, 149–50, 153, 163–5, 172, 176–7; gender constraints 32, 144, 161, 164–5, 179; *see also* plague

Yazd 108, 110, 117, 120, 126, 132, 136, 173

Yemen(i) 30, 31, 41, 49, 70; textiles 26, 31, 35, 36, 57, 60–1, 76

al-Zahir *59*, 59

Zand 108, 113, 125; textiles 147

zandaniji 40, *42–3*

zarbaft 8, 26, 110; *zaribafan* 109

Ziegler 144–5, *146*

Zoroastrian(s) 13, 108, 140, *142*; *see also dhimmi*